PRACTICING
FOR LOVE

The contents of this work including, but not limited to, the accuracy of events, people, and places depicted; opinions expressed; permission to use previously published materials included; and any advice given or actions advocated are solely the responsibility of the author, who assumes all liability for said work and indemnifies the publisher against any claims stemming from publication of the work.

RoseDog Books
585 Alpha Drive
Suite 103
Pittsburgh, PA 15238
Visit our website at *www.rosedogbookstore.com*

ISBN: 978-1-6453-0505-7
eISBN: 978-1-6453-0481-4

Library of Congress Control Number: 2019917116

PRACTICING FOR LOVE:

A MEMOIR

By

Nina Kennedy

RoseDog Books

PITTSBURGH, PENNSYLVANIA 15238

ACKNOWLEDGEMENTS

To bless this work I must, first and foremost, honor the ancestors. The first Kennedy whose name I know in this country was George Washington Kennedy, an enslaved African who lived on a plantation near Andersonville, Georgia. His wife, Emma Bolah, was also enslaved. Their tenth child was a son, Royal Clement Kennedy, my grandfather, who married Mary Magdalena Dowdell. He was a mail carrier and she was a school teacher. Their third child was my father, Matthew Washington Kennedy, who married the former Anne Lucille Gamble, my mother.

My mother's mother, Nina Hortense Clinton, was descended from free African Americans. Her mother, Cecelia A. Lett, was a direct descendant of the founders of the Lett Settlement in Zanesville, Ohio, which was a self-sustaining community of mixed-race families. The families of the Lett Settlement were landowners and tax payers in Ohio before the Civil War, and challenged the State of Ohio for the right to vote and for access to education during the 1840s, 1850s, and 1860s. Nina's father, my great-grandfather Martin Clinton, owned an ice cream "depot." My grandmother Nina Clinton married Dr.

Henry Gamble of Charleston, West Virginia, who was descended from Scotch-Irish settlers, Native Americans, and enslaved Africans. Born at North Garden, Albemarle County, Virginia, Gamble's mother, Willie Ann Howard, had been enslaved on the Howard's Neck Plantation in Goochland County Virginia. Her father was her master and her mother, Eliza Howard, was also a slave. Henry's father, Henry Harmon Gamble, was a foreman on the same plantation, whose father was Scotch-Irish. Henry Harmon's mother was from the Powhatan tribe. My grandfather was born during the Civil War, received degrees from Lincoln University and Yale School of Medicine, and set up his practice in Charleston, West Virginia. My mother was born when he was sixty-two years old, and was the daughter of his third wife.

My grandmother had traveled the world as a Jubilee Singer under the directorship of Frederick Loudin, and was in London for the coronation of King Edward VII. She wrote beautifully and eloquently about the coronation in her letters and diaries, and assisted a photographer in developing the film of the photos of the coronation, thus being able to bring photos of the coronation back to the United States in 1902. She was just twenty-one years old at the time. Upon her return, she taught at a Colored high school. Her English was flawless!

My grandmother died just a few months before my mother learned that she was pregnant with me. I was born to a woman in mourning, a woman who had been too close with her own mother because her father had died when she was a child. Early in my life I felt the pressure to act as the parent while my mother behaved like a child. It would take many years to come to grips with the reality of this pathological role-reversal.

My parents were both classical pianists, and they were determined that I would become a pianist as well. They both had felt that racial discrimination had prevented them from having the careers that they felt they deserved. All of their hopes and expectations fell onto me, to realize their dreams and become a concert pianist in the post-Civil Rights era. Not only did I become a concert pianist, I was also a child prodigy, presenting my first complete recital at age nine and appearing as piano soloist with the Nashville Symphony – before an audience of over four thousand people – at age thirteen.

It was important for me to write this memoir as a testament to what women experience in a field run and dominated by men. For centuries, men got away with denying women opportunities because it was taken for granted that they would inevitably get married and have children, and that was the end of their careers. The women who did not marry were called "spinsters" and were pitied as such. They were supposed to know nothing of passion. So why would anyone choose to hear a chaste version of the great romantic works? It was okay to let women teach, but keep them off of the stage.

Even when I performed the most romantic piece ever written – the Liszt transcription of Wagner's *Liebestod* – I was told after my audition for then associate conductor of the Philadelphia Orchestra William Smith, "Don't play this. Play Mozart or Schubert." He wrinkled his face, "But don't play this." What is so wrong with a woman relating the heights of ecstasy to an audience? Is a respectable woman not supposed to know anything about ecstasy? Is she supposed to be a vessel lying in wait for her husband's pleasure while experiencing none of her own? Or is a woman's passion too intimidating? Does it make a man feel like her sexual servant?

Mind you, this wasn't some kind of half-hearted, weak, feminine performance. Pianist John Pennick had the courage to tell me the truth, "You play it like a man!"

I'll put it this way: I was never one to pull back from a climax.

It was important to me to write about my romantic life as well as my career because my quest for love has been inextricably linked with my quest for success as a musician. Of course, keeping the double standard in mind, a woman must tread lightly where romantic details are concerned lest she be called a whore, slut, etc. I could never go through the motions of flirting or sleeping with a man to get a contract, though I've known some women who did. And now since we have learned from the scandals involving conductors such as James Levine, evidently some men have done so as well. However, in that particular case, some of the males involved were too young to consent.

I must acknowledge that I was inspired by Arthur Rubinstein's *My Young Years*, as well as Anaïs Nin's diaries. Gertrude Stein's *The Autobiography of Alice B. Toklas* was also a huge influence. The writings of James Baldwin, Maya Angelou, and Alice Walker also inspired me. I also must acknowledge the lover of writer bell hooks who said, "If you want to read books that focus on black women, you better start writing and keep writing."

Some of the names of persons in this book have been changed to protect their privacy and anonymity.

I am eternally grateful to Susan Seltzer for showing me how to love and supporting me unconditionally. To quote Michael Jackson, she was "gone too soon."

Most of this book was written while I was living in the suburbs of Cologne, Germany. I must thank Gerda Neurauter for her love and support during that time.

My sincere thanks go to April Gibson for inspiring me to share portions of my memoir for a blog spot she created. At the end of the blog I wrote, "For the juicy details of my romantic life, you'll have to wait for the book." Well, here's that book. Enjoy!

Nina Kennedy
New York City, 2018

I never dreamed of a big wedding, of a white dress, or adoring husband. Instead, I dreamed of playing Carnegie Hall.

Part 1

1

I was born in the American South in a segregated Colored hospital in Nashville, Tennessee. The year was 1960. Many civil rights struggles took place in Nashville during the early 1960s. There was the bombing of the home of Dr. Z. Alexander Looby, a prominent African-American attorney and activist, just three months before I was born. Segregationists were responsible for the bombing. Then there were the sit-ins at downtown lunch counters conducted by black students at Fisk University, who were simply demanding to be served. "Whites only" signs greeted customers at all of the lunch counters in the department stores downtown. These students – some of whom were from up North – had had it with segregation, so they sat in silence and studied while the police were called. Angry mobs of whites gathered to spit on them and pour glasses of water over their heads. Some of the poor students were severely beaten, so the resulting protests were quite dramatic. I remember my father lifting me onto his shoulders at one of the rallies outside of City Hall so that I could see what was going on. I still didn't know what was really happening. I just knew that we were surrounded by black people. There had been some chanting, some singing, and now we were just standing in silence while some individuals spoke.

With all of the turmoil going on out in the streets, we had our own little private race war going on in our house. My father was a dark man, descended from enslaved Africans who lived on plantations near Andersonville, Georgia. My mother was comparatively light-skinned, descended from free, mixed-race settlers in Ohio. Her birth certificate however clearly stated that she was "Colored." Occasionally she ordered him around like a servant and he cheerfully obeyed her commands. When I turned out to be as light-skinned as my mother, I became a convenient target for my father's pent-up frustrations. Everything he was never able to say to a white person, he said to me. Later my mother would tell me stories of how he would leave the safety pins to fasten my diapers stuck to my skin. He claimed not to hear my screams. She would laugh when she told the story.

My father believed in the old-school parenting rules and set out not to "spoil" his child. He felt that a baby needed to be taught that no one would come if she or he cried or screamed. Eventually it would learn that its needs would be met. It just had to wait. He didn't bother to distinguish between whimpers of loneliness or screams of pain. He simply would tune out if there were any sounds coming from the nursery.

My parents were members of the music faculty at Fisk University. Both of them were professors of piano. In addition, my father directed the famed Fisk Jubilee Singers for thirty some years. My mother served as the piano accompanist for the

My parents, Anne Gamble and Matthew Kennedy

group. Soon after I was born, my parents resumed touring with the Fisk Jubilee Singers and also toured as duo-pianists. I was left with babysitters for long, extended periods during the first years of my life. I imagine I tried desperately to figure out ways to make my parents stay home. But I guess I learned – once I figured out exactly what it was that was taking them away from me – that nothing was more important than performing and traveling.

A word about the Fisk Jubilee Singers: Founded in 1871, this group of student singers initially traveled to raise money for the founding of Fisk University, or the "Free Fisk Colored School" as it was named by the American Missionary Association in 1866. General Clinton B. Fisk had been a Union Army officer during the Civil War. Classes were held in what had been Union Army barracks which were erected on what used to be land where slave auctions were held. Keeping in mind that it had been illegal for slaves to read and write until the

The Fisk Jubilee Singers

Civil War, students of all ages enrolled at the Fisk School. Since the KKK didn't like the idea of blacks being educated, they repeatedly burned down the buildings. With the money from their concert tours, the Fisk Jubilee Singers are credited with building Jubilee Hall, the first permanent structure built in the United States specifically for the purpose of educating freed slaves. The building was surrounded by a high, thick stone wall designed to be impenetrable by the Klan. The Victorian Gothic building still stands today, and is a monument to higher education in Nashville.

The repertoire of the Fisk Jubilee Singers consisted primarily of Negro Spirituals, the old slave songs that were sung on the plantations of the Old South. The subject-matter of these songs was primarily religious on the surface, but they contained deeper meaning. While slave-owners sanctioned biblical passages that emphasized obedience to masters, Spirituals would refer to "a great camp meeting in the Promised Land," meaning the North, or "Go down Moses, way down in Egypt land. Tell old pharaoh to let my people go!" substituting "Egypt" for the South and "Pharaoh" for the slave-master. Most of these songs reflected the longing for freedom felt by all enslaved Africans.

It is because of the Fisk Jubilee Singers that Nashville is called "Music City" today. When Queen Victoria heard them sing in 1873, she proclaimed, "With such beautiful voices, these young people must be from the Music City of the United States." Hence, Nashville's nickname was born. The queen commissioned a life-sized portrait of the group which hangs today in Jubilee Hall. It should be pointed out that in the painting, the woman seated at the keyboard, Ella Sheppard, was the matriarch of the original Fisk Jubilee Singers. She had studied composition and was therefore able to arrange and notate most of the Negro Spirituals sung by the group. It was her arrangement of the Spiritual "Swing Low, Sweet Chariot" that was utilized by Czech composer Antonín Dvořák in his *Symphony from the New World*. It should also be pointed out that as a slave, young Ella Sheppard was sold for $350.

Matthew Kennedy and the Fisk Jubilee Singers

My mother, Anne Gamble

My father, Matthew Kennedy

Portrait of my mother by Aaron Douglas

My parents both attended Fisk as undergraduates. They saw each other as rivals while they were piano students. Both went elsewhere for graduate school – he to Juilliard, she to Oberlin. When they both returned to teach at Fisk, the sound of wedding bells was not far off.

My father took the role as director of the Fisk Jubilee Singers in 1957 when his predecessor John W. Work III fell ill. Before then, he had served as piano accompanist for the group when it was directed by Mrs. James A. Myers while he was an undergrad. When my father served his country in World War II, my mother was piano accompanist under John W. Work.

When my parents married in 1956, it was the talk of the campus. Charles S. Johnson – grandfather of the former Secretary of Homeland Security under President Obama, Jeh Charles Johnson, and the first black president of Fisk – gave my parents their wedding since my mother's father had been killed when she was a child. The Johnsons admired my mother's playing and were pleased and honored to have her on the Fisk faculty.

When I was born four years later, my parents later told me that I had to be placed at the front of the display room for newborns in the hospital because so many came in asking to see "the Kennedy baby." Jokes and insinuations that I would be a child prodigy abounded. When asked if they had a boy or girl, their answer was, "It's a pianist."

And so it was. I would observe them teaching their students during their lessons and would memorize the pieces they were learning. My ear was so overly-developed that no one realized that I could not see the sheet music placed in front of me. I wouldn't get my glasses until I was nine years old, because a teacher from school called to tell my parents that I couldn't see the blackboard. For the first nine years of my life, I had never seen the stars.

Already practicing

My parents were the kind of socially responsible citizens who felt it necessary to integrate previously segregated restaurants. We, as a family, attempted to enter Morrison's Cafeteria when I was very small. The first time, the manager of the restaurant blocked the door with his body and bellowed, "You can't come in here! This is a *Southern* chain!" Such intimidation did not stop my parents. They kept coming back until we were finally allowed to order our food and sit at a table. I'm sure that some of the staff were happy to see us, and some of them weren't. Morrison's was close to the Fisk campus, so it was convenient for us to be able to go there for dinner. I don't remember the exact details of all that was happening. However, I do remember the stress my parents were feeling based on their body language and their insistence that I be on my absolute best behavior, which meant no loud talking and no getting up and running around. Other white children were running around and playing, but I was not allowed that privilege. It made me wonder what was so special about them that they got to laugh and play and be loud and I didn't.

Occasionally my mother would bring me into the Fisk Jubilee Singers rehearsals, which took place during the evenings. I was always very popular with the students. They would run over to me and pick me up or put me in their laps. I remember one incident at home when I wanted to sit in my father's lap. He was sitting in a big green lounge chair and I put my hands on his knees trying to climb up. But he looked down at me like I was a stranger. I knew that other people seemed to enjoy lifting me up and placing me in their laps, but evidently he was uncomfortable with that kind of affection. I never saw him display any physical affection toward any child.

I was always an only child. My parents were both forty years old when I was born, so the children of their friends and colleagues were much older than I was. They lived in a house on campus when I was born and then moved to a house in the suburbs when I was three years old. My mother had bought that house during one of her many emotional breakdowns, which would put her in the hospital for "a rest." She had seen the ad for the house in the newspaper and made a down-payment without consulting her husband. She felt that the way their old neighborhood had deteriorated was a contributing factor in her breakdown. Their marriage suffered greatly as a result of her insistence on moving.

I started going to nursery school when I was too young, I believe, so that my mother could resume her teaching schedule. Many of the boys were much older than I was and thus bigger and stronger. I came home with the cuts, scrapes, and bruises to prove it. It felt like a daily struggle for survival. I was too small and meek to be thrown in the lions' den with such rough kids. One of them pulled me into the bathroom with him and locked the door. He put me on the floor and tried to act out what he must have seen his parents doing, though we were fully clothed. The teachers helplessly stood outside waiting for him to unlock the door. By the time he did, practically the whole school was waiting outside. He was always getting into trouble, so how did the teachers allow him to pull me into the bathroom in the first place?

When I entered kindergarten, my parents enrolled me in a school that was close to the Fisk campus and was in a neighborhood where affluent African Americans lived. I remained in that school through first grade, when the school board informed my parents that I was not allowed to attend the school because it was outside of our district. The school to which I was assigned was closer to our house but in a rough, poor neighborhood. By my arrival in second grade, the students there had already formed friendships that would last a lifetime. I came in as an outsider. I didn't understand their slang. I wasn't used to their rough behavior. It marked the beginning of years of social isolation.

My father was also suspicious of the children who were my classmates. He made it perfectly clear that I was not to share with them any details of our travel schedule with the Jubilee Singers.

"They'll come in here while we're gone and rip us off!" he yelled.

At this school I became bilingual. I had to speak the slang the kids spoke to keep them from calling me "Oreo" – black on the outside and white on the inside. They already called me yellow or "yella" to make me self-conscious about my skin-color. After a day of speaking ghetto slang, I would come home and speak the King's English to satisfy my mother. My parents had no clue of the amount of stress I was under.

Just as my father claimed not to hear my distress at being stuck with safety pins, he was also deaf to my distress from being bullied at school. The black kids at school were extremely mean to me. I spoke correctly, which my teachers appreciated. But the kids gave me hell! I was terrified. I would come home in tears daily because of the ridicule, verbal attacks, and threats of physical violence. I saw children beaten and bloodied on the playground. My stress level was extremely high for a child my age.

The one place where I was not bullied was at the music conservatory on the white side of town. I was enrolled in a piano class for children ages seven through ten, taught by William Higgs at the Blair Academy of Music. I was the youngest in the class. Playing the piano had always been easy for me. I could memorize Mozart sonatas at seven years old. As the years went by, the white kids respected and admired me. We all grew up together.

For fun, my father and I would split up a Liszt *Hungarian Rhapsody* or the Rachmaninoff Prelude in C-sharp minor into four hands. I would play what was written for the treble clef with both hands and he would do the same for the bass clef. This music was really too difficult for me but because of my excellent ear, I could "fake it." I did not know at the time that my father had heard Rachmaninoff perform live in a segregated balcony at a concert hall in Macon, Georgia when he was a boy. Introducing me to this music while I was still a child was very important to him.

When I was in elementary school – say, fourth or fifth grade – I made a friend at the beginning of the school year, a little white girl who would sit with me to have lunch and hang out with me in the halls between classes. Our friendship developed for a few weeks. Then one day she approached me in the hall with a horrified look on her face.

"What's wrong?" I asked.

In all seriousness, she said, "Somebody told me you were a nigger!"

I didn't know what to say. I didn't know whether or not she knew that "nigger" was the wrong word for a "black person." It was clearly a word she had heard spoken in her parents' house. At the time, I didn't have the language to say, "That word is inappropriate," etc. So I just shrugged. Judging from the shock on her face, one would have thought that I had just told her that I was a leper. She shook her head and whispered, "No!" then walked away. Later when I saw her in the hall and waved hello, she pretended she didn't see me. She never spoke to me again.

With my mom and Marian Anderson

The lesson for me was this: regardless of how light-skinned I was, or how articulate I was, or how well I played the piano, whites would still see me as a nigger. Luckily the famed contralto Marian Anderson was a friend of my mother's and I knew that she had dignity and respect in other parts of the world. Miss Anderson had stayed in my grandfather's home in Charleston, West Virginia whenever she was performing in the area because at that time she was not allowed to stay in hotels. My mother had met her when she was a child and they remained friends for the rest of Miss Anderson's life. In fact, their correspondence can be found in *The Marian Anderson Papers* at the University of Pennsylvania Library.

My father had a sister who lived in Long Island with her husband and two children, and we often drove up from Nashville to visit them during the summers. Since their home in Brentwood was not so far from Marian Anderson's home in Danbury, Connecticut, we would occasionally drive to see her as well. She lived in a sprawling mansion on multiple acres of land. Her husband was a cattle rancher, ergo the acreage.

During some of these summer excursions we would visit Miss Anderson in her Manhattan apartment. Even her speaking voice was velvety and rich.

Via Miss Anderson's role-modeling, the seeds were planted for my dreams of living in Europe and enjoying success as a concert artist. That is… if living in America didn't destroy me first.

It was around this time that my mother started straightening my hair with a hot comb to make me look as white as possible. It couldn't get wet or it would go back to its natural curly state, so that meant no swimming for me in the summer. A side note:

when the federal government decreed that public pools in Nashville could no longer be segregated – in other words, for "Whites only" – the local city government closed the pools, which made the whites even madder, so they blamed the blacks.

I knew that I was not allowed to languish in the sun, the reason being so that I would not get any darker. In the 1960s when afro hairstyles became popular, my mother was the kind of self-hating black person who would send her female students back to their dorms if they came into a lesson wearing an afro.

"Go home and put a comb through your head," she demanded.

The boys, of course, did not receive the same reprimand. My mother's hair was always perfectly straight. The only time I saw her hair in its natural state was when it was being washed.

As the Anti-War/Black Militant Movement grew on Fisk Campus, some black students demanded that the university get rid of all white faculty. My mother's best friend was a history professor, Dr. Pearl Bradley, who was white. The two of them would laugh at imagining the Black Militants' reaction to hearing Bing Crosby's "White Christmas."

My parents were married in the Fisk Memorial Chapel in 1956. I was christened in that church. We attended Sunday services there regularly until some of the Fisk students wanted to form a gospel choir. They would call it the Black Mass Choir. My parents were vehemently opposed to the formation of such a group because the kind of singing it called for was bad for the voices of members of the Jubilee Singers or the University Choir. My mother often complained about the "hollerin' and screamin'" coming from the throats of the Black Mass

Choir singers. The students won the battle, however, and gospel music became a regular part of the Sunday service. In protest, my parents joined the congregation at Nashville's First Baptist Church Capitol Hill, where I was baptized.

There was great excitement in the black community when performers like The Supremes and The Temptations appeared on *The Ed Sullivan Show*. I and my parents were glued to the TV screen for those events. Unfortunately, after watching The Temptations my mother had to comment on what a negative representation it was for whites to watch these men "... dancing around like monkeys." At times, you would think you were listening to a racist white person when my mother spoke. The pain from the racism she had experienced ran deep to the point where she truly felt that her duty as a college professor was to "whiten" her black students as much as possible.

At Fisk I was lucky to be in the audience for concerts given by Jessye Norman, Nina Simone, pianist Leon Bates, Benjamin Matthews, jazz pianist Don Shirley and his trio, Geoffrey Holder, and Duke Ellington (as a soloist) among others. Plus, the dance and theater departments presented recitals and productions annually, to say nothing of the annual concerts given by the Fisk Jubilee Singers. On top of all of that, there were the student recitals. As a child I sat through endless student recitals given my parents' students, which were required for them to be able to graduate. The Nashville Symphony would come to Fisk campus to collaborate with the University Choir and other ensembles. For one of those collaborations, my mother appeared as piano soloist in a performance of Beethoven's *Choral*

Fantasy, for which I had to sit on stage as her page-turner.

I was not allowed to listen to popular music on the radio supposedly because the lyrics were too risqué. But when I was transferred to Haynes Elementary, the black children introduced me to the local soul music station, WVOL. Suddenly I was quoting lyrics sung by Aretha Franklin and James Brown. I found the radio channel on our stereo at home, but my parents were quick to discourage me from listening. My mother seemed to be eager to create new rules for punishment so that my listening privileges could be revoked.

I, like other young black girls my age, was fascinated with The Jackson 5. I observed their success and wondered why it was so important to my parents for me to pursue a career in classical music. These boys were making millions! Even though I had no allowance, I convinced my father to purchase tickets for a Jackson 5 concert when they came to town in 1970. Michael Jackson was my idol. I didn't want to marry him (even though we were the same age). I wanted to *be* him. I wanted to sell millions of records and have adoring fans all over the world. He was my professional role-model. My parents also saw to it that I had several books on the life of young Mozart. The only reason why more blacks aren't into classical music was because they weren't exposed to it, or so I thought. I truly believed that my parents were preparing me for a successful, affluent life. They had joined "Jack and Jill" so that I could socialize with affluent black children. When other parents would host events, I saw that other black families lived in clean, organized houses. So why was our house so junky? I suppose, in the back of my young mind, I thought that all my work and practice would result in our being able to live in a large clean house, perhaps with servants, so that my mother wouldn't be so unhappy. Michael Jackson had made millions as a child, so why couldn't I?

So, I practiced. My parents insisted that I practice at least two hours a day, every day. There was a Steinway studio grand in the living room of my parents' house, plus they each had two Steinway grands in their piano studios on campus. My mother's perfect pitch was most annoying as she would call out to me from the bedroom when I played wrong notes. She always knew what the correct notes should be. I was still overly reliant on my ear since I had never fully developed the skill of sight-reading. I would struggle with the score until I could manage without having to look at it. As long as my pieces were prepared to perform for the faculty evaluation at the end of the semester, all was well.

My first complete solo recital at nine years old

• • • • •

The year was 1970. My father was preparing for a recital at George Peabody College as part of the requirements for completion of his Ph.D. My mother was preparing for a faculty recital at Fisk and I was preparing for my first complete piano recital at Riverside Church. All of us were practicing furiously. The repertoire for my parents' concerts was permanently implanted in my memory and I would end up using several of those works in the concerts I gave as an adult. All of our recitals were enormously successful and I received an array of flower bouquets and congratulatory telegrams from my parents' friends. My parents were very happy and the message was clear that this was what I needed to do in order to please them. There was no turning back.

2

As I neared the end of my time in elementary school, the bullying I experienced simply increased. My classmates were older and more vindictive in their attacks. As Nashville schools were officially integrated, white students from distant neighborhoods were bused to our school, Haynes Elementary. Along with the white students came white teachers and newer books and materials. The quality of education definitely improved.

Meanwhile, in 1971 the Fisk Jubilee Singers celebrated the centennial anniversary of their founding. (That year Mathew Knowles was a student at Fisk, along with his buddy David Lombard. This was twenty years before Knowles' daughter Beyoncé would set the world on fire with Destiny's Child and Lombard's group En Vogue would sell millions of CDs.) My father was still director of the Jubilee Singers during the many tours that year and I was lucky to be allowed to travel with them. There were major concerts at Nashville's War Memorial Auditorium and at the John F. Kennedy Center for the Performing Arts in Washington, D.C. I observed firsthand the nuts and bolts of practice and preparation, of promotion and publicity, of worries over ticket-sales, etc. We traveled throughout the country to California and the Bahamas.

Around the same time, Fisk University was recovering from a scandal involving embezzlement of funds committed by the former president. Eye-witnesses testified that when he was traveling he was "living like a king." Faculty were being asked to take pay cuts. My mother was extremely frustrated and made it clear that she wanted to leave Fisk. My father, however, was deeply committed to Fisk University. His doctoral studies were geared toward fulfilling qualifications for a full professorship. Unfortunately, he feared that racism played a part in his being kept from receiving his degree. He would have been George Peabody College's first recipient of a Doctor of Musical Arts degree, and he was convinced that the school would not give this honor to a black man.

George Peabody College hosted a wonderful piano festival annually during the summers. Many established artists would come to Nashville for the festival. My own teacher, Enid Katahn, presented a beautiful recital for the festival. I remember playing Chopin's Ballade in G minor in a master class conducted by famed pianist Lili Kraus during the festival. Her advice was very insightful and entertaining. At one point while I was trying to execute a very difficult passage, she suddenly clasped my face to her bosom to stop me. The audience laughed as I scrambled for notes I couldn't see. It was a light-hearted moment that certainly broke the tension. But the audience acknowledged that I played the hell out of that piece, considering I was just fourteen.

Unfortunately, I don't remember any recitals given by African American pianists during that festival.

For junior high school, I was forced to ride a bus to the school to which I was assigned: Ewing Park. This meant that in addition to having to sit in class with students who made my life hell, I'd be trapped on a bus with them twice a day for thirty minutes each way. The boys sitting in the front would kick me when I got on the bus and again when I tried to get off. They called me "white girl," which was clearly intended to be an insult. My hormones were changing, my mother's drinking and mood-swings were increasing, and my father stuck his head in the sand. I started having crying fits that would go on for days. My parents would not allow me to stay home by myself since they were at work, so I would go to school and sit in the guidance counselor's office all day.

After weeks of this, the guidance counselor called my father to see if anyone could pick me up to take me home. I could hear him yelling at her through the phone while sitting across from her desk. She held the receiver away from her ear, then hung up. He had apparently already hung up on her. She looked at me apologetically, not knowing what to do. It was no surprise to me that he was unconcerned about my well-being at school. But he rarely lost his temper. Oh, he would throw tantrums maybe once a year, yelling and cursing at the air. He never directed his rage at my mother or me. He'd go off for a few minutes, go into another room, then come back like nothing had happened. He never apologized or showed concern. It may have been another personality that took over.

But I was very much afraid of him. I never knew when it was safe to relax after one of his outbursts.

Throughout junior high school, Franz Schubert was my best friend. He was part Golden Retriever, mixed with other stuff. When the bus approached my stop at the end of the day, he'd be sitting there with clouds of dust rising behind him from his wagging tail. He was already full grown when he came to us, though his ribs were protruding through his skin. He used to come and play with the neighbor's dog so I'd bring him some table scraps which he'd gobble down. Soon he was waiting at the back door for me to come out. Pearl Bradley was the one who said to my mother, "Why don't you let her keep him." So my parents took him to the vet for a checkup, bath, and shots. Then he became my constant companion. Since he stayed outside during the day, he was only allowed to stay in the kitchen when he came inside.

I always LOVED dogs. As a child I spent more time outside with dogs than I ever did with other children. At the height of my canine popularity, nearly a dozen dogs would come into our yard to hang and play with me and Franz. They were my buddies and my protectors.

As Franz got older, he was starting to lose his vision. Sometimes when I walked toward him, he would bark as if I were a stranger until I got close enough so he could see and smell me. Then he'd wag his tail and come over and lick my hand. As the weather got colder, he would take naps under the car when the engine was still warm. The older he got, the longer it took him to wake up when the ignition turned on. I would always look to make sure he wasn't under the car before we got in.

Franz Schubert, my buddy

Meanwhile, I noticed that I was not developing crushes on boys. Some of my female classmates talked about thinking this or that boy was "cute." I never saw them as cute. They were just rude, smelly, mean boys. However, I did think that some of the ladies in the Jubilee Singers were pretty. If I had any crushes, it was on them.

I can't really say exactly when it was that I began to notice my mother's "thirst." I knew that she was always happier when we left the Works' house after dinner and an evening of drinking. I began to notice that my mother would spend her evenings alone in the kitchen after my father and I had gone to bed. They always slept in separate beds because he would have nightmares which caused him to toss and turn in his sleep. My mother claimed she was an insomniac so any sleep disturbance was intolerable. Later I learned that during those nights in the kitchen, she would feast on snacks and wash them down with multiple glasses of sherry. I was in the seventh grade when we started to learn about the effects of alcohol on the body. Soon after those lessons I happened to be cleaning out the kitchen cabinets and found dozens of empty sherry bottles. Why didn't she just throw them away, you ask? Well, I think she didn't want us to see the empty bottles in the garbage can so she just shoved them in the cabinets and forgot about them.

In the early 1970s, we would watch a then sixteen-year-old Oprah Winfrey delivering the local 6:00 news. She was the first African American news anchor in Nashville. My father was a regular customer of Oprah's dad, Vernon, at his barbershop. Nearly forty years later, Vernon Winfrey made a significant contribution toward helping us complete the documentary film I was producing on my father's life.

In the summer of 1973, my father was invited to join the piano faculty at the Interlochen Arts Academy's National Music Camp at Interlochen, Michigan. It was the first time in my experience that my father was the faculty member and my mother was just his wife. We drove to Michigan in the family car with Franz Schubert and attempted to make a summer of it. It was clear that my mother resented being introduced as just the wife. She would go out of her way to explain to the various white people we met that she too was a member of the piano faculty at Fisk University back home. They would nod and say, "That's nice," and then go back to conversing with my father.

That summer marked a turning point in what would become my career, since that was when I decided to learn and memorize Gershwin's *Rhapsody in Blue*. One of my father's graduate students had learned and performed it the year before, so it was thoroughly in my ear. That student, Carol Elligan, was my favorite of his students. I thought of her as my best friend in spite of the fact that I was twelve and she was in her mid-twenties.

At Interlochen, while my father taught individual lessons in his piano studio, I sought out practice rooms where I could work. Soon I noticed that white students would gather outside of the window of my practice room to listen to me play. I would finish long passages and look up to find groups of strangers applauding me.

There were concerts every night, which were amazing. We heard pianist Van Cliburn playing Brahms' Second Piano Concerto and visited with Duke Ellington after his concert with his orchestra. Duke had met my mother during her student days in Charleston, so she was especially delighted to see him.

That summer I took swimming lessons in Lake Wahbekanetta with other kids my age and enjoyed splashing around with them after class. One day, the surf was unusually rough and 1 was quickly carried out by the current. Soon I was swallowing lots of water and called to the lifeguard for help. I had to be rescued by the lifeguard. By then I already knew not to tell my mother when I got home. It would have upset her too much.

At Interlochen, my parents and I would eat breakfast, lunch, and dinner in the school cafeteria. My mother complained about all of the bread, potatoes, rice, and pasta that were served and often shed tears over how difficult it was for her to lose weight. Frequently I was on the receiving end of her outbursts and had no idea of what I had done wrong. I started to avoid her as much as possible. I took babysitting jobs, visited with kids my age, practiced, anything to stay away from our cabin. I think that part of the reason for my mother's moodiness also had to do with the fact that she didn't have easy access to a liquor store, and our living quarters were so small that she wouldn't have been able to hide the bottles without our noticing. Also, the two of them had to sleep together in the same bed. And to top it off, my body was maturing. I was becoming a woman.

Meanwhile, unbeknownst to me, my father was pleased and impressed with my progress and spoke highly of me to his colleagues. One of those colleagues was Dr. Thor Johnson, who was the conductor of the Nashville Symphony. That summer, he was conductor of the Interlochen World Youth Orchestra. I would often pass him on my bicycle and wave hello. He always gave an exuberant response. One day my father invited Dr. Johnson into his studio to hear me play the *Rhapsody in Blue*. I didn't really think of this as an audition, so I wasn't nervous at all. I played well for him and he said that he wanted to hear it again after we got back to Nashville.

I would celebrate my thirteenth birthday that summer. My father took us to an ice cream parlor in town as part of the celebration. He and I ordered black cherry ice cream cones. My mother didn't order anything for herself. While walking to the car, we were contentedly licking our ice cream, commenting on how delicious it was. Suddenly my mother

Thor Johnson

lost her temper. How dare we enjoy ice cream in front of her while she was trying so hard to lose weight, she bellowed. I went into my usual numbed state that took hold whenever she threw a tantrum. Suddenly, I heard my father say, "Okay, Anne. That's enough!" I couldn't believe what I was hearing. Was my father actually standing up to my mother? I never thought he had the nerve to do such a thing. All these years I thought that he had condoned her outbursts and agreed that I deserved to be verbally abused. He himself had been the target of her tirades and usually he would just bite his tongue and take it. But this time, away from Nashville and their colleagues at Fisk, he actually stood up for me. She looked at him in disbelief, closed her mouth, and pouted all the way back to our cabin. My whole perception of their relationship had changed forever.

I always wondered if the fact that I was excelling at the piano had any effect on his newfound ability to stick up for me. I was going to need an enormous amount of self-esteem to be able to stand in front of crowds of strangers and perform. My mother had seemed bent on destroying my self-esteem, so that I wouldn't "argue" with her. In hindsight, it became clear that most of the time I was on the receiving end of her unfinished business with her older half-sister. I may have begun to resemble my Aunt Katherine as I matured, in my mother's eyes. But at the time, all I could do was shut down emotionally and tell myself that my mother's yelling was a sign of love. At least – that was what my father said. Little did I know that I was being set up for emotionally abusive relationships in my adult life.

Back in Nashville, Dr. Johnson came to my mother's studio on Fisk campus that fall to hear me play again. This time I was a little nervous. He asked for additional repertoire, and I wasn't sure if I would be able to impress him enough to secure an engagement. He was very kind and supportive, and assured us that he would be in touch.

A few months later, Dr. Johnson called our home one evening and asked to speak to me. He asked if I would be available to perform the *Rhapsody in Blue* with the Nashville Symphony in June. It would be an outdoor concert at the bandshell in Nashville's Centennial Park. I ecstatically accepted the invitation.

A few weeks before the concert, I became quite the celebrity. I was interviewed for the local TV news and was the subject of various newspaper articles. The fact that I was thirteen years old made quite the headline. I was well-practiced and prepared

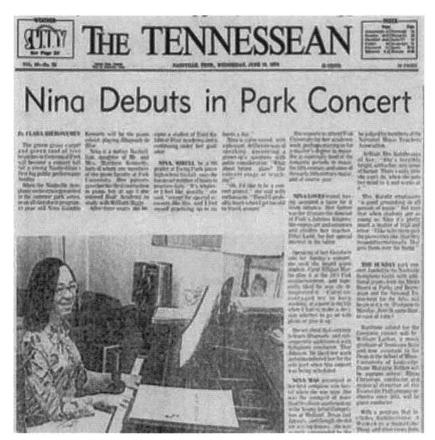

Tennessean article

Performing the Rhapsody in Blue with Nashville Symphony

Publicity photo taken when I was 15 years old

and was looking forward to my official debut in Nashville. My mother had bought me a red, white, and blue sleeveless gown, appropriate for a warm summer day. On June 23rd, the day of the concert, four thousand people showed up to partake in this Gershwin celebration.

While waiting backstage, I noticed that my mother became particularly demanding. The only word to describe her behavior was infantile. She needed me to find the bathroom for her and take her there. She needed me to find a seat for her. She needed me to get her a glass of water. Her demands seemed endless. I was so busy running around catering to her needs that I didn't have time to be nervous. In fact, it was a relief to get them out into the audience and be free of her.

The audience of four thousand gave me a standing ovation. Carol Elligan and another Fisk student presented me with bouquets of red roses. My godfather Dr. George Redd hosted a private reception for me in his home on Geneva Circle, the street where many of Nashville's well-to-do African Americans lived. The critics were most generous with their praise. All in all, it was a wonderful experience.

I would learn several years later that one of the reasons for my mother's meltdown during that park concert was, in the 1950s, she had been invited to appear as piano soloist with the Charleston, West Virginia Symphony in a performance of the first movement Rachmaninoff's Second Piano Concerto. She would have been the first African American to do so. Just a few months before the concert, the conductor who had engaged her died suddenly. His replacement, who was "a vicious racist," according to my father, cancelled her contract.

My father felt that she had never fully recovered from this heartbreak. As it turned out, I became the first local African American to appear as piano soloist with the Nashville Symphony, and their youngest soloist ever – up to that point. My mother surely wanted to be able to be happy for me. But she just couldn't. The memory was too painful.

The fact that my mother named me after her own mother gave a clue when it came to searching for reasons for her infantilism. Her father had grown children from two previous wives before he married my grandmother. Katherine, the first-born, used to beat and slap my mother and her brother when they were small. Floyd, the son of the second wife, would often drink and then carry around my grandfather's shotgun when he wasn't at home. My mother told a story of a time when Floyd was listening to the radio, but my grandmother had told my mother to practice the piano. Evidently the piano-playing was too loud for Floyd, so he told her to stop. Then my grandmother told her to continue. At that point, Floyd grabbed my grandfather's gun and pointed it at my grandmother, screaming, "You're not my mother!" etc. etc. Panicked, my mother jumped up from the piano stool and stood between her mother and the gun. When her father came home that night, he threw Floyd out of the house. My mother must have been nine or ten years old when this happened because her father was killed in a car crash when she was eleven. There was clearly an unmet need for parenting, and she intended to force her own daughter into that role.

• • • • •

Dr. Lee Minton, an ophthalmologist in Nashville, a patron of the arts, and a dear friend of Dr. Johnson's, would host musical evenings in his home during the summer. After the symphony' concert, he invited me to participate in these evenings. Dr. Minton lived on the rich, white side of town, so it was a big deal when we were invited to his home. Later, when Dr. Minton retired and moved to London, he continued the tradition of hosting recitals for young artists. But this time, instead of hosting them at his home, he rented the prestigious Warwick Arts Trust and filled the hall with invited guests – one of whom was the famous Russian pianist Shura Cherkassky, who became a lifelong friend.

Shura Cherkassky in his London Apartment

The following season I received an invitation to appear as piano soloist with the Savannah Symphony Orchestra, also in a performance of Gershwin's *Rhapsody in Blue* for their Black History Month concert. I immediately informed Dr. Johnson, who was so pleased.

In Savannah one afternoon, when I was finished with rehearsals, we pretended we were tourists and went on a tour of the old port area. A significant part of the port was used during the Slave Trade. The tour guide told us that chains, manacles, and even bones were unearthed in the holding area where enslaved Africans waited to be auctioned off. My mother went on and on about how it made her shiver to think about the treatment these people endured. It always amazed me how she was the only one who was free to express her emotions in public. She was so light-skinned, anyone would have assumed she was white. My father was the obvious descendant of slaves, yet he said nothing. I was just so nervous, worrying about all that took place during the rehearsal and hoping I could incorporate all of it into my interpretation of the Gershwin. I was also hoping that my mother wouldn't have a melt-down on the tour bus.

This was my first formal evening symphony engagement, in a formal concert hall, with the orchestra players and audience in evening attire. The concert was a huge success. My mother often told people about how emotional she became while walking up the aisle before intermission, and seeing "all these white people with their programs on their laps opened to the page with my baby's picture!"

Dr. Johnson passed away not long after the Savannah

concert. After his death, Dr. Johnson's sister informed my parents that he had been talking about me on his deathbed, about how he had been "in a dark place, and suddenly I see light," and he was so happy to hear that I had just been engaged to perform with another symphony orchestra. Music critic Louis Nicholas recounted this story in his book *Thor Johnson: American Conductor.*

After Savannah Symphony concert

3

Not long after the concert in Centennial Park, the Nashville Symphony temporarily made its home at the brand-new home of the Grand Ole Opry, which stood in the Opryland theme park in the suburbs of Nashville. Songstress Roberta Flack was invited to solo with the symphony for a special concert and of course we had gotten tickets. We had backstage privileges since the symphony staff knew us well, and my mother spent the second half of the concert backstage – probably because of the luxurious, spacious bathrooms there. I remained in the audience for the rest of the concert and was thoroughly smitten by Ms. Flack and her silky, sultry voice. I was still a celebrity among the regular symphony concert-goers, so several stopped me to talk to me after the concert. When I finally got backstage to Ms. Flack's dressing room, she and my mother were chatting animatedly. As I approached her, Roberta Flack said to me, "Oh, I'm so happy to meet you!" I almost didn't know what to say. Here she was one of my idols and she was happy to meet *me*? Wow!

My parents would receive flyers announcing piano competitions at their offices on Fisk campus so I figured, with this major success under my belt, that I would apply to compete. First prize usually included a decent amount of cash and some concert dates, to say nothing of the publicity and prestige. Each competition required that you submit a photo for which my mother insisted that my hair be straight. Not only did I not voice my opinion to her, but I didn't even have an opinion. She was in complete control of my physical appearance.

I had a very strange experience at a competition in Cincinnati, Ohio. I had included the *Rhapsody in Blue* in my repertoire for the first round of competition. When I got on stage, the judges asked for Bach. I played a couple of pages of it and then they stopped me. They then asked for a Haydn Sonata. I knew that the repertoire they were requesting would not show off my chops. I had the feeling that they were doing this on purpose. After I was finished, I sat in the audience to listen to other competitors. Sure enough, the boys were asked to play showy, bombastic pieces. I didn't have a chance. It also seemed like the judges gave me half the time that they gave to the others. It almost felt like they were rushing me off the stage. They had taken my money for the application fee, but once I got there they treated me like crap. Was this racism? Or was it sexism? Or both?

I played in the junior high school band during my years at Ewing Park. In three years, I managed to learn to play the clarinet, flute, oboe, and bassoon. I even played the piano for the jazz band that met for rehearsals after school. Of course, my highest grades were in music but I remember also receiving effusive praise for my writing. Hmmm... If I had had any choice in the matter of career direction, who knows?

By the end of junior high I was inducted into the National Junior Honor Society and had scored in the 98th percentile of the PSAT.

For senior high I chose a school that would take me away from the mean, abusive kids who had made my life hell for so long. McGavock High School was a comprehensive high school, meaning that students could prepare and be trained for jobs that didn't require college degrees. It was way out in the white suburbs, near the Opryland theme park. It was a highly competitive school. If I had not gone there, I would have been forced to go to the school in my district, which was not competitive at all.

I still needed to take the bus, however, and the bus stop was too far away for me to walk. One of my parents would have to drive me to the bus stop in the morning and pick me up at the end of the day.

I was still going to the Blair Academy of Music on full scholarship and studying piano with Enid Katahn. I also had weekly classes in ear training and music theory. The only other African American in my music theory class was Anthony Williams, who eventually took a position as organist at Fisk University. He even directed the Jubilee Singers for a few semesters.

My concert career was still in full swing. I learned and performed the MacDowell 2nd, Beethoven 4th, Rachmaninoff 2nd, and Grieg concerti. I still, however, received more orchestral engagements to perform the *Rhapsody in Blue* than any other works. One orchestral engagement was for the regional Governors' Conference in Jackson, Mississippi. I was

Enid Katahn

With Lewis Dalvit and the Jackson Chamber Orchestra

engaged to perform Beethoven's 2nd Piano Concerto with the Jackson Chamber Orchestra for a live concert. The second performance would be taped for broadcast at their local PBS studios. This was my first official concert TV taping. After realizing that any serious mistakes could be edited out, I flew through the performance like a breeze.

I was fourteen. That year I had won first place in the Tennessee Music Teachers' Association piano competition. As part of that prize, I was scheduled to give a concert at Middle Tennessee State University in Murfreesboro. It was a school night so I would have to be picked up at the bus stop after school for the two-hour drive. My mother met me at the bus and we drove in silence. We arrived at the music hall on the campus in plenty of time. I played the concert without a hitch. We stayed for a short reception where I received compliments and praise from members of the organization. Then we hit the road back to Nashville.

About thirty miles outside of Nashville, my mother broke the silence.

"Well, I may as well tell you. I was rushing to pick you up and... well... Franz was still under the car when I pulled out."

I sat in stunned silence.

"I think he's okay. He ran off, so I couldn't get out and look for him. I didn't have time." Her voice was cold. There was nothing to do or say until we got home.

We pulled into the driveway and I ran out of the car to look for him. I called and called for him. No response.

My mother was looking for him in the bushes where he would sometimes hang out, "Oh, there he is. Come on, Boy!"

But he didn't move. My mother asked our neighbor Mr. North to come over and help us get him out. He used a hoe to pull on his collar and pulled his lifeless body out from under the bushes and onto the driveway. My mother started wailing and boohooing and ran into the house.

"I was rushing! I didn't have time to get down there and look. He yelped and screamed and... I didn't have time!" she whined.

She ran into their bedroom and threw herself onto the bed. After thanking Mr. North, my father went in to comfort her. No one said a word to me. I held my breath and bit my lip until I drew blood to keep my tears from falling. When I was emotional, all I'd ever heard from my father was, "You stop that crying!" Meanwhile, he had all the patience in the world for my mother's crocodile tears. I really wanted to ask her how much she'd been drinking before she got in the car, but I didn't dare. My best friend was gone, all because of some stupid concert. We buried him under his house in the backyard under the sprawling plum tree.

In my parents' house, I was basically biding my time until I left home for good. My mother wasn't pleased with anything I did. My father accused me of not doing enough chores around the house. The real question was: how was our house ever supposed to get clean when he was such a hoarder? Junk was everywhere! Even in what was supposed to be my bedroom, his stuff filled the drawers and closet. There was no place for me to put my things, so I just threw them on the second twin bed. Meanwhile, my mother would cry and complain to her friends that I wouldn't clean my room. I was in a no-win situation. All I could do was count the months, days, hours, and minutes until it was time for me to go to college.

Meanwhile, my repertoire was developing. I was winning scholarships from the John W. Work III Memorial Foundation, the Nashville Chapter of Links, Inc., and the National Association of Music Teachers. Our church, First Baptist Church Capitol Hill, often engaged me to perform. I even had a few piano students.

And then there were the concerts. Friends of my parents invited me to perform in Nassau, the Bahamas. It was my first encounter with a society where blacks ran everything, even at the highest levels of government. The music, the food, the dancing, the weather, the tropical plants, and palm trees... all of it was wonderful! My concert had been well publicized in the local papers and the media. One young man was so excited to meet me that he had cut out my picture from the newspaper and taped it onto his mirror. He was a doctor, and a friend of my hosts who were well-respected college professors. He asked them if he could take me out to dinner one evening after the concert. He wanted to treat me to the kind of nightlife that was usually reserved for white tourists. But before we went to the casino, he took me to meet his mother. It was a lovely evening. He was a perfect gentleman. I enjoyed the best meal I'd ever had (up to that point) and a Las Vegas-style show complete with elaborate costumes and topless dancers. Ooh la la!

Socially, I didn't have close friends at school or at conservatory. But in high school I found the drama department and the gay boys. They told me about the gay bars in Nashville and took me with them when I was old enough to drive. They opened my eyes to a whole new world.

Our high school was invited to send representatives to participate in the Friendship Force, a program organized under President Jimmy Carter to encourage fellowship between regular American citizens and the people of Venezuela. The head of the drama department was asked to select talented students and I was chosen to perform. Between the many gatherings, cocktail parties – one was at the President's Palace, no less – and concerts, I made many friends and came out of my shell so to speak. It was also my first encounter with fresh black coffee brewed from fresh coffee beans. I couldn't get enough of it.

It struck me as odd and unfair that the young gay boys who came with us on the trip were able to hook up with strangers so easily. Girls didn't do this. I had no idea of how to pursue a romantic tryst with a lady. I was attracted to many of the women I met in Caracas, which was not always the case in Nashville. So many of the women in Nashville wore jeans and cowboy boots and hats in the clubs. The boys taught me that I was attracted to femmes, but most femmes already had a butch on her arm. The whole thing seemed way too complicated.

The most significant relationship during my teenage years outside of the relationship with my parents was with Enid Katahn. She was the only one it seemed who was genuinely concerned about my happiness. She could tell if the kids at school were getting me down or if my mother was on my case. I could speak honestly with her about what was going on at home. There was a time when my mother was in and out of the hospital to have three or four cysts surgically removed from her breasts. They all turned out to be benign, but the stress and worry were enough to affect my studies. Enid explained my situation to the jurors at the end of the semester and totally put me at ease before I played.

I spent the summers of 1976 and '77 as a student at the Aspen Music Festival in Aspen, Colorado. Another one of Enid's students, Jeni Slotchiver, had studied there and highly recommended it to me. My mother, of course, made a fuss that, "This is what the *white* kids do!" Eventually I was able to find some scholarship money to help with the expenses. I applied and was accepted, and had requested Aube Tzerko as a primary teacher. Tzerko was a former pupil and assistant of the great Austrian pianist Artur Schnabel.

Each year I entered the piano concerto competition. The Beethoven second was the selected concerto for the first year and the Grieg was the war horse for the second. I performed for several master classes, including one given by Edith Oppens. That first summer, the daughter of pianist Rudolf Serkin lived down the hall from me. She and I became dear friends and are still in contact as I write this. Pianists Claude Frank and Lillian Kallir (who are married) had invited Margie over to their home for dinner one night and she brought me along. The following concert season when Claude Frank was soloist with the Nashville Symphony, my parents introduced themselves to him after the concert. At first, he didn't remember who I was, but when they reminded him that I was Margie's friend, then he remembered. Margie had also told her father about me, whom I would meet two years later in Philadelphia when he appeared as piano soloist with the Philadelphia Orchestra in a performance of Beethoven's "Emperor" Concerto. I will never forget that performance.

My roommate for the first year was violist Lois Landsverk, who is now a violist for the Bamberg Symphony in Bamberg, Germany. It was delightful seeing and visiting with her in New York just recently after the orchestra performed at Lincoln Center.

I was able to meet and mingle with several celebrities in Aspen, including André Watts, Itzhak Perlman, Yo-Yo Ma, and even Henry Kissinger.

Aspen was where I tried smoking marijuana for the first time. There were always bongs being passed around at parties. It took quite some effort to learn to keep my finger on the hole, light the bowl, suck, let go of the hole, and inhale. And don't spill the water on the carpet! At one of these parties I experienced my first kiss from a white man. He clearly wanted to do more, but politely said goodnight when I made it clear that I was not interested. It wasn't a first kiss since I had already been kissed by a boy in Nashville. Boys were much more insistent about kissing me than girls were, it seemed. But I kept looking, waiting, and hoping. One day...

Up until that first summer, I had never really understood how sex worked. I had certainly never overheard or walked in on my parents doing it. I don't think they ever did it while I was in the house. I'd had a classmate in junior high school who had gotten pregnant – a white girl. She had taken some time off from school, so she was a little older. I tried to get the details from her, but she was no help. Well, at Aspen there was an international film festival which included some adult films. Finally, I got clear about the mechanics, at least from the male perspective.

As a scholarship student, I was required to sing in the choir for performances of Mahler's "Resurrection" Symphony and the Verdi Requiem. Thus began my relationship with and love for these great works. African American soprano Carmen Balthrop was the soloist in the Mahler and tenor Seth McCoy was one of the soloists for the Verdi. After that summer I sought out his manager and began a delightful correspondence with him.

It was such a pleasure connecting with Ms. Balthrop and Mr. McCoy because there were hardly any African Americans on the faculty at Aspen. There were maybe five or six black students among hundreds of whites and Asians, so the experience could be rather isolating. One of those black students was Nathaniel Ayers, the subject of the Jamie Foxx film *The Soloist*. Ayers was playing the double bass in the orchestra that summer and word had spread that he was very talented. He even sought me out for a dance at one of those infamous parties.

It was Jeni who informed me of a rumored practice at Juilliard involving requesting private lessons with faculty members (and many of the Aspen faculty were also on the faculty at Juilliard). After spending a few thousand dollars to study privately with a member of the faculty, you improved your chances of being admitted to the school. I knew that we didn't have that kind of money, but I thought I could at least impress a teacher with a private audition. I filed away the information for future use.

I was also getting the idea that the classical music world seemed to be a closed social club. Membership was eighty percent white with a few Asians, and it seemed to help matters if you were Jewish. Jeni was Jewish and her family seemed rich! I seriously thought about converting for a while – Sammy Davis Jr. had done it – but saw that it called for more reading than I had time for.

I also noticed that several young females took advantage of their close proximity to male conductors by sleeping with them. Some were able to secure contracts as a result, but this was not something I was willing to do.

That second summer, my mother insisted that I return from Aspen early to perform for the National Medical Association convention which was being held in Nashville that year. I was to play in the middle of a longer program of speeches and other presentations. The fee hardly covered the price of the plane ticket. I really did not understand why it was so important to my mother for me to play on this program. Years later I would learn that her father, Dr. Henry Floyd Gamble, had been a past president of the NMA (which was founded in 1895 because African-American doctors at that time were not allowed to join the "white" organization, the American Medical Association). Dr. Gamble also founded the local chapter of the NMA in Charleston, West Virginia.

My mother also may have been thinking in terms of attracting a husband for me among those distinguished medical doctors. The dress she had me wear, however, was entirely too conservative to attract a man. Mind you, she never expressed any of this to me. I was baffled by her strange, staring-off-into-the-clouds behavior, but I did what she said without argument. And, by the way, not one of those distinguished men asked me out on a date.

After that second summer in Aspen it was time to prepare for college auditions. I had put together an impressive program including the Beethoven Sonata Opus 2, No. 3; Chopin's B minor Scherzo and Mazurka in A minor Opus 17, No. 4; a Bach Prelude and Fugue, the Aaron Copland *Passacaglia*, and the Debussy Prélude *Jardins sous la pluie*. Several southern colleges invited me to perform concerts on their campuses so that I felt thoroughly prepared for my auditions. That semester I auditioned at Indiana University (where Jeni Slotchiver was studying), the Juilliard School, and the Curtis Institute of Music.

I took the bus to Bloomington and stayed with Jeni for the audition at Indiana. When I came to New York to audition at Juilliard, I stayed with a friend I'd met at Aspen and her parents. While in town, I called other gay friends I had met that summer who took me out to the gay discos. There I saw gay men using "poppers" for the first time and watched their wild, extravagant dancefloor behavior. After the disco closed, some of us ended up in a cab going down to The Village to an after-hours club where I witnessed more wild behavior, including seeing people falling over after taking Quaaludes, and activities in one of those infamous back rooms. When my eyes adjusted to the darkness, I saw that people were actually having all kinds of sex in all combinations – boys on boys, boys on girls, etc. I didn't see any girl on girl action though, unfortunately. One gay man desperately wanted to prove to me that he was in fact heterosexual. I politely declined his offer.

When I came to Philadelphia to audition at Curtis, I stayed with friends of my parents. So no partying this time. At Curtis, all of the students were on full scholarship provided by the Curtis-Bok foundation. Piano majors also had grand pianos delivered to their apartments. That year there were three openings in the piano department. Seventy-two pianists came to audition. I was selected as one of the three. I was also accepted at Indiana University, but I figured it would be easier for me to come out of the closet in a big city like Philly.

The day the acceptance letter from Curtis arrived, I was afraid to open it. As long as I didn't know the results, there was still hope. The letter was waiting for me in the car when my mother picked me up from the bus stop that day. I opened it to find that I had been accepted. My mother shed a few tears and then told me to call my father as soon as we got home. She actually dialed his number and said that I had something to tell him. When she held out the phone for me, I yelled across the room "I was ACCEPTED!!"

He then said to me, "You've just made my... *life!*"

4

One night during my final semester in high school, I met a female couple at a disco who happened to be seated at my table. Rico and BJ were supposedly out on a date, but Rico was very friendly and chatty. She introduced herself to everyone at the table. Rico was twenty-two years old; BJ was a few years older. Both of them were very beautiful. Rico had long, straight black hair, perfectly chiseled features, and an androgynous sexiness. BJ was more feminine, wearing a large afro and tight-fitting colorful clothes. Rico ordered a round of drinks and was enthusiastically bouncing to the music, her nipples protruding prominently under her thin spaghetti-strapped top. We danced to a few songs while BJ posed in her seat. At some point during the shouted conversation we learned that BJ's apartment was not far from my parents' house. We exchanged numbers and promised to stay in touch. The next day Rico called my parents' house and asked what I was doing, and offered to pick me up. My melodious laughter filled the house during our short conversation, which was something my mother had never heard.

"Who was that?!" my mother demanded after I got off the phone.

"Oh, a friend." I avoided her gaze.

"What friend? What's her name?"

"Rico."

"Rico? You haven't mentioned any 'Rico' before. Who are her parents?"

"Oh, Mom..." I got up and headed for my room. "I have to get dressed."

"Get dressed for what? Where do you think you're going? You don't have permission to take the car, young lady." She was bent on sabotaging any little bit of happiness that might come my way.

"I don't need the car," I yelled from my room. "She's picking me up."

That seemed to silence her for the moment. At least she knew better than to try to forbid me from leaving the house. I ran into the front yard as soon as I was dressed to avoid my mother's interrogation. A few minutes later, I heard a loud car engine approaching the house and then saw a white Stingray with red flames painted along the sides. The car slowed as it pulled in front of my parents' house. Sure enough, Rico was driving. She was alone. She motioned for me to get in. I'm sure my mother was watching from the front door, but I couldn't bring myself to look to see if she was there. The disapproval on her face would have ruined my afternoon. As we pulled away, I closed my eyes and imagined her smiling and being happy for me – something that, for whatever reason, she was incapable of doing.

We took a drive to Centennial Park, which had a reputation as a cruising-ground for queers. We parked the car and went for a walk around the lake and watched the heteros and their kids feed the ducks. Rico told me she was born in Mexico and her real name was Esther Peña.

"Folks around here can't say it right. They call it 'Peena' or 'Penne,' so I just tell 'em to call me Rico."

She was cute in the club, but she was absolutely breathtaking in the daylight, the sunshine sparkling off of her thick black hair, her nipples straining against her tight, skimpy top.

"That's a nice car you have there."

"Thanks. It's BJ's. D'you wanna go by her place later?"

"Sure. Why not?"

Was I feeling a slight tinge of disappointment that she didn't want to go somewhere to be alone with me? Or was that jealousy I was feeling? I couldn't really read her signals. She didn't touch me or make any kind of moves on me. She seemed to genuinely enjoy being outside in the open air, free from BJ's annoyed looks. I figured this was the time to get the scoop. "So BJ's your girlfriend?"

"Sometimes."

"What does that mean?"

Rico hesitated. "Brenda's okay to be around... when she's good," she gave a devilish smile. "But when she's had too much to drink, I don't wanna be around her."

"And how often does that happen?"

"Damn near every day!" She laughed and slapped her thigh. "She starts drinkin' malt liquor for breakfast." She was silent for a moment. "But Brenda's okay though. She lets me take the car whenever I want. Half the time she's too drunk to drive it."

While walking next to her I wondered if she could tell how lonely I was, how desperately I was craving her touch. I'd never had a boyfriend. Didn't want one.

"You stay away from those boys," my mother's hairdresser used to say to me. She was the one who straightened my hair with a hot-comb. "Those boys are just nuthin'. You hear me?!"

The braces had just recently come off of my teeth and I was still getting used to my new contact lenses. The kids at school had called me "ugly" for so long, I really had no sense of my own attractiveness. Whenever a boy asked me for "a chance," I thought it was a big joke and everyone was just waiting to laugh at me.

We eventually walked back to the car and headed to BJ's. By the time we got there, girlfriend was feeling no pain! When we walked in the door, she looked us up and down obviously assuming that we had already done the deed.

"So, where you been?" she snapped accusingly.

"We went to the park," Rico replied. "And can't you be polite? Invite her to sit down or something?"

BJ sauntered into the living room and pointed to the sofa.

"Ain't you got nothin' else to drink?" Rico called from the kitchen, the sounds of bottles clinking in the refrigerator filling the air.

"All I got is beer," she yelled back, then looked at me. "You wanna beer?"

"Sure. Thanks."

"Bring us two beers!" she yelled to the kitchen.

The sounds of rummaging continued.

"Ain't you got no chips or nuthin'?" Rico yelled.

BJ glared at me. "Now that bitch knows damn well I don't keep no food in this house. No, gyaddammit!" she yelled. "I ain't got no gyaddamn chips!! And hurry up with them beers 'cause I gotta go to work!"

So here was a nice segue into some potential conversation.

"So, what kind of work do you do?"

BJ looked at me, then giggled to herself.

"I'm in entertainment," she mumbled.

"Oh, the music business?"

Almost every other person in Nashville had something to do with the music business, but I hadn't met anyone who was black and in the biz. Country music was a white people's affair.

"No," she said. And that was it. Her tone made it clear that I wasn't supposed to ask questions.

Rico came in with the two bottles and put them on the coffee table. "So who you takin' care of today?"

BJ shrugged. "I dunno."

I eyed them back and forth, hoping I could figure out the mystery.

Rico observed me. "She has to go and take care of her girls. Whenever Junior calls..."

"Girl, shut up!" BJ spat. "This chile don't need to know 'bout my business."

But after two more beers, BJ was ready to spill the beans about her career. "See, when Junior's girls get horny, he calls me to... take care of 'em."

"And Junior is..."

"He a pimp! That fool ain't nuthin' but a nasty-ass pimp!"

"I see."

"And he be sittin' there wantin' some pussy so bad! Ha!"

I was horrified. "You mean he sits there and watches?"

BJ looked at me like I was from another planet. "Well if he payin', then he sho as hell gonna watch! And he be wantin' some pussy so bad!"

She cracked herself up again. Rico shook her head disapprovingly.

"Don't you be shakin' yo head at me! I think it's about time *you* went out and made some money!" Again, she looked at me, "And that bitch'll go out in the street. At least I ain't walkin' no streets!"

I was in way over my head with these girls. They couldn't have cared less about my piano playing or the fact that I'd been accepted at Curtis. I tried to be as polite as I could and waited for Rico to take me home. She got up to go to the bathroom and left me alone with BJ.

She took another swig of beer. "You know she shot a girl, don'tcha?"

I had just taken a swig and almost spat it out. "Uh... who?"

"Rico."

"She did? Why?"

"She don't like to talk about it, but yeah, she almost killed a girl. Don't tell her I told you."

I couldn't believe what I was hearing. My head was swimming and I felt slightly faint, then I realized that BJ was still talking.

"Yeah... she'll ask me, 'You want me to put on a dress and go out and make some money for you?' She crazy! She bought that car though."

At that moment the bathroom door opened and the sound of the flushing toilet drowned us out. Rico came into the room, took one look at me, and grew concerned.

"What are you talking about?" she asked BJ.

"Nuthin'," BJ shrugged.

She looked again at me. "What?"

I shrugged, suddenly afraid that my tongue was stuck to the roof of my mouth. She gave a dismissive wave and walked toward the kitchen.

"Don't listen to everything she say," she called out. "She a liar."

I soon learned why Rico was BJ's on again/off again girlfriend. It was because she had another girlfriend. This girl was still in high school and lived with her single mom in the projects. She was a tall, chocolate brown basketball player who was the star of her high school basketball team. When she didn't have BJ's car, Rico needed me to drive her to her other girlfriend's house in my father's car. Soon I was even picking BJ up from her job on the night shift at a shoe factory.

One day, out of the blue, Rico asked me during a phone conversation, "So... do you... uh... like me?"

After saying, "Of course I like you. What kind of question is that?" etc. etc., I asked her what she meant and she said, "Like, do you wanna have a relationship?" I was stunned. I knew she already had two girlfriends. What could she possibly want with me? (For God's sake! Say something, Nina!)

"Well... I know I'm leaving town soon for college, so... whatever we might have, it would have to be short."

"I know," she said. "I was just laying here, naked, thinking about you."

OMG! I didn't know what to say.

"Okay, Rico. I think I have to go now. It's late and I have school tomorrow."

"Okay, Baby. You sleep tight. And be sweet."

"Uh... okay. You too."

I was walking on air. Here this girl didn't even have a high school diploma and she had the power to make me feel ten feet tall. I invited her over for dinner and set up the TV trays outside to spare her from having to sit at the table with my mother, who would've chewed her up and spat her out. She would've blown a gasket if she had known the truth about Rico and BJ. I turned keeping my mouth shut and leaving the room into an art form.

• • • • •

The Nashville Youth Symphony sponsored a concerto competition during my senior year and I was picked as one of the winners. Up to this point I had performed the *Rhapsody in Blue*, Beethoven's Second Piano Concerto, and the MacDowell Piano Concerto with orchestra. This time I would perform the Grieg. Another prize winner was chosen to perform the first movement and I closed the program with the second and third movements. The concert took place in the auditorium at McGavock High School so it was gratifying to have so many of my high school colleagues in the audience as well as my clas-

sical/Blair colleagues, where many members of the Youth
Symphony studied. Our performance received a standing ovation and shouts of "Bravo." Backstage after the performance,
my mother was weeping because "the music was so beautiful." I guess it was supposed to be a compliment, but the sight
of my mother weeping was a frequent occurrence. I was tired
of her tears by that point.

As the day of my high school graduation approached, I was
ecstatic. Finally, the end of my imprisonment in my parents'
junky house was in sight. That day I wore a white dress (since
our caps and gowns were white) and a little bit of makeup. My
classmates had never seen me so dressed up. Some of them
barely recognized me. On my gown I also wore the gold rope
indicating my membership in the National Honor Society. During the course of the ceremony I was one of four students presented with a Faculty Award in recognition of my work as a
concert pianist. I thought surely my mother would be proud.
But no, she wasn't. She was full of complaints and criticisms
that day. I could not believe the intensity of her displeasure and
meanness. Here this was a day that I would remember for the
rest of my life, and she had to ruin it. It brought back memories
of the concert at Centennial Park when I was piano soloist with
the Nashville Symphony. Again, that was supposed to be my
big day, and she became so infantile backstage that I had to devote all of my energy to catering to her whims. The day of my
departure could not come soon enough.

Even today when I look at the pictures taken on that day,
my parents have beaming smiles and I'm looking confused
and bewildered. She put on that fake smile specifically to keep

anyone from thinking that she had done anything wrong. She was a master of manipulation.

A few days after my high school graduation, Rico and I went out to the club. We danced and drank and partied, and had a wonderful time. At some point during the evening she revealed that she and BJ had had a fight, and she asked if she could stay over at my place. I figured my parents would be asleep by the time we got home, so I told her it would be fine.

At the end of the evening we made our way home. I was always super cautious while driving after I'd had a few cocktails, so I drove at 30 MPH all the way home, even on the expressway.

The house was dark when we pulled into the driveway. We tried to be as quiet as possible but inevitably bumped into things and giggled our way into my bedroom. I cleared off the other twin bed and tried to make her comfortable. She sat on her bed, I sat on mine. We chatted and laughed and chatted some more.

Suddenly she said, "Oh! D'you still wanna see the gun?"

"Sure," I said.

Without hesitation she grabbed her bag, pulled the gun out, emptied the bullets from the chambers and threw them into the bag, closed it, and handed it to me. The reality that I had just brought an armed woman into my parents' house hadn't sunk in yet. I was still full of alcohol and enjoying the buzz. Leave it to my search for love to bring me into my first direct contact with a firearm. I held it and examined it, then quickly handed it back to her.

"How's the girl doing?" was all I could think to ask.

"What girl?"

"The girl who was shot."

"Oh, her. She's fine. You can hardly see the scar."

That was a relief. At least she wasn't a murderer, or at least as far as I knew.

She let out a yawn.

"You're tired," I said. "I'll turn out the light so we can get undressed."

"Okay," she said.

In the darkness, I giggled my way back to the bed. "Okay. I'm taking my top off now."

"Turn the light back on! I wanna see!"

We both laughed. "Okay. My jeans are coming off."

"That's not fair! I wanna *see!*"

After the laughter subsided, silence.

"What would you do if I came over there?" I shocked myself with my own boldness.

"I dunno," she said. More silence. Then she said, softly, "You can come over here if you want to."

If I want to?! I thought to myself.

"Okay," I said and jumped out of my bed and into hers.

As we lay side by side, naked, my mother's voice rang in my head. All she had ever said to me about sex was, "It's painful at first, but eventually it can become pleasurable." My mind raced with all of the rules I had heard about butches and femmes. I guessed I saw myself as a butch because I was attracted to femmes. But BJ was much more of a femme than Rico, yet Rico certainly was not a butch. And her other girlfriend – the high school basketball star – was much butcher than Rico.

She didn't do anything, so I asked, "So... whadya wanna do?"

"What do *you* want?"

"Well..." I thought for a while. "I'd really like to hold you."

She said, "Okay," and turned onto her side to face me.

God! She's gorgeous! I tried to put my arms around her and got momentarily confused trying to figure out which arm went underneath her and which went over or under hers. But eventually we figured it out. We fit. I was worried, embarrassed, and surprised at how much I was trembling. Once I finally got into her arms, I didn't want to let go. I felt I was holding on for dear life. Suddenly she pulled her head back and I saw that her lips were searching for mine. The softness of her lips, the slight brush of her tongue, the softness of her body, all of it was overwhelming me. My head started to swim. I was panting.

"Wait a minute. I gotta catch my breath."

She looked concerned. "You okay?"

"Yeah, I'm fine. I just need to catch my breath."

"Okay." She giggled to herself. "You know... you're so innocent." She sounded guilty.

"Really? What does that mean?"

"You're just ... so innocent."

I calmed myself enough to get back to what we were doing. I had always wanted to kiss a woman's breast and here was my chance. I leaned over and kissed her neck, her shoulders. It sounded like she was enjoying what I was doing as the little sounds indicative of pleasure escaped from her throat. I inched down further to the soft mound of flesh and rested on an erect nipple that slipped right into my mouth. She let out a deep moan. I kissed and licked lightly. Her breath quickened. I felt her hands on my back and on the back of my head, urging me to continue to apply more pressure. It was probably way too soft for her, but I was in such rapture and bliss. It was totally and completely overwhelming. This was the moment I had been waiting for, the act of physical love that I felt, in that moment, was giving me life. I had been walking around in a numbed-out haze up to this point. No more. Never again!

She shifted. "I wanna ask you a question." I was all ears. "I wanted to ask you... how do you feel about oral sex?"

Her voice brought me back to earth from my cloud. "Uh... I don't know. I've never done it. You don't have to."

I certainly didn't know the details of what oral sex entailed, but the sensation in my gut was so confusing and uncomfortable that I didn't feel I was ready for it. In truth, I was as ready as can be. But I didn't know at the time that this sensation actually meant that I was ready to have an orgasm. I probably assumed it was some kind of digestive trouble or that my period was coming. I kept holding her and holding her until finally I heard her slow, steady breathing and light snores. I didn't want to let her go, but my own exhaustion soon took hold. As the sky began to lighten, I returned to my own bed for a deep, sound sleep.

The next day I showed her some of my articles and awards. (Could this woman possibly *love* me?) She even tried on my cap and gown. "Maybe it'll make me smart," she said as she looked at herself in the mirror. As I was falling deeper and deeper in love, I guess she was realizing that she didn't fit in my world and was already planning her exit.

A few days later, Dr. Minton was hosting another one of the musical evenings which he was calling "Eine Klein Nacht Musik" (A Little Night Music) and again I was scheduled to play. But this time, after having made love for the first time, I thought that I could hear the difference in my playing. People even commented that I looked happier, more relaxed. If my mother overheard, she just frowned. I more or less kept my distance from her since she was complaining about one ailment after another. Her numerous prescriptions did not prevent her from drinking several glasses of champagne, however.

I tried to hang out with Rico or at least set up a time when we could be alone. She seemed to be keeping her distance. Then she finally confessed that she and BJ had made up and had gotten back together. I didn't know whether or not this meant that she and I could no longer see each other. I offered to pick both of them up. BJ wanted to stop by the liquor store. When she got out of the car, I asked Rico for a kiss. She just shook her head while staring straight ahead and then looked down at her lap guiltily. It looked like she had already been through the wringer with BJ. The last thing she needed was for this kid to be making more demands of her.

Suddenly a fury rose in me. I didn't say anything, but was totally shocked at the intensity of my feeling. BJ came back to the car and chatted in full self-absorption. Rico and I sat silently. I took them where they wanted to go and then drove home. I kept calling her and leaving messages which went unreturned. It was time to start thinking about what I would take with me for college, so I distracted myself with packing. We never said goodbye.

5

Arrival in Philadelphia

That summer while we were on our way to Long Island to visit my father's sister and her family, we stopped in Philadelphia to look for an apartment. After looking at a few expensive studios in rundown apartment houses, we decided on a studio in the Sylvania House just off of lower Broad Street. It was four blocks from Curtis and very affordable. My parents paid for one month's rent in advance of my planned arrival to hold the unit for me.

Later that August, they packed a U-Haul trailer full of stuff I didn't need and drove me to my first taste of freedom. I had already discovered that the neighborhood gay bookstore was right around the corner from my apartment. Three women's bars were within walking distance. I was ready!

One of my early memories of that bookstore (called Giovanni's Room) was a reading presented by Rita Mae Brown. I'd already found a copy of *Rubyfruit Jungle* in Nashville and here was my chance to have her sign it. She held my hand a little too long while shaking it, enough to make me blush. Thanks to Giovanni's Room, I discovered the writings of Alice Walker, Ann Shockley, James Baldwin, et al. I was so naïve when I arrived in Philly that I didn't even know that *Giovanni's Room* was the title of one of James Baldwin's books.

When I first arrived in Philly – home of the world-renowned Philadelphia Orchestra – the word on the street was that the famed conductor Leopold Stokowski was on his deathbed. It was Leopold who turned the Philadelphia Orchestra into a world-class organization and will be forever known as the Maestro who shook hands with Mickey Mouse in the Disney movie *Fantasia*.

Eugene Ormandy was conductor when I arrived and held the position until his retirement in 1980 when he was succeeded by Riccardo Muti. Often I would pass Maestro Ormandy on Locust Street on my way to school and would say "Good morning" to him, hoping he would remember my face and engage me one day to be a future soloist with his orchestra.

Soon after my arrival at Curtis, I was approached by a tall black female violist who would become my best friend. Sharon Ray picked up a viola while in high school to play in the local youth orchestra in her hometown of Kansas City, and then held the first chair position in the Curtis Symphony Orchestra. Sharon had floor-to-ceiling stereo speakers in her downtown apartment and turned me on to Wagner and Strauss operas, Mahler symphonies, and Oscar Peterson. Since she was very social with the orchestra players, I was invited to parties where the bong was passed, the lights were inevitably turned off, and Brahms, Mahler, and Tchaikovsky symphonies were blasted from the speakers. All of us swooned in silence. One of our friends upon graduation only auditioned for a post in the Columbia, South America Symphony. The reason why, you can guess: He intended to live out his professional life in a land where he would have easy-access to top-quality weed.

Sharon had a membership at a nearby YMCA, to which she invited me for an afternoon. I was fascinated with the workout equipment and promptly threw out my back while doing bench-presses. I found a chiropractor who took some X-rays and snapped my spine back into place. This was the first time I saw an X-ray of my spine. The doctor pointed out to me that I had a severe curvature in my lower spine. He said it was indicative of bad posture from a young age. The "S" shape of my spine had grown with my body as I matured. I immediately thought of all of those years of sitting on the piano bench as a child with no back support. No one observed my posture. They were too busy listening for wrong notes.

Sharon was booked for several freelance gigs in Philly and Atlantic City. One booking was for the back-up orchestra for the Donna Summer concert at the Academy of Music. Donna Summer was at the height of her fame, so this concert was a big deal! I went backstage to visit Sharon after the concert and was approached by a large black man who started chatting with me. (Little did I know that he was actually hitting on me.) He offered me two tickets for the show the following evening. Later I learned that this man was actually Donna Summer's brother. Even Teddy Pendergrass was in the audience that night. He walked right past me with his very large, black female bodyguards.

The décor of the Common Room of the Curtis Institute of Music reflected Old World money and attitudes. The oriental rugs and Dutch paintings served as constant reminders of why we were there: to uphold Old World values. As usual, I was the only black female piano student enrolled at Curtis. There was one other black female soprano, Daisy Newman, in the opera division and two black female string players – Sharon and violinist Diane Monroe, who is now an amazing jazz violinist and has toured widely with the Diane Monroe String Quartet. Her quartet – then called the "Uptown String Quartet" – appeared and performed on an episode of *The Cosby Show* in the 1980s.

Wednesday afternoons, all students would meet in the Common Room for tea poured by the elderly daughter-in-law of founder Mary Curtis Bok. Every time she saw me, she asked what instrument I played and how long I had studied there. And I saw her every week!

I noticed early on that most of the female piano students were very expensively dressed. Many of them were Korean and I would learn later that they came from very wealthy families. I had never really developed any sense of style while living in Nashville because my parents rarely took me shopping. My mother had always picked out my clothes based on what was on sale. The first time I set foot in a department store in Philadelphia and saw how much some of those dresses cost, I couldn't believe my eyes! There was no way I could afford to dress like those girls. As much as my parents went on about how little money we had, I thought it would please them that I wasn't interested in clothes. I would find out later that they weren't always truthful about their financial status, to me, at least. It was just another manipulation designed to keep me from asking for material things.

My class schedule was intensive. I had my weekly piano lesson with my primary teacher, Eleanor Sokoloff, Keyboard Studies and Score Reading with Dr. Ford Lallerstedt, Music Theory with David Loeb, and Ear Training with Miss Klar. Having the grand piano in my studio apartment meant that I never had to worry about finding a practice room. I took advantage of the opportunity to learn copious amounts of repertoire, including Beethoven's "Appassionata" and "Waldstein" Sonatas, Chopin's F minor Ballade, the Tchaikovsky and Brahms D minor concerti.

I thought that studying at the Curtis Institute meant that I was well on my way to establishing a solo career. However, my primary teacher, Eleanor Sokoloff, had other plans. She made it clear in my first lesson that she would not listen to any repertoire. She would only hear me play scales, arpeggios, and Pischna exercises, which were some of the most boring exercises ever written. Mrs. Sokoloff had a very loud, almost screeching voice that I found to be very intimidating. Her comments could be quite rude at times. No one had ever spoken to me this way before. I was quite disheartened at the thought of having this woman as my teacher for the next four years.

Welcome to Curtis!

That year there was a story being whispered among the students about a female piano major who had practiced and learned the Brahms Second Piano Concerto over the summer. Her teacher was Mieczyslaw Horszowski. When she brought this piece into her first lesson of the school year, Mr. Horszowski refused to hear it.

"A woman cannot play this piece," he said.

At the time, the man was eighty-six years old. Did he not know that Johannes Brahms composed the piece for Clara Schumann to premier and perform? The poor student had no recourse. There was no one to whom she could complain. One can only hope that the students at Curtis today are not subjected to such sexism.

I didn't have a TV in my little studio apartment, so I listened to Mumia Abu Jamal's sultry, sexy voice and Donna Summer's new disco hits on the radio. I also listened to the classical music station and heard lots of the recordings by the Philadelphia Orchestra.

Being a student at Curtis meant that we were given free tickets for orchestra concerts, so my repertoire of orchestral scores blossomed. I attended those concerts religiously. I still had not seen a woman conduct, but it never occurred to me that the field was closed to women. I naïvely assumed that with enough training and preparation, the doors would be wide open to me. Since I had sat in on so many orchestral rehearsals – both as a piano soloist and in the audience – I was well aware of the kind of personality it took to command the respect of so many accomplished musicians. They needed to know that their conductor respected and cared for them, but they also needed to be slightly fearful of his or her wrath. It was a delicate, delightful balance. I couldn't wait to get my hands on an orchestra.

As it was Riccardo Muti's first season as music director, I even had the opportunity to speak with him backstage after the concerts. It was during one of those backstage visits when pianist Rudolf Serkin told me, "Oh, yes! Margie told me about you."

I made friends quickly and easily at Philadelphia's women's bars. There was a place called Sneakers not far from the river, a place on Front Street, and the PBL Club just four or five blocks from my building. Since I was totally inexperienced at dating, it took me a while to pick up on the signals someone may have sent out indicating that she was interested. One young lady, a model and also a newcomer to Philly, invited me to her apartment for a visit. She had a gay male roommate whose boyfriend happened to stop by. She had gone into the bathroom to take a shower. Afterwards, she was standing at the sink combing her hair, stark naked. I must have been staring at her for quite some time because when I looked back at her roommate and his guest, they had begun making out and gradually taking each other's clothes off. The next thing I knew, Lori, still naked, came over, sat next to me on the sofa, and placed her hand on my thigh. She was a femme, so I guessed she was waiting for me to kiss her. As her face inched closer to mine, I summoned my courage and placed my lips lightly upon hers. Yep! I was right. She clasped my head with her hands and kissed me passionately, pressing her naked breasts against me. We re-positioned ourselves so that I was on my back and she on top of me. Quite some time must have passed because the next time I looked over at the boys, they were totally naked and fully at it. I had never seen a man perform fellatio on another man before, so it was quite a learning experience for me. Suddenly I realized that I was sweating profusely, so my own clothes started coming off. What an afternoon that was! Lori and I would make love for a while, then take a break and watch the boys for inspiration.

I'm sure they watched us too, when they took a break. They stayed on the floor mat and we stayed on the sofa, so there was no co-mingling of bodily fluids. But all four of us felt that we had bonded somehow after that day.

Lori and I met a few more times after that. She knew I was preoccupied with school so I really didn't have that much time for a full-blown romance. During our affair however, I became aware of the fact that I was not having orgasms. I really didn't know what a female orgasm was but I knew that I was not experiencing what the adult film actresses were pretending to experience. I set out to read every book I could find on the subject, including *Our Bodies Ourselves*, *Sapphistry*, *The Joy of Sex*, and *The Female Orgasm*.

One evening while I was on my way to Lori's apartment, a young man started following me. He was calling out to me while walking with his bicycle. I tried to ignore him until he came up next to me and put his hand on my body. I smacked his hand away and said, "Leave me alone!" and started walking faster. When I got to Lori's building, I ran up the steps and into the vestibule to ring her buzzer. He was right behind me. He dropped his bike on the steps and came in after me, where I was trapped waiting for Lori to buzz me in.

He slammed me against the wall with his body and proceeded to grope me and grab at my crotch. This had never happened to me before. My first instinct was to fight him off. It took a few seconds before I realized that I could scream. When I released the sound from my throat, he let me go and ran off. I stood there in stunned silence, picked up my white hat from the floor, and hit the buzzer for Lori's apartment again.

They both took one look at me when I came inside and grew concerned. I hadn't realized when I put my hat back on that it was dirty and smudged. When I told them what had happened, he called the police right away. Lori and her roommate were both white, so they had no qualms about calling the police. I wasn't particularly emotional or hysterical at all. Just numb. Stunned. I couldn't believe I had just been attacked, in fact almost raped. I described my assailant to the police. Within a few minutes they were at Lori's apartment. Her roommate had quickly removed all of the bongs, pipes, and weed paraphernalia that happened to be laying around. I felt bad for causing them so much trouble. The policemen asked me to come with them. They walked me to the back of a police van and opened the door. There was my assailant with his bicycle, crying like a baby. A policeman told me that they had seen us on the street, and they had seen that I was clearly scared because I was walking so fast. When the call came in, they knew exactly who they were looking for.

They took me to the police station to file the report. I sat alone in an office for what seemed like hours until a tall, beautiful black woman walked in to take down my account of what happened. She was dressed – there is no way to say this politely – like a hooker. It was already well after midnight so I guess she had been "walking the beat" as they say. She wrote down the details and then a kind policeman drove me back to my building. I never made it out to the club that night. I wrote down everything that happened as soon as I got home in case I had to testify. On the day we were scheduled to appear in court, I informed my teachers that I'd have to miss class that day, gathered up my notes, made my way to the court house, and sat and waited for my case to be called. One of the staffers told me that my case was being postponed. I would receive a notice in a few days telling me the new date and time.

Weeks later I received the notice, went through the whole rigmarole again, all for nothing. Three times my case was postponed and all three times the defendant and his attorney hadn't shown. The fourth time, he was there cleanly shaven in a coat and tie along with his shifty, twitching defense attorney.

I was glad I had my notes, but I really didn't need them because the events of that evening were branded on my brain. The defense attorney took my notes as "evidence." It really shocked me how much time he focused on what I was wearing and the fact that I'd been wearing contact lenses that night. (I was wearing my glasses in court that day.) There was an audience of creepy voyeurs. I was by myself because it hadn't even occurred to me to ask anyone to accompany me. Even my parents didn't know about what had happened.

The female judge found my assailant guilty of indecent assault, asked him to apologize to the court, and sentenced him to counseling and probation. He was a juvenile (which I didn't know before that day), so his sentence took his youth into consideration. Never again was I able to take it for granted that I should be able to walk from here to there without being assaulted. I immediately bought myself a can of mace.

• • • • •

With contralto Marian Anderson

That year Marian Anderson was a Kennedy Center Honoree and would receive the medal from President Jimmy Carter. The event was being broadcast live from the Kennedy Center in Washington and Miss Anderson actually called me in my little studio apartment to tell me to watch. She asked how it was going at Curtis. I guess she could tell from my voice that I wasn't terribly enthusiastic. She told me to wear pretty dresses and to keep my chin up. I didn't have the heart to tell her that I didn't wear pretty dresses.

Marian Anderson had enjoyed success and fame in Europe in the 1930s and was almost worshipped as a goddess in Sweden, where she met and sang for famed pianist Arthur Rubinstein. He wrote in his second autobiography *My Many Years* just after he had signed a contract with concert impresario Sol

Hurok for a third American tour, "Suddenly at that point I thought of Marian Anderson. My enthusiasm for her had had great results. She had an immediate overwhelming success wherever the managers engaged her on my recommendation. I told all that to Hurok. 'You ought to present her in America,' I said, 'I vouch for her triumph. She is the greatest Lieder singer I have ever heard.' He made a sour face. 'Colored people do not make it with the box office,' he said in his professional lingo. But he was visibly impressed by my insistence. He left for Amsterdam to hear her sing and signed a contract the same night."

Sol Hurok secured the engagement for Anderson to sing on the steps of the Lincoln Memorial before an audience of over 100,000 after the Daughters of the American Revolution had refused to allow her to sing at Constitution Hall – which they owned – because of her race. That concert marked the turning point in Hurok's career.

The year was 1937 and Rubinstein had already noticed tensions and violence perpetrated by Hitler's Nazis against the Jews throughout Germany, Poland, Hungary, and Romania. As he lived in France, he himself would be directly affected by this surge in hatred only a few years later. I don't know if Rubinstein was aware of the fact that audiences in our nation's capital were segregated until Marian Anderson's groundbreaking concert at the Lincoln Memorial. President Franklin Delano Roosevelt used this concert as a propaganda ploy to solicit "Negro" participation in and enthusiasm for the Second World War. After all, how could he justify sending black troops to defeat the Nazis while racism prevailed at home? Mrs. Roosevelt resigned from the DAR after witnessing their embarrassing behavior.

Violinist Fritz Kreisler was on the side of the Germans during World War I, so it should have come as no surprise that Kreisler played for segregated audiences. In the 1920s there was outrage in the black community of Charleston, West Virginia – my mother's birthplace – when Kreisler was engaged to give a concert but blacks were not allowed to purchase tickets. My uncle Howard, who was still a young boy and burgeoning violinist, was given a ticket and was thus able to attend. My maternal grandparents, along with other African-American community leaders, took out a full-page ad in the local newspaper protesting this blatant discrimination. Kreisler brought his racist leanings to the United States where racism, segregation, and discrimination were already flourishing but on a different level than his German anti-Semitism. He was one of a few individuals who spread their racist filth all over the globe.

When African-American soldiers liberated the German and Polish concentration camps, they were praised as heroes by the Jews. But when these men returned to the United States hoping that their patriotism would grant them equality in their homeland, they were greeted with the same indignities that they had endured before they left. My own father told a story of being mistakenly put in charge of a group of white soldiers during the Second World War and being responsible for getting them from Boston to Virginia. He sat panicking for the whole train ride, wondering what he would do when they reached the Mason-Dixon Line where he would be required by law to sit in a segregated "Jim Crow" car. He continued to panic until they disembarked without incident. But this was the kind of humiliation American soldiers had to endure well into the 1940s and beyond.

Now the Trump administration and the Republicans are bent on destroying the gains African-Americans have made over decades. To watch them in action is truly nauseating, and many of his followers don't even know why they need to hate scapegoats so much. Such people seem to need to feel superior to someone else in order to feel secure. They haven't even bothered to figure out why they have chosen a particular target. It is most unfortunate. But I digress.

• • • • •

I saw on the Philadelphia Orchestra schedule that operatic tenor Seth McCoy was scheduled to appear for a concert, so I wrote to him to ask if he'd like to meet. He invited me to lunch at one of downtown Philadelphia's most expensive restaurants. We had a lovely chat and a delightful meal. When he saw that Curtis was getting me down, he became angry.

"Don't you let those people break you down. They make me sick!" he hissed under his breath.

He then gave me the whole story about how some American opera houses refused to cast him as the romantic lead with a white soprano. His anger surprised me, since he was a success. My father had never shown such functional, targeted anger. He would waste so much energy on talking himself out of his anger that he was totally blocked. Then his anger would spew out in uncontrollable, dysfunctional tantrums, usually directed at females. I never saw my father go off on a man.

Sylvia Olden Lee was a premiere vocal coach who was on the faculty at Curtis. In 1933 she was invited to play at the White House for the inauguration of President Franklin Delano Roosevelt. In 1942 she toured with baritone/film star Paul Robeson as his official piano accompanist, and in 1954 she was hired as vocal coach for the Metropolitan Opera. She coached opera stars Kathleen Battle and Jessye Norman. Her husband, Everett Lee, was an internationally acclaimed orchestral conductor who made his home in Sweden. He was the first African American to conduct a Broadway musical, the first to conduct an established symphony orchestra below the Mason-Dixon Line, and the first to conduct a performance by a major U.S. opera company. I had heard him conduct the Nashville Symphony before I left there.

Sylvia Olden Lee was also a dear friend of my mother's. Her father, James Clarence Olden, was a member of the Fisk Jubilee Quartet, which included tenor Roland Hayes. She and my mother were both Oberlin alumni and her daughter Eve had accepted a faculty position at Fisk for a semester. Mrs. Lee came to Nashville to visit when her daughter was establishing herself there and I remember her as having a delightful sense of humor.

During one of my boring lessons of playing Pischna exercises, Mrs. Sokoloff blurted out, "That Sylvia Lee has been asking me and the director why you and Graydon Goldsby [the other black piano student] aren't participating in the concerto competition."

Every year the Philadelphia Orchestra would sponsor a concerto competition for young artists. The winners would perform with the orchestra.

Mrs. Sokoloff continued, "When she goes off the deep end, watch out! I told her you weren't participating because you weren't ready."

Well part of the reason why I wasn't ready was because you only allowed me to play scales and arpeggios and Pischna exercises! How dare you?! Sylvia Olden Lee was reacting to the racism that we encounter every day. I kept my mouth shut because this woman had complete power over me. But I never forgot how this white woman felt totally free to disparage this family friend without fear of complaints or reprimand.

And by the way – Graydon Goldsby was a genius. He studied piano with Jorge Bolet and was one of the most talented musicians I ever heard. I had heard a while ago that he had moved to Sweden or Norway where he was enjoying success (and he was a very dark man). Just recently, when I Googled him, I saw that there was an outstanding warrant in Philadelphia for his arrest. The Philadelphia Police Department had seen him as just another black male deserving of arrest and incarceration. No wonder he left this country.

Sharon Ray graduated at the end of that academic year. After graduation, she went on a series of auditions for various American orchestras but no one would hire her – the first chair violist of the Curtis Symphony Orchestra! The resulting frustration – along with physical struggles to adjust to a different-sized viola assigned to her by her teacher – took its toll on her body and morphed into a full-blown case of tendonitis to the point where she could barely pick up her instrument. Years later, she taught herself to play the electric bass and slayed globally with rock and funk bands in addition to having regular gigs in Las Vegas and Los Angeles. Within the past few years she picked up the viola again and has been performing with orchestras and chamber groups in the Los Angeles area.

Toward the end of the school year, Eleanor Sokoloff informed me that she was not going to renew my scholarship for the following year. In other words, she was kicking me out. She allowed me to prepare to audition for other faculty members before the end of the year, but I'm sure she made it clear to them that I was not to be re-admitted. Since I was preparing a program, she submitted to listening to repertoire. Thank God! If I'd had to play another Pischna exercise, I would have passed out. I prepared the Chopin F minor Ballade and the Beethoven Waldstein Sonata for performance. Mrs. Sokoloff agreed to listen to my program one last time before I played for Horoszowski and Bolet.

When I finished the Chopin, she said, "I could kick you in the stomach!"

"Excuse me?"

"I could kick you in the stomach! If I had known you could play like that, I never would have revoked your scholarship."

I couldn't believe what she was saying to me. *She* was the one who had refused to listen to any repertoire all year. And now she's shocked that I can play?!

"Well it's too late now. There's nothing I can do," she said.

I left her studio hoping that I would never have to look at her old, wrinkled face again. Later I would learn that she had made a habit of kicking young girls out of Curtis. She had ruined so many careers and no one ever questioned her actions. My mother had even come to ask her face to face exactly what the problem was. I observed them from a distance in the Common Room. My mother told me that all Mrs. Sokoloff could talk about was what I wore. She was a pro at this so she totally dominated the conversation. I was quite surprised that my mother was so quiet.

I had read in Arthur Rubinstein's *My Young Years* of his encounter with a teacher in Berlin who was so embittered that he set out to sabotage careers of young pianists. Whether it is conscious or not, such creatures exist and school administrators should be very careful when hiring teachers who literally hold the futures of these young artists in their hands. Eleanor Sokoloff had been a fossil dating back to the days of the Curtis founder, Mary Curtis Bok. Most of the people of that generation did not believe in civil rights or equality for African Americans. Such people got their kicks out of taking on a student just to destroy him or her, and they know full well that the shame of being kicked-out would force the victim to keep his or her mouth shut. It took a lot of work for me to overcome Sokoloff's mistreatment and verbal abuse. Unfortunately, I have heard that she set out to ruin many more careers. As I write this, she is over one hundred years old and still torturing students.

Mrs. Sokoloff did have some students who weren't necessarily so talented, but she liked them nonetheless. I learned later that these students had wealthy parents who often wined and dined both of the Sokoloffs. Her husband Vladimir was also on the faculty and supervised much of the chamber music at Curtis, so I saw him there often. He was very chummy with then director John de Lancie. These parents often paid for private lessons and also made of habit of presenting Mrs. Sokoloff with expensive gifts. Since my parents could not afford to play this game, it was clear that I was going to have to find someone who could.

Years later, I would learn of the heartbreak suffered by pianist/songstress Nina Simone inflicted by the Curtis Institute of Music. She came with her family to audition for admittance to Curtis, but was rejected. As a result, she was forced to take a job in a nightclub in Atlantic City to support her family. At first, she played the piano wearing concert gowns, but the manager forced her to sing and threatened to fire her if she didn't. She was an extremely talented pianist and had said that she wanted a concert career. The National Association of Negro Musicians gave her some support, but it was not enough to launch a classical career in a field where whites made all of the decisions. It should come as no surprise that she sang the Blues so well.

6

Since Curtis did not have a bachelor's degree program, my parents insisted that I pursue a degree at Temple University, where the esteemed African-American pianist Natalie Hinderas was on the faculty. I was still giving concerts and performing with orchestras, but for my academic parents, a bachelor's degree was absolutely necessary. It was at Temple where I stood before an orchestra as conductor for the first time, as a student in Jonathan Sternberg's Orchestral Conducting class with members of the Temple University Orchestra. The very first time I stood on the podium conducting Schubert's "Unfinished" Symphony, the professor commented that I had the right "look" for the position. I was home!

Returning to Nashville for the Christmas holidays and the summers was always an ordeal. In my absence, my parents' hoarding got out of control. You couldn't even walk through the den or their bedroom. Magazines and newspapers and junk were everywhere. We couldn't host any guests because there was no place for them to sit. I had to meet my old friends outside of the house, which meant that I was often at the club or at Fisk or Blair, just to get away. I would spend the holidays

Natalie Hinderas

cleaning my parents' house. I never knew what the phrase "Coming home for a rest" meant.

Not long after I met Lori, I met another young lady at the women's bar in Philadelphia, let's call her Joan. I had begun to notice familiar faces at the bar on the weekends and Joan was one of them. I don't remember who approached whom or how we started that first conversation, but we kept running into each other. She revealed that she had a car and would offer to drop me off at my door.

Since Philadelphia was so close to Atlantic City, Joan offered to drive me and some other friends to spend an evening there. I had never been to Atlantic City, so I was curious to see the famed Boardwalk. That particular weekend the Miss America Pageant was taking place, so the hotels and restaurants were filled to capacity. There was a popular women's discotheque in Atlantic City to which Joan had planned to take us, so she parked the car and all of us made our way to the club. To my surprise, many of the pageant contestants were there on the dance floor having a good ole time. They were embracing and kissing, and bumpin' and grindin'. If I hadn't witnessed it with my own eyes, I wouldn't have believed that the future Miss America could have been a lesbian!

Toward the end of the evening, Joan was visibly annoyed and moody. I had no idea of what her problem was. Maybe it was because she had to stay sober because she was driving. The rest of us were drinking and dancing and flirting, but Joan sat in a corner by herself, clearly in a funk. Weeks later I would learn that she was more interested in me than she had ever expressed. Joan was very feminine and stylish, but rather cold. She was dropping me off at my apartment for months before she hinted that she wanted to be more than friends. I had had no idea. She had given me no indication that she was interested. But one night, during our regular good night kiss on the cheek in the front seat of her car, I noticed that she was trying to kiss me on the lips. I was already pulling away when I noticed this and she just looked embarrassed. But when I leaned in again for another kiss, it became a very long, full on, deep tongue, French kiss. I remember saying to her, "I didn't know you could do that."

Joan had studied photography at the Philadelphia School of Visual Arts. When I met her, she was running a photography studio at a suburban department store. She was still living with her parents and drove for nearly an hour to get home after leaving the club at 2:00 am. She had a very large

Labrador Retriever who needed to be walked when she got home, so there was no possibility of her spending the night anywhere else.

Joan had a close friend who lived just a few blocks away from me in Center City. Deb had also studied photography at the SVA and was living with her boyfriend. She used Joan as a model for some of her photography projects. I guess Joan and Deb had spent a lot of time talking about me, since Deb was full of questions for me when we met. She knew that Joan was not an aggressor, so she would need some help.

The three of us would go out to the club and I could have sworn that Deb was the one who was actually hitting on me. She was even more stylish than Joan and very flirtatious. Joan always struck me as being rather sad. She had lived in New Orleans for a while, working as a waitress in drag bars. She had told me something about being coerced into a sex act by a so-called male friend. Later I realized that she was trying to tell me that she had been raped. At the time, I didn't really know how to respond to such information. But looking back, it is clear that she was still affected by the trauma.

Deb also had her share of trauma. She and her boyfriend decided that they would have both of us over, get us drunk, and push us into the bed. Well, all of us ended up getting drunk and all of us ended up in bed. Ted had a hunch that Deb was fantasizing about being with a woman, so it turned him on to watch his girlfriend play with Joan and me. I don't think Deb did very much with Joan, but she was sure as hell all over me. I looked up to see her breasts in my face and her nipple being pressed into my mouth. She was moaning and sighing and having a great time. Then suddenly, she went somewhere else. All of a sudden she was crying and calling out some man's name (a name of someone who was not there) and whimpering, "Stop! Please stop!" I was too drunk to fully comprehend what was happening, but Joan and Ted were shaking her and calling her name. Later I would learn that she had gone into flashback and that she had been molested as a child by a man with that name.

After such an inauspicious beginning to our intimate relationship, Joan made arrangements to spend the night at my place, which meant that someone else had to walk her dog. We began a relationship that lasted maybe ten months until she cheated on me with another employee at the department store. I was really too young for her; she was twenty-six and I was eighteen. She liked having the illusion of control by virtue of being so much older than I was. But intellectually we weren't on the same page. I wanted to go to Philadelphia Orchestra concerts and she was content going to a jazz club. She was snippy and sarcastic and I was hopelessly and youthfully optimistic. She also insisted on calling herself "bi," even though we were supposed to be in a monogamous relationship. Her only ambition was to be an "escort" for rich men and to be taken to fancy parties and formal events. I hoped that she was joking when she said this, but something told me that she wasn't.

When I moved out of my studio apartment at the Sylvania House, I moved into Joan's parents' house for a few weeks. Her mom was pleasant and her dad was very funny. Of course, I fell in love with the dog. It turned out that her uncle had a small house that he was renting and he agreed to let us take it. Within a month of our living together, she started her fling with her work colleague. This butch girl had a flashy sports car and Joan liked being driven around in it. When I found out about the affair, of course it was a big drama. She wanted to go off and spend the night with her, which meant that she intended for me to walk her dog. I wasn't having it. So she put me out of the house and took my keys. I went next door and called the police. I got back into the house that night, but moved out within a week. Later I heard that she and the new girl had broken up violently within a month. I never saw her again.

I temporarily moved into an apartment house with Sharon Ray and her housemate for a while. Thanks to Sharon and Helena, I was invited to so many house parties that it was hard to keep up. These women were culturally diverse. There was a women's choir that gave regular concerts annually and the after-parties were always extravaganzas. After the first relationship left such a bad taste in my mouth, I pretty much steered clear of them for the rest of my time in Philly. Mind you, I had plenty of flings, but no steady girlfriend.

Then I found a live-in babysitting job with a friend of the daughter of friends of my parents in Nashville. This lady was a widow and had two teenage daughters. They lived in a large stone mansion in Germantown. Her husband had turned the third floor of their house into his office. He was an attorney. He had been dead for several years and they still had not cleaned out the space. I cleaned it in less than a week. My room had a fireplace and I had a private bathroom at the end of the hall. There were also a swimming pool and tennis court on the grounds, and a grand piano in the living room. There were two dogs and two cats. The dogs usually left piles of crap on the living room rug, which I had to clean. One cat had turned the fireplace in my room into his own personal litter box. There must have been two years' worth of dried poop in that fireplace. Even after I had cleaned it out and put up the screen, the cat had to try one last time to make his mark, and wounded himself in the process when he knocked the screen down. I cleaned it again, fastened the screen more securely, and made sure that the door to my room was closed when I left the house.

Even though the two girls were fatherless, they were extremely privileged. They were part of a prominent Jewish family in Philadelphia. Their mother and grandmother would give them everything they asked for, and they were told repeatedly how beautiful they were by both women. I often wondered what kind of personality and self-esteem I could have developed if I had been raised like this. It was a constant struggle to remind their mother that I was there because I was a full-time student and my class schedule interfered with my ability to be on hand to pick up and drop off the girls at their whims. They had a full-time maid, yet I was expected to cook (sometimes) and clean the kitchen. The mother was quite comfortable with throwing tantrums, which made my situation even more precarious. Once she made a "joke" to a friend of hers about how "Nina does the work and I crack the whip. Right, Nina?" I was setting the table and pretended not to hear. She was right in that I received no pay for my work – just room and board.

There were no union rules or workers' manual for my labor. My "employer" was free to use me however she pleased.

After moving into my new living situation, I soon learned that my house was not far from the home of Dr. Maurice Clifford, then-president of the Medical College of Pennsylvania. Dr. Clifford's wife, Patricia Johnson, was the daughter of former Fisk president Charles S. Johnson and the aunt of Secretary of Homeland Security under President Obama, Jeh Johnson. She and my mother were dear friends. The Cliffords had a grand piano in their living room and invited me to come and practice as often as I needed. They also provided some greatly appreciated meals.

During that first year at Temple, my friend Rene Swartz asked me to act as music director for a stage production of Ted Tiller's *Count Dracula*, which she was directing. I had not done much composing since there were so many notes written by other people swimming around in my head. But Rene asked me to compose the music for a choir of vampiric "angels" praising their leader. Since I grew up sitting in on Fisk Jubilee Singers rehearsals, four-part harmony arrangements were a piece of cake for me. I molded a melody around the Latin text of a chorus in praise of Lucifer, as Rene requested. I also directed the choir during rehearsals. Shortly before opening night, a camera crew from the local television news station came to cover the dress rehearsal and promote the production. It was truly an honor to hear my own music broadcast on TV that night.

Meanwhile, I was establishing myself at Temple University. I was learning bushels of repertoire and taking a full academic course-load. They had even designed a required physics class for music majors: Acoustics. Freshman Composition helped my writing skills and an African-American Literature class turned me on to the likes of Countee Cullen and Zora Neale Hurston. My inability to sight-read made life difficult for me because, as a piano major, I was required to accompany voice majors and instrumentalists every semester. Some of the white faculty didn't want to believe that my difficulty with sight-reading was real, since they all had heard me perform. The only one who tried to help me was Lambert Orkis, who went on to enjoy international fame as piano accompanist for violinist Anne-Sophie Mutter.

Saxophonist Grover Washington Jr. was a student in the graduate program at Temple while I was there. He was a tall, beautiful man, and I'm sure that he usually avoided eye-contact with black females out of fear of not being able to get rid of them. Eventually, as he began to recognize mine as a familiar face, he and I would say hello to each other. He had an absolutely gorgeous saxophone case with a beautiful African design made from black and brown leather. The rumor was that the white faculty was extremely rude to him when it came to scheduling his audition. He was on tour during the regular audition dates and some were trying to delay his admittance. He was credited with the line, "They can go and buy my records."

I knew that pianist Leon Bates had been a protégé of Natalie Hinderas' and was living in Philadelphia. We had remained in contact since his concert at Fisk, so once I was settled in at my new live-in babysitting position, I gave him a call. He came over for lunch and some tennis, revealing his bulging muscles in a tight-fitting t-shirt. We had a delightful time. We even played some pieces for each other. He was a very serious musician and was very devoted to producing a top-quality sound on the instrument. Years later I was happy to see his music video of the first movement of the Gershwin Concerto in F with the Basel Symphony Orchestra. So they made him out to be a boxer and put a concert grand in a boxing ring. So what! At least he had a classical music video. Later that year Leon was asked to fill in at the last minute for pianist André Watts, who could not present his recital at the Academy of Music that night. It was a huge opportunity for Leon Bates and he performed masterfully.

My relationship with my parents improved greatly after I left their house. At least I was no longer bombarded with having to look at all of their junk. I was free to go to the club whenever I wanted and to pick up whomever I wanted. I could practice without her criticisms and corrections being shouted from the back room. And, I think, the fact that I was no longer there meant that they were left to take their frustrations out on each other.

Unfortunately, it became clear to me that my parents really weren't interested in how I was. Their weekly phone calls were geared toward gathering as much information as they could on my concerts and contracts so they could brag to their friends at church about my activities. I was so accustomed to keeping my personal life a secret that they simply took it for granted that I didn't have one. Little did they know that I was building a very large circle of friends within Philadelphia's women's community.

I began sharing with some of my closest friends about my struggles with achieving orgasm. They were very sympathetic, and the project of "Nina's First Orgasm" became a community affair. One friend had just bought a new vibrator so she gave me her old one – just the external kind, not the kind you insert. Then another friend gave me some erotica and sexy magazines, and another friend gave me some silk scarves and feathers and oils. I put all of my gifts to use and set out to conquer this obstacle. The first night, I came close. My breathing quickened, I started sweating, and that sensation took over my pelvic area. The feelings were so intense that it frightened me. I stopped myself, but knew I was on the verge of something new and dangerous. The next night, the same things happened and I was determined to ride it out, "to see what the end will be," to quote the Spiritual. The sensation mounted. I rode the wave and came out on the other side. OH MY GOD! It was a full-on, earth-quaking, soul-shaking, gut-trembling orgasm! So this was what all the excitement was about. Suddenly I understood Wagner operas – all of the build-up and anticipation, then it would pull back and start up again, etc. I lay there and wept. Within a few seconds I had vivid memories from when I was in nursery school. I remembered being shamed by the cook who caught me during nap time with my hands in my pants. She scolded me and said, "You stop that!" with a stern, almost angry expression. Yet she was almost smiling. It was very confusing. I was separated from the rest of the kids and forced to take my nap in an isolated hallway. The memory was as clear as if it had happened yesterday. Never mind all of those sterile, clinical, physiological books I was reading about orgasms. What worked for me was erotica!

It was during my first semester at Temple that I started psychotherapy. It all began in the aftermath of finding out that Joan was cheating on me. I signed up for a counseling session and the young intern was so concerned at my level of emotional upset that she signed me up to see the psychiatrist, who immediately gave me a prescription to calm me down. After a sufficient amount of time passed and I seemed emotionally stable enough, the psychiatrist suggested that I start seeing an older psychotherapist who specialized in LGBT issues. I am forever grateful to this woman.

For the first time, a total stranger helped me put my mother's behavior in perspective. I had never admitted to anyone else just how outrageous her behavior had been. In fact, I hadn't even been able to admit to myself that her behavior was indeed outrageous. The more her drinking intensified, the more she had put me in charge of running around to find public toilets for her. I remember running in a panic through grocery stores, department stores, banks, wherever we might have been, praying to find the bathroom for her in time. Often it was too late and she would wail and boohoo while telling the graphic details to my father, who would pity and comfort her. I was thoroughly disgusted. This therapist actually said to me at one point, "It's a miracle that you can find women attractive at all."

I remembered an incident that took place while my mother was shopping for dresses at a department store in the mall. She had come out of the changing room to show us the dress she was trying on. Unbeknownst to me at the time, she was so drunk that she forgot that she was in public and started taking the dress off before she realized that she wasn't in the changing room. She was always too exhibitionistic with us, undressing in front of us while we were in the room, so I can see how she forgot where she was. But all of a sudden it struck her that she was in public and people were watching. I remember saying, "Not here, Mom!" Then she panicked, ran back to the changing room, and looked behind her to see if anyone was following her. *Why would anyone want to follow her?* I wondered. She was extremely overweight and looked even older than she was. Had she had a flashback, perhaps?

7

Meanwhile, I had met an older gay male couple through Bob Cole – a friend of my parents' – who introduced me to a descendant (through marriage) of the Pitcairn family, whose compound was in the outskirts of Philadelphia. Pianist John Pennick had married the daughter of a Pitcairn. She raised horses on a large estate. He had converted an old cow barn into his piano studio and apartment, which housed two nine-foot concert grands. We hit it off so well that he eventually would host private concerts for me, inviting all of my friends.

The two gay men, Mike and Mike, were antiques dealers and one of them was a public school teacher. He invited me to come and perform at several public schools in the area. One young lady was especially interested in hearing me play and meeting me. She was an aspiring beauty pageant contestant and played the piano for the talent portion of the competition. In fact, she was already Miss Delaware County and was preparing to compete for the State Crown. When Mike brought her over to introduce us after my performance, I took one look at her gorgeous smile and body and I knew that I was smitten. Amy told me that she wanted to study at Temple starting in the fall, so I offered to take her under my wing.

It became clear that my new friend Mike was playing matchmaker with me and Amy. He'd invite me over for dinner and Amy happened to be there. Then he'd offer to drop us off at the club. Amy revealed to me that she had a boyfriend, an Italian stallion who would always promise to pull out and then would forget at the last second. "Oh, I'm sorry babe," he would whine, and she would tolerate it because he was good-looking, her mother liked him, and he had a nice car.

Easter weekend of my junior year at Temple, the Fisk Jubilee Singers were scheduled to give a concert at Carnegie Hall on the preceding Saturday night. I invited the beauty queen to join me for the weekend. We took the train from Philadelphia and stayed in the same hotel where my parents were staying. Her parents would meet us the next day to take her back to Philadelphia and I would stay in New York to visit with my parents. She had never seen the Easter Parade on Fifth Avenue so she and her parents were excited to be able to witness the festivities.

After the concert, while my parents and the Jubilee Singers were meeting fans and well-wishers in their dressing rooms, Amy and I remained in the hall to see if we could get on the stage and touch that piano. The white staff had left and the black staff began to clean. Amy and I were able to have our way with the piano and try out our repertoire in that acoustically perfect room. I had never sounded better.

Jazz pianist Don Shirley (subject of the film *Green Book*) was in the audience for the concert and invited us over to his apartment for a night cap. Little did we know that he actually lived in the Carnegie Hall building. I hadn't known that there were apartments above the concert hall. He had a beautifully decorated apartment complete with oriental rugs, priceless paintings, and a nine-foot concert grand. He was excited to play for us and educated all of us to the fact that the theme of the second movement of the Scriabin Piano Concerto was actually the melody of the Negro Spiritual "Were You There (When They Crucified My Lord)?" He played painfully beautiful passages of it and I was smitten enough to include the work in my repertoire. He then invited "the young people" to play. I offered some Rachmaninoff Preludes and even Amy played. It was the first time my parents heard her play. Let's just say that her playing paled in comparison to her beauty.

After leaving Don Shirley's place, my parents returned to their hotel and Amy and I hit the town. I remembered the disco where my friends had taken me when I came to audition at Juilliard as a senior in high school, which was not far from Carnegie Hall. We came to the entrance and the bouncer suddenly stopped us.

"You can't come in," he announced.

"Uh... why? We have I.D.," I said.

"It's not that. *You* can come in. *She* can't."

This was crazy. I asked to speak to the manager, who explained to me that they didn't want straight girls coming into the disco because they attracted straight boys. There must have been some kind of incident recently, which certainly wasn't our fault. But we suffered the consequences nonetheless.

After saying goodbye to Amy and her parents the next day,

I spent another couple of days with my parents and his sister's family in Long Island. Inspired by my experience at Carnegie Hall on the piano, I looked forward to perfecting my repertoire for my senior year.

That fall, Amy and I were spending more and more time together alone. She poured out all of her complaints about her boyfriend's behavior. She even invited me to her parents' house for dinner. I remember taking my time when it came to coming out to her. I knew that I liked her a lot and I didn't want to risk losing her friendship. When I finally did tell her, she said, "Do you really think I didn't know?!" and she laughed at my worry and concern. In fact, she had been waiting for me to tell her. We would joke about when she was going to try it with a woman. She would laugh and playfully slap my behind. After months of friendship and listening to her complaints about "the stallion," I decided that it was time for it to happen. I invited her to spend a holiday weekend at my house. I knew the girls and their mom would be away, so I'd have the place to myself. I got logs for the fireplace, chilled a bottle of champagne, played the piano for her and invited her to play for me, and set out to make her as comfortable as possible. At the end of the evening, I came into the guestroom to kiss her goodnight. This was when she asked me to stay with her a little while longer. That was it. It was on!

It started so softly, with soft little kisses. Then the flame of her desire ignited quickly and suddenly. Next thing I knew we were in flagrante delicto, and I knew that this woman had stolen my heart. I was in love.

The next day we took a long walk in the woods. She held

my arm while we were under my large yellow umbrella, the light rain freshening the air. I felt so happy and at peace. This woman could truly appreciate my musicianship and what I could do with my fingers. I started to imagine what life with a beauty queen would be like. Lots of closet time, that's for sure!

Amy went back to her parents' house that Sunday night and I didn't see her again for a couple of days. The next time I saw her in the music building, she was super-excited.

"Nina, come here! I have to tell you something!"

She took my arm and pulled me into a practice room. We sat down facing each other. Her face was full of excitement. She grinned and opened her mouth, waiting for the words to come out.

"It... it happened!"

I was flustered. "What happened?"

"*It!*" she exclaimed.

I shrugged my shoulders.

"You know..." she was exasperated, "I was with my boyfriend last night and... It happened! I..." she whispered, "... came with him!"

I was dumbfounded.

She was still going on and on, "I mean... I didn't really know it hadn't happened before. I mean... sex with him was... okay... But, WOW! *Nothing* like this! Oh my God!"

She hadn't even noticed the look on my face. I think I managed to say, "Well, I'm happy for you," then told her I was late for class.

My friends had warned me about straight girls, how they'd use you as an experiment and then drop you like a bad habit.

I thought Amy and I had a bond, especially after that wonderful weekend. I couldn't believe that it didn't occur to her that this news would be painful for me to hear. She ran straight from my bed to her boyfriend's. So what does that make me? Some kind of warm-up tool?

I avoided her for weeks. Finally, we almost bumped into each other in the hallway one afternoon. We both had time between classes, so we ducked into a practice room to talk.

"Okay. What's wrong?" she asked.

I struggled to find the words. "I just... I couldn't believe that you would go and be with your boyfriend right after being with me."

She looked down, embarrassed.

"I know," she said softly.

"And then you had to *tell* me about it. I mean... I didn't wanna hear *that!*"

"I know. I mean... I realized... I'm sorry."

There it was. She apologized. So what more could I expect to get out of this conversation? It was my own fault that I fell so hard for her, knowing that she called herself straight. I'd have to lick my own wounds. It hurt too much just to look at her.

"I have to go," I said and left the room.

• • • • •

In 1981 a concert was arranged for us as a family to be presented at the Fisk Memorial Chapel. My father had been dreaming of the three of us being presented in concert and now it was finally happening. My parents opened the program with their traditional repertoire for two pianos, including the Mozart D major Sonata and an arrangement of the Gershwin Preludes. Then I closed the first half with the Chopin *Andante Spianato and Grande Polonaise Brillante*. I don't think the audience was prepared for what they were about to hear when I came out onto the stage. My reputation had preceded me since my performance of the *Rhapsody in Blue* with the Nashville Symphony. When I finished the last octaves of the Chopin, the audience erupted in thunderous applause and sprang to their feet. Since it was intermission, I figured I could go backstage and start to relax but they would not stop applauding until I returned to the stage.

My parents returned for the second half with the *Concert Piece for Two Pianos* composed by their colleague and mentor John W. Work, and a delightful piece called *Scaramouche* by Milhaud. My mother and I then closed the program with the first movement of the Tchaikovsky Piano Concerto, with my mother playing the orchestral reduction on the second piano. Again, we received thunderous applause. My father joined us on the stage and then we offered an arrangement of Scott Joplin's *The Entertainer* with my mother and me on the second piano and my father as the star. He was in his element and the audience loved it. After the concert, we were presented with a plaque and a Certificate of Recognition signed by then-Governor Lamar Alexander. The Reverend Kelly Miller Smith Sr., then-pastor of First Baptist Church Capitol Hill and a disciple of Dr. Martin Luther King, made the presentation.

● ● ● ● ●

I always was a die-hard Horowitz fan. One of my favorite recordings to listen to during my childhood was the one of his historic return to Carnegie Hall. I imitated his interpretation of Chopin's Ballade in G minor on that recording for many years. My favorite recordings during my days at Temple were his Rachmaninoff Third Piano Concerto with the New York Philharmonic, and the Rachmaninoff Second Sonata. When I finally found a score of the second sonata, I was disappointed to see that most of the notes from the Horowitz recording were missing. That was when I learned that there were two editions – one from 1913 and a revised version from 1931. Supposedly, pianists had complained that the original version was too difficult and had too many notes. There were some lovely passages in the revised edition, so Horowitz decided to combine the two using the best stuff of both editions. Unfortunately, the 1931 version was the only one I could find. The older one was out of print.

It was the summer of 1980 when I finally got my hands on a copy of the original edition of the sonata. Friends of Miss Hinderas' arranged for me to attend the Chautauqua Summer Festival where Ozan Marsh was on the piano faculty. Ozan was also a Rachmaninoff fan, so when I told him of my desire to learn the second sonata and my difficulties finding the first edition, he told me that he had a copy. I would have to make photocopies myself, but I was finally in possession of a copy of the original version.

Chautauqua was a wonderful place, similar to the Aspen festival. There was a large outdoor arena covered by a permanent roof but without walls. Concerts took place every night and lectures, talks, and other presentations took place during the day. The music school was in a scenic, picturesque area, so we were able to hear everybody's repertoire and practice through the open windows. That summer I met fellow African American pianist Richard Alston, who was also studying with Ozan. Richard and I performed in a master class conducted by André Watts, who gave me an hour's worth of private instruction the following day.

That summer I worked intensely on the Rachmaninoff Second Piano Concerto, and performed the third movement in the auditions for appearing with the youth orchestra. I was chosen as one of the winners, so Nathan Gottschalk conducted a concert of portions of works, including operatic arias. My Rachmaninoff closed the program and received a thunderous standing ovation.

Singer/songwriter Melissa Manchester had come to Chautauqua to give a concert. Because I was one of the winners/performers for the awards concert, I had backstage privileges and was able to meet and visit with Melissa. She was such a sweet, dignified lady. We exchanged several warm hugs and kisses and she wished me much success. Her song "Midnight Blue" had helped me get through my teens. I was so grateful to be able to hug her and thank her for that song.

Later in the summer, there was the concerto competition for a performance of a complete work with the Festival Youth

Orchestra for the following season. I participated using the complete Rachmaninoff, and was informed immediately after the competition that I had won first prize. This meant that I would return the following summer as guest soloist with the orchestra.

The ovation after that performance sounded like an eruption. I thoroughly enjoyed rehearsing and performing with the orchestra. I ended up being engaged for several concerts as a result of that performance. Individuals throughout the northeast invited me to present recitals for their performing arts organizations.

When I returned to Temple for my senior year, I knew I had reached a new level of artistry after the summer at Chautauqua. I was so happy to have a copy of the first edition of the Rachmaninoff Second Sonata in my clutches and couldn't wait to get to work on it.

Even today I am amazed at the amount of repertoire I studied and performed while at Temple. On my concert programs alone I found performances of the Bach G minor English Suite and D major Toccata; Beethoven Sonatas Opus 2 No. 3 and the "Appassionata"; all four Chopin Ballades, the *Barcarolle*, several Études, and the *Andante Spianato and Grande Polonaise Brillante*, as well as the famous A-flat Polonaise; five Rachmaninoff Preludes, Ravel's *Gaspard de la Nuit*; and Schumann's *Carnaval*.

My final semester at Temple I won the piano concerto competition, which meant that I appeared as piano soloist with the Temple University Orchestra in a performance of Rachmaninoff's Second Piano Concerto. Music majors of course were required to give recitals, but since I matriculated as a sophomore, I didn't get the memo that we were required to attend a minimum number of recitals as well. My last semester, I had to sit in the audience for at least twenty recitals before I could graduate.

I remember performing the Saint-Saëns Second Piano Concerto with an accompanist, Stacie Comstock, who played the orchestral reduction on second piano. I had initially met Stacie in Aspen and found that she was also studying with Miss Hinderas. The audience predominantly made up of students gave us a thunderous standing ovation. They were whistling and whooping and kept calling us back to take more bows. It warmed my heart to receive such an ovation since most of my audiences in Philly had primarily consisted of elderly little white ladies with white hair. I had also played in a few nursing homes for very appreciative audiences. Some of these kids were required to sit in the audience as well, but word had begun to spread that when I was on the concert schedule, they should try to catch my performance.

Gaby Casadesus gave a master class that year and Stacie and I played the first movement of the Saint-Saëns concerto for her. We closed the program and Madame Casadesus said to the chair of the department while pointing to me, "This is a *real* pianist." I guess this was her way of distinguishing me from the pianists who had played before me. Leon Fleisher also gave a master class that year. For him I played the Liszt Sonata. For my senior recital I gave them the Four Inventions by Ulysses Kay, the Liszt Sonata which closed the first half, "Ondine" from Ravel's *Gaspard de la Nuit*, four Rachmaninoff preludes, and I closed the program with Chopin's *Andante Spianato and Grande Polonaise Brillante*. The ovation was tremendous! My mother had performed the Liszt Sonata on her faculty recital in 1970, so this piece had been more or less memorized for twelve years. It is a tour de force and I played the hell out of it. The hall was packed for my concert and both students and faculty came up to me for weeks afterwards to compliment me and tell me how moving it was. Even Amy came to the concert with her mother. She was so moved she couldn't speak. She hugged me and kissed me on both cheeks.

Soon afterwards, my primary teacher Natalie Hinderas wrote the following:

> "NINA KENNEDY was my student for two and a half years during which time she demonstrated evidence of a superior musical talent as a pianist. She is capable of working diligently and thoroughly in her learning procedure of notes and interpretation. She has the combination of inner fire and poetry in performance which captivate audiences.
>
> Ms. Kennedy is worthy of consistent and available support and encouragement whenever and wherever possible.
>
> Natalie Hinderas, Concert Pianist
Professor of Piano
Temple University"

Graduation was approaching and I had no plans for what I was going to do in September, so on a whim I decided to apply to Juilliard for the Master's program. Again, I came to New York to audition, but this time I was armed with Ravel's "Ondine" from *Gaspard de la nuit*, the Chopin *Andante Spianato and Grande Polonaise*, and the Liszt Sonata. They had me open with a Bach Prelude and Fugue, and then they asked for a little Chopin. Then they heard the entire Ondine. After the final chord of the Ondine I heard Abbey Simon say, "Good!" They were saying their thank you's and goodbyes, and I was shocked that they hadn't asked to hear any Liszt. Evidently, they had already made their decision because I was awarded a full scholarship to study at the Juilliard School for the fall semester of 1982.

I made a few trips to New York during the summer to search for a live-in babysitting job near Lincoln Center. I had gotten a list of families who were looking for live-in babysitters in the Student Activities office at Juilliard. I called a few of the numbers and made appointments to apply for the jobs. I remember feeling a bit overwhelmed with all that I had to do. It would have been nice to have a brother or a sister, or both, who could have helped me with moving and finding a living situation. I knew it was pointless to ask my parents for help because I would have ended up taking care of them. My father was such a cheapskate. The prices for hotel rooms in Manhattan would have been astronomical for him, and my mother's last visit in Philadelphia had turned out to be a nightmare. She complained about food. She complained about my apartment. She needed me to run around and find bathrooms for her. She was more of a pain than she was a help.

Finally, I found another Jewish family with more pampered children. They lived on the Upper East Side of Manhattan, which would be a forty-five minute bus ride to Juilliard. They called my last employer – the widow with two daughters – for a reference, and then hired me for the job. I would have the maid's room just behind the kitchen, which had a private bathroom.

The last days in Philly were filled with saying goodbye to my friends and several bon voyage parties. Eventually I finished packing, loaded up my little Subaru, and drove to New York City all by myself. Somehow, I made a wrong turn on the way to the Lincoln Tunnel and ended up approaching the Holland Tunnel. The Twin Towers, magnificently illuminated, stood to greet me on the occasion of my arrival to my new home.

8

Start Spreadin' the News...

My first full day in the Big Apple, I had filed the paperwork for the transfer of funds from my bank accounts in Philadelphia to my new account in New York. A couple of days later, I had run out of all the cash that I had and attempted to make a withdrawal at the bank, when I was informed that the transfer was not complete and the funds not available. When I asked the teller when I would be able to withdraw cash, she said it would be within the next couple of days, hopefully. As I didn't have a credit card, this marks the only time in my life when I did not know where my next meal was coming from. It was the only time I went to bed hungry. The next day, the transfer was complete. So I treated myself to breakfast at a traditional New York City diner.

One of the first things I did after settling into my new home was to find my way to the nearest women's bar. The Duchess used to be on the corner of Seventh Avenue and Christopher Street in the West Village. I had even made my way there when I came to town on one of those preliminary trips to search for housing. I remember seeing a young, tall, beautiful black woman usually standing toward the back of the bar. I didn't know her name, but she was there frequently.

A few years later when I ran into one of the bartenders from The Duchess, she said to me, "Yeah. You used to come in back when Whitney Houston used to hang out there. She used to be there all the time."

Whitney Houston. I knew her face looked familiar when her first album came out, but when I'd see her at the bar she wasn't wearing any makeup. In fact, she looked a little butch in her leather jacket and hair pulled back. It was such a tragedy to lose her the way we did. Several have said – including her ex-husband – that if she had been free to live her truth, she might not have become addicted to drugs in the first place. The pressure to be married to a man and stay in the closet took its toll on her psyche daily. Robyn Crawford was her support system and never should have been forced to leave her side.

I learned just recently that young Vladimir Horowitz used to put on makeup and hang out in sailors' bars in the port cities of Europe. His friend and mentor Sergei Rachmaninoff used to give him a hard time about being gay, and told him to stop. It always amazes me how some heterosexuals think that being gay is a choice. The only actual choice is: be gay and be happy or pretend to be straight or celibate and be miserable. Which would you choose?

I fully took advantage of being so close to the Theater District and Lincoln Center. That first semester I would treat myself to a Broadway play per week, purchasing discounted tickets for students. I attended New York Philharmonic concerts as often as I could. One evening, pianist Alicia de Larrocha was giving a concert at Avery Fisher Hall. I had gotten a last-minute student ticket for a seat in the second box on the left – keyboard side. At some point during the intermission, several people on the main floor were pointing up to the first box next to mine. I asked a woman sitting next to me what they were pointing at. She said, "That's Vladimir Horowitz sitting over there."

I couldn't believe my ears. Horowitz! My idol! I sprang over to him without hesitation. His bodyguard came over right away.

"Oh, Mr. Horowitz, I'm so happy to meet you," I gushed. "I'm studying at Juilliard. You know I've studied your arrangement of the Rachmaninoff Second Sonata and found a copy of the original edition. So, I'm putting the two versions together, like you did."

The old man then peered up at me and made no response.

"Uh... may I please have your autograph?" I handed him my program and a pen.

The bodyguard then put his arm between my program and Horowitz's shoulder.

"Mr. Horowitz does not sign autographs!" he barked.

"Oh. Well, may I shake your hand, then?"

The old man slowly raised his finger for me to hold, which I did. Later I learned in one of his biographies that Horowitz refused to shake hands with strangers because of an incident early in his career when a man shook his hand so hard that it affected his playing that night. I began to think about erecting my own boundaries where hand-shaking was concerned.

At the end of the concert, while she was still receiving her ovation, Madame de Larrocha looked up to the first box and acknowledged the presence of Mr. Horowitz, who waved back at her. After the concert, I went backstage to congratulate Madame de Larrocha and learned while overhearing her conversations with friends that her husband had just died recently. The tears would well up in her eyes as she spoke. I could see that she didn't have much patience with autograph-seekers and fans, but I made a point of looking into her eyes and complimenting her work from one pianist to another. She took the time to engage with me, which was most gratifying.

Life in Manhattan was super expensive. Fortunately, I was still engaged to give recitals throughout the country, but it wasn't bringing in enough to cover all of my expenses. By then it was clear to me that the various conductors with whom I had worked did the hiring as far as soloists were concerned, so I made the logical decision to enroll in the conductors' program while completing the requirements for the master of music degree in piano performance, which was how I was able to participate in Leonard Bernstein's master classes. I am also indebted to Professor Mary Anthony Cox for teaching the toughest ear-training/score-reading class I've ever had. Her advanced level course was required for the composers and conductors, and all of us left her feeling thoroughly prepared for our future careers. I was one of two females in the class, the second being Maria Rojas, a harpsichordist from South America. As a young girl she had studied with a German refugee and was very well prepared for a classical career.

Trombonist Richard Kelly Young and I met in Mary Anthony Cox's Ear Training class for first year graduate students, and soon became close friends. Many of us trembled with fear in the hallway before entering the classroom. Ms. Cox was a hard task-master! She devised various forms of what we called torture, demanding that we perform our assignments before the entire class. Score-reading exercises consisted of singing one line while tapping the rhythm of another and conducting the whole time. As a trombonist, Kelly had an amazing diaphragm. He could spit out long phrases without taking a breath. I always knew when Kelly was practicing on the fourth floor. I could hear his "Ride of the Valkyries" echoing through the halls as soon as I got off the elevator, and simply followed the sounds of his music until I found his practice room.

The infamous practice rooms within the Juilliard building are a source of myth and legend. When the elevators opened on the fourth floor, the cacophony of sound was an experience in and of itself – dozens of extremely talented musicians on various instruments playing the hell out of whatever it was they were practicing. One heard fragments of solo repertoire, orchestral passages, arias, you name it... all being torn apart and slowly put back together flawlessly! The rule regarding the practice rooms was: if you leave a practice room vacant for ten minutes, you lose it. Well, there was a famous "Korean mafia" of young girls who would appear exactly at nine minutes and fifty seconds to reclaim the room – sometimes for themselves, sometimes for their friends. There were also stories of pianists leaving razor blades hidden between the piano keys. I remember hearing something about someone doing a glissando. The result was quite messy.

One day while having lunch in the Juilliard cafeteria, I saw a handsome young black man who looked vaguely familiar, so I sat down at his table and introduced myself. Turns out he was

Damon Evans, the actor who portrayed the character "Lionel" on the TV show, *The Jeffersons*. Damon was in the opera program and was putting his energy into his first love (since his television career had given him a bit of a financial cushion). When he learned that I was from Nashville, he asked if I had met a Dr. George Redd, who was his uncle. That same Dr. Redd had been the dean at Fisk University, and was also my godfather. Needless to say, Damon and I became fast friends. We were practically related! I recently saw Damon's name in the credits of the Glyndebourne production of *Porgy and Bess* conducted by Simon Rattle. The clip of his performance is also shown in the PBS documentary *Broadway Musicals: A Jewish Legacy*.

During my first year at Juilliard, I was invited to appear as piano soloist with the Nashville Symphony Chamber Orchestra in a performance of Beethoven's Second Piano Concerto, which I had performed with the Jackson, Mississippi Chamber Orchestra. Conductor Kenneth Schermerhorn had been recently appointed music director of the Nashville Symphony. At the same time, he was music director of the Hong Kong Philharmonic Orchestra and was guest conducting the New Jersey Symphony Orchestra. We met for lunch near Lincoln Center to discuss the proposed concert. It would be a special non-subscription event that would take place in the new Tennessee Performing Arts Center, which was built with the support of billionaire business woman Martha Ingram. Her philanthropy supported my career throughout the years. Visual artist Earl Hooks was commissioned to draw a "Portrait of the Artist by an Artist" for the promotional fliers and commemorative posters. His drawing of my face also appeared in the program.

NASHVILLE SYMPHONY ASSOCIATION
Kenneth Schermerhorn, Music Advisor

and

TENNESSEE PERFORMING ARTS CENTER

present

Nashville Symphony Chamber Orchestra
Peter Schaffer, Conductor
Nina Kennedy, Piano Soloist
Sunday, March 20, 1983, 3:00 p.m. - Polk Theatre, TPAC

Portrait of the Artist
By An Artist

The handsome pen and ink drawing of Nina Kennedy in the program, was done by widely acclaimed Black American artist Earl J. Hooks, head of the Fisk University Art Department.

The drawing is also used on Special Posters which are for sale in the lobby, and will be personally signed by the artist.

It was most gratifying to see the support of Nashville's black community for this event. The members of our church alone practically filled the hall. The headline for the review of that concert read: "Nina Kennedy Shows Her Fine Piano Technique."

I knew that the Nashville Symphony was going through some financial difficulties at the time, but imagine my dismay when, over a month after the concert, I still had not been paid. Everyone else – including the staff at the Performing Arts Center – had been paid. They just forgot, I guess, to pay their soloist. I called Maestro Schermerhorn to express my disappointment. He apologized profusely and promised that I would receive my check within a few days. He kept his promise.

Again, I was in a living situation with a demanding family, and this time there were three kids – two girls and a boy. The mother also expected me to bathe the boy during his nightly bath, which felt very uncomfortable to me. They also seemed to forget that I was a full-time student – at Juilliard, no less – which meant that I had a full class schedule and needed to practice. These people also had a full-time maid who came every weekday. It was a large, sprawling apartment on East 86th Street. These people enjoyed a lifestyle that I hadn't even imagined, complete with weekend trips to the country house, priceless paintings on the walls, etc.

One night toward the end of the semester, I was overwhelmed with preparing for exams and lost track of the time. I knew that my employers were expecting me to babysit that night so I rushed home as fast as I could. By the time I got back to the apartment, their two Kosher guests were there sitting in the living room, but they had not been able to eat anything since the household was not Kosher. I was maybe thirty minutes late. The four of them left for the evening and I continued to study in my room. The next day, my female boss took great pleasure in firing me and asking me to leave. She couldn't have cared less that I was preparing for exams and was under enormous stress already.

I scrambled around, putting up signs in apartment buildings in the Lincoln Center area. A few days later I got a call from a woman who was legally blind and had a sofa-bed in her one-bedroom apartment. She was getting older and simply wanted to have someone in the apartment with her. The price was right so I moved in immediately. It turned out that because her vision was so bad, she could not see that her ground-floor apartment was infested with ants. I cleaned and exterminated the place myself. There were just a few weeks left of that semester and the apartment was just a few blocks from school. I figured I could stick it out.

During my last year at Temple, I had given a concert in Albany and met a lovely black couple afterwards who had been in the audience. The two of them, Juanita and John Jackson, wanted to introduce me to an older black lady, a widow, who lived alone in Albany and also had a house in Oxford, Pennsylvania. Her name was Geraldine Mowbray. She was a retired medical doctor and owned a gorgeous seven-foot Bösendorfer. I ended up coming back to Albany to visit this couple and they were very excited to be able to introduce me to Dr. Mowbray, who hosted a musical evening for me in her home.

Dr. Mowbray was planning a trip to her house in Oxford that summer and needed help cleaning it out. She was bringing the Bösendorfer with her. There was also a swimming pool behind the house. She invited me to spend the summer with her, so at the end of my second semester at Juilliard, I moved out of the ground-floor apartment and made my way back to Albany. Dr. Mowbray was packing up her possessions and directing the movers on how to handle the piano. These movers were not professionals and the piano ended up with a large scratch on the side of the keyboard. She took it in stride. This elderly black woman had enormous courage. I watched her order those white men around and yell at them when they dropped the piano. In hindsight, I realized that she wanted me there in the house whenever those men were there. I drove her in her car down to Pennsylvania and the moving van came a day later.

Dr. Mowbray had had a daughter who had passed away several years before while in her early twenties. Her daughter had been diagnosed with terminal cancer.

"But she was so practical that she decided to kill herself instead of enduring years of chemotherapy and radiation and wasting all that money," Dr. Mowbray said.

After a few weeks, she was calling me by her daughter's name. I could tell she was really enjoying my company, and she was a much more functional mother than the one I had been born to. She knew a little something about clinical depression and explained to me how mothers who are inattentive to their infants can affect our moods for the rest of our lives. I wished someone had explained this to my mother *before* I'd gotten here.

And what a wonderful summer that was! It didn't take long to clean the house to the point where it was livable. I even learned how to completely take care of a swimming pool, complete with back-washing and placement of the diatomaceous earth. After a long day of working on the Rachmaninoff Second Sonata, we'd usually have dinner in a restaurant and then, after Dr. Mowbray went to bed, I would swim naked under the stars.

Some of my Philadelphia friends came out for a Sunday afternoon picnic. It was delightful seeing Sharon Ray again and soprano Melody Breyer, who had left Curtis before I arrived but was a dear friend of Sharon's. I played some of the Rachmaninoff for them. The deep, rich tone of that Bösendorfer completely spoiled me. After that summer, it wasn't often that I was able to perform the sonata on such a responsive instrument. But when I did get the chance, I was ready for it.

9

When it was time to return to Juilliard in late August, I rented a room in an apartment in Spanish Harlem. A women's bookstore was around the corner from where I lived, and on their bulletin board I saw an announcement of the New England Women's Music Retreat (NEWMR) which was taking place over the Labor Day weekend. Women left signs offering and asking for rides, so I took down a few numbers and contacted them.

I didn't have much camping equipment; in fact, all I had was a sleeping bag. Soon after we arrived and set up the communal tent, I saw a woman I had met a few months earlier strolling through the woods in her little purple shorts, topless. She was out to have a good time! We had met and danced at Ariel's bar in New York earlier that year. When I said hello to her, she told me later that she actually hadn't recognized me. I reminded her of our dance and conversation at Ariel's and she said of course she remembered. But in fact, she hadn't. She just said that she did because she thought I was cute. By the end of the weekend, Susan and I were definitely an item. Back in New York, I would go to school during the day while she was at work and we would spend the nights together at her apartment. I gave up my rented room and moved into Susan's place after paying for three months of rent and spending maybe ten nights there.

Susan Seltzer was a Systems Programmer at the Metropolitan Life Insurance Company when I met her. Later she would take a position at Morgan Guaranty Trust on Wall Street. She loved the fact that I was a classical musician and knew that her parents would be impressed by this as well. In fact, soon after I met her father, we discovered that we both loved Mahler Symphonies. At her parents' house, her dad and I would sit in the living room blasting the music, or we would take off for the golf course. In a way, I was the son he never had.

Susan's mother, however, was another story. She was a very controlling woman and Susan was terrified of her disapproval and her anger. She made it clear that she was going to be the boss of Susan's life regardless of who her significant other was.

Meanwhile, Susan was teaching me what it meant to be loved unconditionally. I didn't even need to ask for material things. She would anticipate what I needed and buy it without question. I had never experienced this kind of love from my parents. Every little thing I had asked them for, the immediate answer was "No!" Eventually it may have shown up in some way or other, but they seemed to feel the need to teach me that I would not receive what I asked for. To this day, I still struggle with asking for what I need.

Susan was a fascinating woman. She had spent several years living on a kibbutz in Israel, where she studied at Hebrew University. She was an avid reader and enjoyed foreign

With Susan Seltzer in St. Lucia

films. She was one of the smartest people I had ever met. It was 1983 and I had never really used a computer before. As a systems programmer, of course she had one, and she completely computerized me. Suddenly I had mailing lists and address labels and a database. I could send personalized letters to conductors and artist management firms all over the world.

Susan socialized with corporate types who did their 9:00 to 5:00 jobs then came home to relax. It seemed my work was never-ending. I would spend my days in class, practice for a few hours in between, and my evenings on the computer adding to my mailing lists, writing my biographical sketches, and composing letters to solicit engagements. Susan was easily paying all the bills; her job as a corporate systems-programmer made this possible. I wanted to contribute something toward my expenses, so I placed an ad in a neighborhood newspaper offering piano lessons. I received several responses, but one stood out. She called during the evening – an elderly woman.

"I really want some voice-coaching in addition to the piano lessons," she said. "That's the nigger in the woodpile."

"Excuse me?"

She was stupid enough to repeat it. "I said, that's the nigger in the woodpile."

I hung up. Days later when I told my parents about the conversation, my father immediately jumped to her defense.

"Oh, you shouldn't have let that upset you!" he cried.

It's as if his brain automatically kept him from feeling any sense of outrage. Perhaps, as a young black male in rural Georgia during the Depression, his lack of any sense of outrage saved his life.

Early that fall I read in the papers that jazz pianist Oscar Peterson and his trio had a five-night engagement at The Blue Note on West 3rd Street in Manhattan. Oscar Peterson was my favorite jazz pianist! I had to get tickets somehow. When I went to the box office, it became clear that I could not afford the price for tickets for two seats at a table, so I reserved two standing-room places at the bar. Susan and I were absolutely mesmerized by his playing, the ease with which he executed those fantastic runs and arpeggios, and the sheer joy he exuded. I went backstage to his dressing room after the concert, introduced myself as a Juilliard student, and asked if I could play for him. He said, "Sure. Come by tomorrow around 5:00." I could barely contain my excitement when I told Susan what had transpired. Both of us were hopping and skipping our way to the exit, squealing with delight.

The next day at 5:00 sharp I was waiting at the entrance of the Blue Note for Mr. Peterson to arrive. Soon it was 5:15, then 5:30... and no Oscar. When he finally came in after 6:30, he barely had enough time to settle in and change for the show. When he saw me, I thought he had forgotten about why I was there. But he instructed the floor manager to give me a ticket for a seat at a table. Again, I was spellbound while Oscar did his thang. Since I was so close to the keyboard this time, I made mental notes regarding his technique and some of the passages. Again, he slayed; the audience was on their feet clapping and cheering.

I went backstage again afterwards, not knowing what to expect. When I got to his dressing room, he and the members of his trio along with some of the staff were drinking champagne. Mr. Peterson was cordial and friendly and he asked someone to hand me a glass of champagne. Later when we were able to chat, he apologized for not showing earlier and explained that he was having some problems with his wrist and had gone to the doctor. I blew a sigh of relief at the knowledge that at least he didn't stand me up. I didn't have the courage to ask to reschedule, however.

I don't know exactly what it was that I hoped Oscar Peterson could do for me. Maybe I simply wanted to have the pleasure of being able to play for a black man who had the power and influence to make a difference in my career. For concert agents and venues, he was their cash cow. I was also impressed with the stand he took back in the 1960s when he refused to perform in the U.S.A. because concert promoters only booked him in jazz clubs. In Europe he performed in lavish concert halls and opera houses. He finally made his return to the States when his manager was able to book Carnegie Hall for him. Of course, the concert sold out within minutes.

I knew I would not have to explain racism to this man. He got it! But unfortunately, I was not yet aware of the sexism which permeated the jazz field. I had not paid very close attention to what was going on in jazz, but hardly any women graced those stages as band members. Sure there were plenty of women singers, but no pianists aside from Mary Lou Williams, whose work I would find many years later.

Susan's parents graciously invited me to spend Thanksgiving with them. Her mother joked about being a terrible cook and even lost one of her fingernails while stuffing the turkey. I volunteered to do most of the cooking from then on. Of course, I would cook Christmas dinner for the family, who squeezed together around our tiny dining room table. Usually they and other Jewish families would go to a Chinese restaurant for Christmas dinner. At least I could provide a home-cooked meal complete with turkey and apple walnut stuffing, candied yams, yellow turnips, collard greens, and macaroni and cheese.

At the onset of my second year at Juilliard, my plan was to win an international piano competition and sign with a major concert artists' management firm. At least that was what the white boys were doing. They were winning prizes right and left and being presented in recital at Lincoln Center, usually in Alice Tully Hall. So in good faith I applied to various international competitions here in the United States, sent out hundreds of dollars in application fees, and prepared the required repertoire. There was only one slight problem: my applications to these competitions were not being accepted. Here I had appeared in concert throughout a good chunk of the United States, the Bahamas, and Venezuela, had won several local and regional awards, and was about to receive my master's degree from The Juilliard School. Yet this was not enough for me to be accepted to compete. The competition organizers always required that you submit a photograph and my picture appeared in many of the newspaper articles about me. Plus, I had presented concerts at many HBCUs (Historically Black Colleges and Universities). So it was obvious to everyone that I was a black woman. Little did I know that black women were not allowed to compete.

Susan witnessed my heartbreak and confusion. She saw all of the preparation that went into submitting materials for these competitions and my hope and optimism when I would send the packages off. I began to ask her to ask her parents to put in a good word for me at the various Jewish arts organizations to which they belonged. But the Jews seemed to have an understanding that they would invest their efforts on the behalf of other Jews. How were they supposed to explain who I was? Their daughter's "friend"? We watched as young white boys were given opportunity after opportunity and I wasn't even being allowed to compete. Disillusionment was taking hold.

Regardless of my disappointments, I still had to do my work for class and give Juilliard my all. I still had an occasional contract for a recital or concerto performance with orchestra.

During this year it was announced that Horowitz was giving a recital at Carnegie Hall and I was one of the first in line to get tickets. The maximum number of tickets that anyone could purchase was four, so I was already in possession of my four tickets when a friend of Susan's mother's asked her if Susan might be able to get a ticket. We were happy to offer our extra two tickets to this friend and her husband. The four of us sat together in the first balcony keyboard side while Horowitz spun his magic. He was certainly past his prime at this point in his life, but in Carnegie Hall, on certainly one of the best pianos in the world, he managed to give us a memorable evening. He himself acknowledged on stage that his encore of the Schubert Musical Moment No. 3 was a perfect performance by pointing to the piano as if to say, "Yeah, that was good!" That encore evoked memories of the old days when he was the best pianist in the world.

My two years at Juilliard had flown by and it was already time to prepare for my master's recital. At that time, I was practicing in the basement of the Steinway building on West 57th Street, which was across the street from Carnegie Hall, on their many nine-foot concert grand pianos. One day I arrived there as usual and was greeted by signs stating that no one was allowed in the basement from 3:00 to 5:00, which was my scheduled time. I marched down prepared to throw out the interloper and heard fragments of Brahms Paganini variations, then some Chopin, then some Rachmaninoff. I peered through the open large, heavy sliding door to find a very old looking Vladimir Horowitz sitting at one of the pianos, surrounded by his goons. After I looked in, the door was closed in my face.

Juanita Jackson, the same lady who had introduced me to Geraldine Mowbray also introduced me to Renate Perls, daughter of famed psychiatrist Fritz Perls. Renate hosted recitals for me in her Upper West Side apartment where she had a lovely grand piano. She also introduced me to a friend of hers who ran a catering service. When I told her of my upcoming master's recital, her friend offered to cater the reception. I was grateful for her kindness until I saw the bill. I was too young and naïve to know that New Yorkers were usually expected to negotiate the price for such a service. I had hoped that, being a friend of Renate's, she would give me a discount. Even if she had, the price was still exorbitantly high. My father said, "You should've just given them cookies and punch." But where was he when these decisions were being made?

My graduate recital at Juilliard was quite the success. My parents came up from Nashville for the event and stayed with my father's sister and her family in Brentwood, Long Island. My teacher William Masselos commented that he had never seen me so "done up." Some of my classmates didn't even recognize me in my concert gown. Herbert Stessin, who also gave me some private lessons while Mr. Masselos was ill, whistled at me backstage.

The standing ovation from my colleagues was most gratifying.

The reception was held in the large backstage lounge behind the concert hall and I was told that some homeless people had gotten in and were stuffing expensive cheeses and patés into their pockets. I was too busy greeting friends and distant

William Masselos

relatives who had come from far and wide to be in the audience. Here again, this was a situation where my father should
have stepped in; but as usual, he pretended not to notice. Several commented that my mother was standing around like a
guest at the reception. Even Susan's parents were more involved in the actual hosting than my mother was. Maybe all
of the white people intimidated her.

Soon after Susan and I were officially together, I noticed a
change in my mother. Gone was the mother of my youth, the
woman who would complain and throw tantrums and cry for
sympathy. That woman was now a watered-down version of
the old one. Eventually I learned that it was because she was
heavily medicated. She had a pill to help her sleep, a pill to
wake up, a pill to calm her down, a pill to lift her mood, and

then there were the pills for her high blood pressure. Her night-table was covered with pill bottles and her drinking was worse than ever. By the time I was in my mid-twenties, my mother was a shell of the woman I had known all my life.

The next day in Ms. Cox's torture chamber... I mean, Ear Training class... she announced to the class, "Ms. Kennedy, I heard you gave a very exciting recital last night."

All eyes turned toward me. I was literally at a loss for words. I think I managed to mumble a faint "Thank you." Some students who had been in attendance nodded in agreement and gave a smattering of applause.

Not long after my recital, my major teacher, William Masselos, wrote the following in his recommendation: "I have come to regard [Nina Kennedy] as one of the most promising pianists in her age group. She has a very fit pair of hands and a solid repertory to build on: we are currently working on the Emperor Concerto and on Rachmaninoff's Second Sonata, in which her execution is as clean as anyone could possibly ask for. I predict, in sum, a very prosperous career for Nina, and am delighted to be playing a part in her formation."

My Ear Training professor, Mary Anthony Cox, wrote: "Miss Nina Kennedy has been a student in my accelerated class in Ear Training since her arrival at the Juilliard School this past September. Her basic musicianship is very strong, and the skills which are needed in my class are in excellent condition. She has maintained a very high level of performance, and her attitude has been marvelous. She is a young lady who should succeed in her endeavors. It is therefore highly appropriate for us to invest both time and money in her future."

I thought I had it made.

Itzhak Perlman gave the commencement address at our graduation ceremony in Alice Tully Hall at Lincoln Center, and spoke of the enormous responsibility we carry as performers to entertain our audiences. He reminded us that the people in the audience have spent their hard-earned money on tickets and are expecting us to distract them from their mundane lives and give them glimpses of ecstasy. He even read some letters he had received from audience members who expressed displeasure with his performance. As far as I was concerned, he was one of those lucky performers who was being paid top dollar for each concert. So what did he have to complain about? I was working just as hard as he was on stage, yet I received barely a tenth of what he was paid. But one day…

Susan was so proud of me. We were so happy.

My Juilliard graduating class (I'm seated on the floor)

PART 2

10

Looking back, I don't know exactly when it began to dawn on me that I was being denied contracts because of American racism. All I knew was that my white male colleagues were being invited to perform by white male conductors all over the country. Some of them were barely qualified, but that didn't seem to matter. What mattered was that they were white men and as such they were being paid at least twice as much as I was being paid for the few jobs I managed to secure.

My friend and patron Dr. Lee Minton had moved to London and had discussed with my parents the possibility of bringing me there for a more public version of his "Eine Kleine Nacht Musik" event. I had graduated from Juilliard and was free and clear with no time constraints. He scheduled the concert for that September. A few weeks after the date was set, I received a call from the U.S. Embassy in Paris. The secretary informed me that the U.S. Ambassador Joe Rodgers was inviting me to appear in concert at the Embassy. Since I was going to be in London, the concert would be scheduled for the following week. Susan and I were ecstatic.

Joe Rodgers was a Reagan appointee and was from Nashville. I believe he had been a financial advisor for Reagan's re-election campaign. I learned later that a dear friend of my mother's, Mary Jane Werthan, had informed l'ambassador of my concert in London. They then made the arrangements to extend the invitation to me to appear at the embassy. Mrs. Werthan had been a great supporter of my career. She had served on the Board of Trustees of Vanderbilt University, and was an officer of the Nashville Symphony. Her husband, Albert Werthan, was known in Nashville as the CEO and Chairman of Werthan Industries, and was a patron of the arts who had served on the Board of Trustees of Fisk University and the Nashville Symphony. In fact, it was their daughter Elizabeth who introduced me to the woman who hired me for my live-in babysitting job in Philadelphia.

Since we were going to be on the continent, Susan requested three weeks of vacation time from work so that we could spend more time in Paris and then take the Orient Express to Vienna, where we would spend another week.

I flew to London by myself; Susan would join me a few days later. Dr. Minton had given me directions for getting from the airport to Victoria Station and then to his flat on Eaton Square. He was spending his time in a different location, so we had the flat to ourselves. He had decorated the place with beautiful antiques and paintings. There was also a private garden in the back. Susan and I had a wonderful time being tourists. At the Changing of the Guard at Buckingham Palace, Susan saw a familiar face in the crowd. It turned out that one of her old colleagues from Morgan was living in London with his boyfriend. They were able to show us around to some of the hot spots. We made a delightful foursome as the boyfriend was also black, and he was British!

The concert at the Warwick Arts Trust was an enormous success. Several other artists performed and I closed the program with Chopin and Rachmaninoff. Susan overheard one elderly lady in the audience saying, "I'll bet she's capable of knocking out fellows." Dr. Minton's friends, pianist Shura Cherkassky and soprano Dame Eva Turner, were in the audience and both joined us for a light supper after the concert. Dame Eva told a delightful story about finishing a performance of *Tosca* and the mattress that had been placed there to brace her fall after she leapt over the parapet was too high, the result being that she bounced high up off of it and was seen by the audience. It was the first "resurrection" of Tosca in history.

That weekend Shura was appearing at the Proms as piano soloist with the London Philharmonic in a performance of the Tchaikovsky Piano Concerto. We met him again afterwards and again he was very warm and friendly.

We left London and took a hovercraft across the English Channel to Calais in France, where we boarded a train to Paris. Susan enjoyed looking through guide books for travel information. Sometimes she seemed to be more interested in reading the guide book than looking at the actual monument or building. She was able to purchase our tickets and order our meals in French. My French, on the other hand, was quite a mess. I remember sitting in a restaurant and trying to order a glass of water. Since I had studied Debussy's *Reflets dans l'eau*, I knew that eau meant water, so I asked the waitress for "un verre de l'eau, sil vous plait." She had an attack of the giggles. I learned very quickly that all I had to ask for was, "Un verre d'eau."

Paris was and still is the most beautiful city I had ever seen. Susan found a small hotel in the area around Châtelet–Les Halles that was closed to traffic. We immediately called the embassy to let them know that we had arrived. The secretary invited us to come over right away to try the piano, so we made our way through the streets of Paris to the embassy's entrance on the Rue du Faubourg Saint-Honoré. The street, the building, the recital hall, all of it was simply fabulous!

The next day the ambassador sent a car to our hotel to pick us up. When we arrived, throngs of fashionably dress women were walking up the steps of the entrance, where military men in uniform were standing at attention and saluting. All of this was for me! I was wearing the gown Susan had bought for me for my Juilliard master's recital. The moment felt surreal. The American Ambassador's Residence is a veritable palace and the ambassador is its king, whose power can only be usurped by the President of the United States. Just walking into the building brought tears to my eyes.

Susan and I were escorted to a beautiful waiting area where I looked over my scores. Ambassador Rodgers came in and gallantly introduced himself. He was a tall handsome man who simply exuded charm. He told me how delighted they were to be able to host this event and to bring a little bit of Nashville to Parisian society.

The Associated Press sent a photographer to cover the concert. After Ambassador Rodgers and his wife Honey gave me

NINA KENNEDY

Nina Kennedy is rapidly gaining recognition as one of today's most exciting young concert artists. She has appeared in recital and as soloist with orchestras throughout the United States, the Bahamas and South America. Born in Nashville in 1960, Nina received her first musical instruction from her parents, Ann Gamble and Matthew Kennedy, who were both members of the piano faculty at Fisk University for nearly thirty years. She then continued her studies at the Blair School of Music in Nashville where she was a recipient of the Myra Jackson Blair scholarship during her entire four years of high school study, and at the Curtis Institute in Philadelphia where she was one of three pianists accepted from a field of 72 competitors. She received her Bachelor's degree from Temple University where she was a pupil of Natalie Hinderas, and her Master's degree from the Julliard School in New York City, where she was awarded the prestigious William Petschek scholarship. Some of her other prizes and awards include first place in the National Society of Arts and Letters northeastern regional piano competition, the first annual Tennessee Arts Commission Artist Grant, and Tennessee's Outstanding Achievement Award signed by Governor Lamar Alexander.

PROGRAM

Jesus Joy of Man's Desiring
Johann Sebastian Bach
arranged by Myra Hess

———

Etude in F major, Op. 10, No.8
Frederic Chopin

———

Ballade in G minor, Op. 23
Frederic Chopin

———

Rhapsody in Blue
George Gershwin

———

NINA KENNEDY
piano

American Embassy
Paris, France

September 19, 1985
4:00 p.m.

U.S. Embassy program

Friday, SEPTEMBER 20, 1985 · THE TENNESSEAN ● 11-D

—AP Laserphoto

On the Continent—U.S. ambassador to France Joe M. Rodgers and Honey Rodgers, right, join Nashville-born pianist Nina Kennedy following her recital yesterday at the American Embassy in Paris. Kennedy's performance, before an invited audience from the Parisian arts community, marked her European debut.

U.S. Embassy in Paris concert article

a short and sweet introduction, I played my heart out for these people. So much was going through my mind: thoughts of Josephine Baker and James Baldwin, the Fisk Jubilee Singers and their first tour of France, the military men out front, etc. It was a wonderful recital, followed by a fabulous reception with canapés, pastries, beautiful fresh fruit, and free-flowing French champagne. Susan and I felt like queens. The large glass doors of the reception hall were open to the rose garden, where we escaped for a moment to share a kiss behind a perfectly sculpted bush.

We gave ourselves a few extra days to enjoy the city. This was the first time in my life that breakfast was brought to me in bed. Fresh croissants and baguettes, cheeses, butter and jam, and coffee were brought to us every morning. I felt I could really get used to this. The food! The wine! Paris is a feast for the senses. The old cathedrals give you the sense that the spirits of the ancestors actually dwell there, unlike the cheap copies of them in the United States. Susan and I were immediately struck by the sheer number of statues of women throughout the city. Whether they were goddesses or actual queens, women held a prominent place in the city's landscape and architecture. It makes one wonder why presidents and military heroes are so important to Americans – that is, to white American men.

Little did I know that an entire day at the Louvre was not enough to see everything. The building itself is a work of art. The time and attention given to the Egyptian exhibits in both the Louvre and the National Gallery of Art in London thoroughly impressed me. It was clear from the sheer number and

Concert hall in the U.S. Embassy

In the rose garden of the U.S. Embassy in Paris

elaborate designs on the coffins for singers that singers held prominent positions in the Egyptian royal court.

As planned, we took the Orient Express to Vienna, which meant that we spent the first part of the trip on cots that hung from the wall in a sleeper car. The train conductor was Austrian, so I tried to speak a little German with him. Most of the German I spoke back then were actually quotes from Wagner operas, so I'm sure it was very amusing. He evidently thought I was too adorable as he pinched my cheeks – the ones on my face, that is. No white American man had ever done that to me. I didn't fully understand his slang, but something told me that it was less than respectful. The train ride was very bumpy, so Susan and I spent most of that night drinking the wine we had brought with us and pulling off pieces of baguette and cheese. The sun was rising as we approached the Alps and the views were absolutely breathtaking.

Susan had made a reservation for us at the Hotel Empire on the Kärntnerstrasse behind the Opera House. We made our way there, did a little bit of sightseeing, had an early supper, and went to bed early since we were quite exhausted from our trip. I was sound asleep when I heard a deafening explosion. I was sleeping so deeply that my subconscious tried to incorporate the sound in my dream in which I saw the mushroom cloud from a nuclear bomb. When I finally woke up, I sat up in bed and looked over at Susan who was already sitting up looking at me. She went over to the window, pulled back the curtain, and saw sheets of glass flying through the air. We learned the next day that the bank directly across the street from us had been bombed because of its holdings in South

Africa. Several had been injured. One poor man lost a leg. We easily could have been out there if we hadn't been so tired. Lesson number one: The Austrians were passionate about their politics.

I absolutely loved Vienna. Again, there were the statues of women, including the huge statue of the Empress Maria Theresia in front of the National Museum of Natural History, which housed the three-inch statue of the Venus von Willendorf – the famous 30,000-year-old fertility goddess. We started out at the Stephansdom, the huge cathedral where Mozart's Requiem had its world premiere, so to speak. Then I had to see the apartments of Mozart and Beethoven, which were a few blocks behind the cathedral. In the apartment where Mozart had lived there was a display of lithographs which were drawings from the first production of his opera *The Magic Flute*. In the opera there is a scene when the animals come out of the forest to dance to the flute's magical music. I had even participated in a production of *The Magic Flute* at George Peabody College in Nashville while my father was in the doctoral program. I was dressed up as one of the animals and danced to the music. Well in these lithographs I saw that originally these beings were not animals. They were supposed to be Africans! In the drawings they were wearing little white loincloths and fancy head-dresses. Why and by whom the figures were altered to become animals, I don't know.

That week we visited the Schönbrunn Palace, The Empress' Imperial Apartments, the Hapsburg family vault (where Marie Antoinette had been entombed after the French Revolution since she *was* Maria Theresia's daughter), and the graves of Beethoven, Mozart, and Schubert. The Viennese had erected statues honoring the great composers as well as their monarchs. They didn't need military heroes. We also enjoyed Sacher Torte and the wonderful Austrian beers. The food was delicious, but heavy. How much Wiener Schnitzel and Bratwurst and Sauerkraut and Gulash and Apfelstrudel and potato pancakes can a girl eat without putting on a hundred pounds?

Too soon it was time to fly back to our country. However, at the airport we saw the front page of the *New York Times* with news of an approaching hurricane. The governor was quoted as saying, "Go home and pray!" Susan and I looked at each other in disbelief. All flights to New York were cancelled until the next day. The airline put us up in a small hotel near the airport.

Perhaps it was a sign to stay in Europe.

11

Back in America, I was immediately back in the grind of trying to secure a management contract. Applying for international competitions was a full-time job. I had to have professional photographs taken, print copies of them, make photocopies of reviews and programs, and in some cases, I had to make an actual tape recording to submit. I had responded to an ad in the Student Activities office for a job involving light secretarial work (i.e., answering the phone, taking messages, getting coffee, etc.) in exchange for free use of a beautiful seven-foot Steinway. The "office" was really my boss' apartment, a sprawling loft in the Garment District. The boss was usually out during the day at his regular office – I believe he worked in construction – so for the most part, I had the place to myself (unless his son was in town). I got a tremendous amount of work done on his beautiful piano which I did not have to share with the Korean Mafia. I was also able to set up my recording equipment – which consisted of a boom-box, a microphone, and mic stand – to produce the required tapes for competitions.

All of this was to no avail. The Cliburn, the Tchaikovsky, and other well-known international competitions would not even accept my application. Here I had a master's degree from Juilliard, concert programs, and rave reviews from all over the country and it still was not enough. How else was I supposed to get a management contract? It was truly disheartening.

The one American international competition that admitted me was the University of Maryland International Piano Competition. This annual event drew contestants and audiences from all over the world. There was a concert series as well as the actual competition. Volunteers offered to host contestants for the week and my hosts were a lovely white family who had a live-in Thai chef. The meals were absolutely delicious, albeit a little spicy for my nervous stomach during the various stages of competing.

When it was my turn to perform in the first round, we were told that we could start with whatever piece we chose. So of course, I opened with the Rachmaninoff Sonata. It was a good way to warm up and get accustomed to the instrument, and the texture was so thick that slight flubs would go un-noticed. No one had told me that the judges would stop me when they were ready for me to move on to the next piece by knocking on a desk. The venue was the large concert hall and the judges were sitting in the balcony, so I wasn't aware that the knocking I heard meant that I was supposed to stop. When the knocking continued and grew louder, I realized that it had been going on for quite a while. I stopped abruptly, obviously startled, to which the audience warmly chuckled. The judges then requested my Bach Prelude and Fugue, which they allowed me to finish. I have heard so many young competitors get lost in the middle of those harmonically complicated fugues. Luckily the piano gods and goddesses were with me on that day. I played it without a hitch. Then they requested some Beethoven, which also went flawlessly. Then I was free to go. I stood, took my bows to enthusiastic applause, and left the stage. I was about to leave the backstage area when my escort gestured for me to return to the stage. The audience was still applauding and I didn't realize that I could take a second bow. This was the first time I actually looked out into the audience. The hall was dark and there was a spotlight right in my eyes, so I couldn't see how many people were out there. But it sounded like a large crowd.

After three days of first round auditions, I was informed that I had made it to the second round. I called Susan that night with the news. She was thrilled and immediately called her parents to inform them.

For the next round, we had to present a full recital. All of us had been required to perform a work by John Cage, which had been commissioned by the competition. Full of avant garde squeaks and squawks, the Cage piece fulfilled the 20th century requirement. Then I gave the audience a Beethoven Sonata and the entire Liszt Sonata. Several commented on my dress after my performance. Now that Susan and her mother were in my life, I could afford to spend time in fashion outlets and department stores. Susan's mother enjoyed having me model gowns and concert dresses for her, and Susan was always waiting with her credit card. I could only imagine what my life would have been like if I'd had this kind of support while studying at Curtis.

After three days of semi-finals and recitals from twelve semi-finalists, the judges decided that I should be given the bottom prize, meaning the smallest amount of money. No management contract. I didn't even get a chance to perform my concerto for the finals. When I returned to my hosts' house, I was weeping openly. They were so sweet to me and promptly poured me a stiff scotch.

Later, I would learn that several African Americans who were present in the audience during the competition embarked on a letter-writing campaign to voice their complaints and disappointment that I was not given a chance to compete in the finals. I did not know this until I received copies of some of the letters weeks later. One such letter came from the dean of the conservatory of the Peabody Institute, Dr. Eileen Cline.

Thank God Susan was waiting at home for me with open arms. It didn't matter to her that I wasn't making money. She made enough for both of us. But I couldn't believe that I had worked so hard for so long with no prospect of earning a decent income. I felt betrayed. I started to doubt everything my parents had told me and began avoiding their calls.

After I graduated from Juilliard, I was on my own when it came to finding places to practice. I had a small upright piano in my little apartment, but I couldn't really develop the nuance required for a full size nine-foot concert grand. I still visited the Students' Activities Office periodically to read the signs posted on the bulletin board listing small jobs and gigs. One listing offered the use of a grand piano in exchange for playing for High Tea once a week at the Dag Hammarskjöld Tower near the United Nations. Diplomats' families lived in the building and the Skyline Lounge was where tea was served. I spent hours there practicing, and the butler was just as kind to me as he was to the residents, bringing tea to me without my having to ask. One day I was asked to provide background music for a delegation from Somalia. Dinner was served, and at one point I noticed that all of the women were sitting on the opposite side of the room from where I was. I clearly had broken protocol, but then again, I was working; so perhaps it was decided that it was more appropriate for me to sit on the men's side. When I took a break, one of the men invited me to have some of their traditional dishes. He was wearing a very expensive-looking suit and gold Gucci watch with very delicate tribal scars along his high cheekbones. He told me about his hundreds of goats, and I think I received a marriage proposal during that conversation. All I could think to say was that I had been booked to play for two hours and it was time for me to leave. The women on the other side of the room clearly did not approve of my sitting and chatting with the men.

Another day in the Skyline Lounge, I was practicing as usual and noticed a beautiful older black lady sitting by herself having tea. The next day I was there, she returned at the same time. This happened for several days. We would nod and acknowledge each other's presence. Finally, she came over to stand by the piano and stared out of the large glass doors. I took a break and introduced myself. She didn't say her name, but she said that she was from Liberia and that she really enjoyed the music. When I asked how she was, she said, "My husband and my sons were just shot and killed two weeks ago."

What does one say?

Some ladies from the Jordanian delegation became regulars at tea. One day they brought along a friend of theirs from Spain, who was very curious about my work at Juilliard. When she discovered that my major teacher had been William Masselos, she squealed with delight. She and Bill Masselos had been childhood friends and both had studied piano at the old Juilliard Institute when it was uptown. There, Bill's teacher was Carl Friedberg, a former pupil of Clara Schumann's. She insisted that I come to her Fifth Avenue apartment for tea.

Elizabeth Brockman had two Steinway grand pianos in her living room. She claimed that Leopold Stokowski had sat in her living room to share his plans to found the American Symphony Orchestra in Washington, D.C. with her. She had photos on top of one the pianos of herself with Leopold, of herself with Kurt Waldheim – former Secretary General of the United Nations and former President of Austria – and of herself with the Shah of Iran. I spoke of my difficulties with practicing and she invited me to practice right then and there. Within the hour, she had called Bill Masselos, gave me money for a cab, and sent me over to his apartment on the Upper West Side. Mr. Masselos was delighted to see me and warned me about Elizabeth's "exuberance." Soon, she insisted that I resume taking lessons with him. Of course, she wanted to supervise my practicing.

Elizabeth Brockman was a delightful lady. She would host dinner parties for her diplomatic friends and invite me to come. Of course, toward the end of the meal she would walk over and whisper in my ear, "Why don't you play." I gladly obliged. The wine was flowing and the food was always delicious.

King Juan Carlos of Spain

My father and the Fisk Jubilee Singers with Princess Irene of Greece and Denmark

Elizabeth had told me that her husband was selling properties on the Costa del Sol, and she was so excited that one of the buyers was none other than King Juan Carlos. She would spend nearly an hour on the phone with the King and would be all giddy after the conversation. Well, one afternoon I was sitting there practicing as usual and the phone rang. Elizabeth was out. The servants were out. The phone just kept ringing, so I answered.

"Hello Elizabeth!" the melodious voice exclaimed.

"Uh, no. Elizabeth is out right now. May I take a message?"

"Well who is this?" he demanded.

"Uh... this is Nina. I'm just here practicing the piano..."

"Oh, *Niiiiina*! Elizabeth told me *all about* you. This is Juan. You know I'm buying her land on the coast. I'm looking forward to hearing you play! When are you coming to Spain?" etc. etc.

The King of Spain was chatting with me like I was an old friend.

Years later, when I was researching the material for my documentary on my father, I found a photograph of the Fisk Jubilee Singers after giving a Command Performance for Princess Irene of Greece in the early 1960s. It turns out that Princess Irene was the sister of the wife (or "consort") of King Juan Carlos, Doña Sofía. This family had been a part of our family's lives for two generations.

12

In 1985, the Delta Sigma Theta sorority had conducted a national talent hunt. The winners were to be presented in a gala event during their national convention at the Dallas Convention Center. CBS Records co-sponsored the affair and sent out a press release announcing the winners, of which I was one. Singer/songwriter Bill Withers was the Master of Ceremonies. I performed Chopin's *Ballade in G minor.* Of course, all of the musicians were hoping that the prize included a recording contract with CBS Records. No such luck, however. We did receive lovely trophies, though.

That same year I was presented as the guest artist for the Tourgee DeBose National Piano Competition at Southern University. I was also presented in concert at the Tuskegee Institute and at Tennessee State University. The classical music radio station in Nashville also presented my live concert on-the-air for their series titled "WPLN In Concert." I also presented concerts at Savannah State and Delaware State Colleges.

The Links Incorporated, founded in 1946, is an African American women's social service organization that is known for numerous annual social activities, including debutante cotillions, fashion show luncheons, auctions, and balls. Members include philanthropists, college presidents, judges, doctors, bankers, lawyers, executives, educators, and the wives of well-known public figures. There are approximately twelve thousand members in 273 chapters in forty-two states. In 1986, their national convention took place in Nashville and I was invited to present the opening night concert to this national audience in the Presidential Ballroom of the Opryland Hotel. The evening opened with greetings from the national president, Dolly Adams, then from the presidents of Tennessee State University, Meharry Medical College, and Fisk University. I then presented a recital of works by Scarlatti, Liszt, John W. Work III, and Gershwin – my own solo arrangement of the *Rhapsody in Blue*. The audience of over a thousand gave me a thunderous standing ovation.

Around that time, we learned that a friend of my parents' neighbors in Nashville had recently acquired a post in the U.S. Consulate in Munich, so I arranged a trip to visit her and audition for conductors and concert agents. It was one thing for Susan to travel to Austria, France, and England, but she and her family refused to set foot in Germany. I would make this trip by myself.

Kathryn Koob had been one of the American hostages held in Iran while Jimmy Carter was president. After she was released, she was given a plum position at the Consulate. She also had a very large, fabulous apartment. I stopped in London on the way to Munich to try my luck with some of the orchestras there. It soon became clear to me that feminism hadn't happened yet in London. The secretaries in the symphony offices had no idea of why I was there. I remember not being able to get through to anyone on the phone, but when I asked a man to call, at least he was able to get to the conductor's secretary. When I arrived at the offices with résumés, press quotes, recordings, and head shots in hand, the secretaries were convinced that I wanted to apply for a secretarial job. I showed them my materials and they still had no idea of what to do. It became clear to me that the men made the decisions, and without a prize from an international piano competition, I was out there floundering on my own.

When I arrived in Munich, I made more appointments but again, most of the secretaries weren't able to schedule auditions with the conductors. One told me that a rehearsal was taking place that afternoon and gave me the location. I made my way there. When I approached the conductor during a break in the rehearsal, the old white man was extremely rude to me. I don't know if it was because I spoke English, if he was offended by being spoken to by a Schwartze, or what his problem was. Eventually one of the violinists took pity on me and pointed me toward his secretary. I left my materials with her.

Kathryn had planned to drive to Vienna for the weekend – where she had lived before moving to Munich – and invited me to come along. I figured it was an opportunity to leave more materials with more conductors' secretaries. She graciously introduced me to her American friends who were living in Munich. We were invited to many parties, openings, premieres, etc. When she would mention that we were planning a trip to Vienna, all of her friends had the same response: "Oh! She *has* to meet Olive!" Eventually Kate explained to me that Olive was an African-American soprano from Pittsburgh who was married to the Austrian Ambassador to Barbados. She had quite the reputation as a socialite and was famous for her soirées at the Ambassador's Residence. In fact, it was just recently – in the age of the Internet – when I learned that Olive Moorefield was a bona fide star of German television in the 1950s and '60s. She was a celebrated actress in the German film *Uncle Tom's Cabin (Onkel Toms Hutte)* and starred in several German language Hollywood-style musicals. Go 'head, Miss Olive!

Again, I hit the ground running in Vienna. I called management offices and left my packets with several receptionists. About a year later I would learn that one of the agents in one of those offices quietly walked over and picked up my envelope. She later engaged me to appear as piano soloist with the Chicago Sinfonietta under the baton of American conductor Paul Freeman. The concert would be the opening night for the Jeunesse Festival at the famous Musikverein in Vienna, from which the annual New Year's Day concert featuring the Vienna Philharmonic is broadcast internationally. The other soloist on the program was soprano Wilhelmenia Fernandez, made famous by the cult film *Diva*.

Vienna at the time was very inexpensive. One could rent a three-bedroom flat for less than half the price of rent in Manhattan. Young people would rent large flats in pre-war (WWII, that is) buildings and install new electrical lines and plumbing on their own. I stayed in an apartment which belonged to a friend of Kathryn's – who was out of town at the time – which was right on the Danube. The young classical musicians I met were actually able to live from their incomes from performing. Granted there were at least ten orchestras in Vienna (including the three opera orchestras) plus various chamber ensembles. The lavish, ornate concert halls were absolutely fabulous and the tickets were actually affordable for young students. (This is what happens when the State supports the Arts!) One frisky young violinist took me on a tour of the Musikverein during a Vienna Philharmonic concert which was being broadcast live on national TV. We went up and down stairwells, leapt over cables, and snuck around corners dodging the security staff. Finally, she looked through a small window of a heavy door, nonchalantly leaned back and said, "Take a look." I peered through the glass and saw a very elderly Herbert von Karajan conducting the Philharmonic mid-performance. She had taken me to the stage door! We stood there spellbound, drowning in the magnificent waves of Bruckner's Eighth Symphony until security made us leave. She feigned a poor, countryside accent and pretended to be lost. I just stood there, mute. The nice man then gave us directions to the smaller Brahms Hall.

My frisky, fearless friend arranged for me to audition for a conductor of one of the many orchestras she played in. He was a young... well, slightly older, man who had a reputation for "auditioning" young girls. I initially had met him at a party and I observed many of the female players in his orchestra sitting on his lap. I wasn't going to do that and he knew it! A few days later when I played for him, he complained about the quality of the instrument I was playing on. But he said nothing about my actual playing. Was I going to have to sit on men's laps to get a contract?

A few days after Kate and I arrived in Vienna, I was disappointed that no one had offered to introduce me to the famous Olive. After a particularly rough day, I bought myself a few bottles of delicious Austrian beer, and went back to the apartment. After the second beer, I started flipping through the phone book. There was the number for the Barbadian Ambassador's Residence. After the third beer, I dialed the number. I don't remember what I said, but Miss Moorefield sounded delighted to hear a familiar American accent. She invited me to her home for tea the next day.

Olive Moorefield became a dear friend and role-model for me. The Ambassador's Residence was located in the most exclusive part of Vienna and she often would entertain the likes of Leonard Bernstein, Kathleen Battle, and Jessye Norman in her home. She also introduced me to the Austrian Heuriger – a restaurant where wine in various stages of fermentation was served, produced from vineyards on the property owned by the restaurateur. Mozart, Beethoven, Schubert, and all of the composers who came through Vienna hung out at the Heurigen, which were famous for their long wooden benches and large tables. You would sit down with strangers but by the end of the evening, we were all best friends, in spite of (or maybe because of) stumbling through broken German and English. I also enjoyed some of the best fried chicken I'd ever had at a Viennese Heuriger! Leave it to Miss Olive to find the best fried chicken in town.

Before I left Vienna, Olive gave me the name and number of a concert agent who was a friend of hers. I stopped by his office on my way to the airport and prayed that *this* was the contact who would make the difference in my career.

I couldn't wait to get back to Susan!

13

At the urging of my parents, I started looking into various doctoral programs in the city. Practicing without being connected to an institution can be a problem in New York, and having deadlines for the learning and memorizing of repertoire is always helpful. Shura Cherkassky had introduced me to pianist Constance Keene, who was then on the faculty at the Manhattan School of Music. With too much time on my hands and no career in sight, I decided to apply.

The audition went smoothly and I was accepted with a partial scholarship. I soon learned that I really was not cut out for the obsession with minute details when it came to doctoral writing. I realized I had had enough of boring academic journals. The biographies were interesting to me, but it was still all about men, men, and more men. I remember presenting a doctoral recital, which meant another opportunity to play before a New York audience. But as far as the coursework was concerned, I don't remember much. I do remember presenting a paper on the utilization of the melody of the Spiritual "Were You There (When They Crucified My Lord)" in the Scriabin Piano Concerto. I also prepared bibliographical notes for a

paper on Dvořák. Soon my concert schedule began to inter-
fere with my class schedule, so I had to withdraw. It was a relief, especially since one of the professors told us that
performers should not publicize the fact that they have doc-
torates. "Doctors are perceived as being cold and sterile," she
said. (That same white woman said something to me along
the lines of: "You people have jazz and rock and roll. Why
can't you leave the classical to us?" Good Lord! Where do
they find these lunatics?)

Still struggling with the dilemma of trying to find a manager, I decided to focus on one thing that I could control. The
organizations that ran the competitions usually asked for a
copy of a *New York Times* review of a New York debut recital,
which I did not have. So I asked the John W. Work III Memorial Foundation in Nashville if they would be willing to sponsor a debut recital for me at Lincoln Center. (Composer John
W. Work and his research of African-American folk music
were briefly mentioned in the film *Cadillac Records*, in which
Beyoncé starred. He had also directed the Fisk Jubilee Singers
before my father took over as director.) They graciously
agreed. So on April 5, 1987, I was presented in my New York
recital debut in Alice Tully Hall at Lincoln Center.

Preparation for the concert was all-consuming. I had to supervise the fundraising, publicity, and ticket sales – with the
help of New York Recital Associates – in addition to preparing
the repertoire. I had scheduled concert tours for months in advance of the actual concert so that my chops would be at their
peak. I resumed practicing in the Steinway basement, where I
had run into Horowitz a few years before. I also found another

piano in an apartment where I could practice. This apartment was on Park Avenue and the hosts were most gracious. Their cat would even keep me company while I practiced.

One day I received a call from *Keyboard Magazine*. They wanted to do a story on me and were asking where their photographer could do a photoshoot with me. I asked my hosts on Park Avenue if we could do the photoshoot at their place. They happily agreed. *Keyboard Magazine* gave me a full-page article in the issue with Herbie Hancock and Chick Corea on the cover.

A few weeks before the concert, my poster appeared in front of the hall. What an experience – to see my face ten times larger than life hoisted in front of Lincoln Center! I observed Japanese tourists standing in front of it and pointing, looking in their calendars and walking into the box office to purchase tickets. This was what it was all about! I was also paying for the salaries and insurance for the box office staff, the stage hands, the lighting personnel, and security. Luckily, an older gay gentleman who was a friend of Damon Evans' offered to provide the Baldwin piano for the concert. Of course, Baldwin was given credit in the program and on all the publicity, so it was advantageous for them as well.

I will never forget walking out on that stage at Alice Tully Hall for the first time. The backstage staff must have been used to performers having the jitters because I remember feeling someone almost pushing me from behind out onto the stage. I was in the most expensive gown I had ever owned. The audience sounded enormous. Some guardian spirit guided my hands and fingers that night. It was the best performance of my life. The huge audience jumped to their feet after the final chords of the Rachmaninoff Second Sonata. I heard shouts of "Bravo!" and was even called back for an encore.

A week after the concert my review appeared in the *New York Times*. The critic was very kind and full of praise. I was honored and humbled to be able to share his review with the world.

At Lincoln Center before my New York Debut

Alice Tully Hall

Home of the Chamber Music Society
Lincoln Center for the Performing Arts

Sunday Evening, April 5, 1987, at 8:00

THE JOHN W. WORK, III, MEMORIAL FOUNDATION, INC.
presents

NINA KENNEDY
Pianist

SCARLATTI	**Four Sonatas** E major, K.380 G major, K.125 D minor, K.52 C major, K.159
BEETHOVEN	**Sonata in D minor, Op. 31, No. 2** **"The Tempest"** Largo—Allegro Adagio Allegretto
CHOPIN	**Andante Spianato and Grande Polonaise** **Brillante, Op. 22**

Intermission

KAY	**Four Inventions** Andante moderato Scherzando Larghetto Allegro
WORK	**Appalachia (1945)** Big bunch of roses Fisher's hornpipe Take me back
RACHMANINOFF	**Sonata No. 2 in B-flat minor, Op. 36 (1914)*** Allegro agitato Non allegro—Lento Allegro molto—Presto

In consideration of the performing artists and members of the audience, those who must leave before the
end of the performance are asked to do so between numbers, not during the performance.
The taking of photographs and the use of recording equipment are not allowed in this building.

My NY Debut recital program at Lincoln Center

• • • • •

In spite of a triumphant concert – a "nine-minute standing ovation" as reported in the papers, shouts of "Bravo!" and encores
and rave reviews – our lives were about to take a turn for the
worst. The next two and a half years became an unimaginable
nightmare.

About one month before the concert, Susan discovered a
lump in her breast. She had had cysts before, which had
turned out to be benign and eventually disappeared. She assumed this one would be the same, so she scheduled a doctor's appointment for after the concert. Within a week, she was
in the hospital for surgery to remove the lump. It was cancer-
ous. The lymph nodes were already affected. Six weeks of radiation treatments, followed by six months of chemotherapy
ensued.

I put my career focus on hold to be by her side. The
chemotherapy treatments, the nausea and hair-loss, and the
sheer terror of feeling betrayed by her own body put Susan
through hell. It was heartbreaking to watch her suffer.

I remember being engaged to perform the Grieg Concerto
with an orchestra in Ohio. This was right when Susan was in
the middle of receiving chemotherapy treatments. Since I
would be away from home for a few days, Susan stayed with
her parents for the days before my scheduled departure and
would stay with them while I was gone. I remember needing
to practice and using a piano in one of their neighbors' homes.
It was such an exhausting time – both physically and emotion-

ally. Just being in her mother's presence gave Susan enormous stress and since I knew this, I did all I could to keep her mom at bay. I think her mom could see the toll all of this stress and anxiety was taking on me, so she was trying to be a little kinder and gentler toward me, which was not in her nature. I think she ultimately appreciated the care and support I was showing toward her daughter.

The concert went well, as usual. My playing was superb, albeit a little stiff. On stage, I wore another gown picked out by Susan's mother.

Months after the radiation and chemotherapy treatments were completed, Susan's cancer seemed to be in remission. A concert agent in Holland offered to arrange a European concert tour for me, and Susan seemed well enough for me to be able to accept. There were concerts in London; Glasgow and Edinburgh, Scotland; Brussels, Belgium; and Amsterdam (which was the pièce de résistance of the tour as the venue was the Concertgebouw – Holland's equivalent of our Carnegie Hall). The agent had made arrangements with swanky hotels so that I could stay in exchange for advertising. Again, there were standing ovations and rave reviews. I felt I was well on my way to a bona fide career. However, there was little money left for me when the tour was over. The expenses and the manager's fee practically did me in.

A few months later, the same agent arranged a concert tour of the western German towns of Saarbrücken, Saarlouis, and Schmelz, where the headline of the review of my concert read, "Eine Meisterin am Piano" ("A Master of the Piano"). Again, I traveled to Germany alone.

At the Concertgebouw

Standing ovation in Amsterdam

Rehearsing in Scotland

In 1989, I was invited to appear as guest piano soloist with the Nashville Symphony in a performance of the Rachmaninoff Second Piano Concerto. When Maestro Schermerhorn asked me which concerto I would like to play, the Rachmaninoff was my first choice.

That year the Nashville Symphony had been on strike, so they were looking to engage soloists who were "less expensive." Since I had such a large following in Nashville, tickets sold quickly when the concert was announced. I would learn later that my concert sold the most tickets of all of the concerts that season.

We performed on two nights in the old War Memorial Auditorium. After my Rachmaninoff, the symphony closed the program with the Dvořák "New World" Symphony. Kenneth Schermerhorn was in his element, pulling all of the drama he could out of the finale of the Dvořák. Of course, my Rachmaninoff received a standing ovation and deafening applause, cheers, and shouts of "Bravo!" I was happy to have the opportunity to perform with him when I did. The Schermerhorn Symphony Center in Nashville is named in his honor, built by the patronage and generosity of billionaire businesswoman and philanthropist Martha Ingram, who devoted several pages in her book titled *Apollo's Struggle* to me, my family, and the Fisk Jubilee Singers.

The headline of the review of the concert in the *Nashville Banner* read: "Guest Pianist Reveals Poet's Heart." In his review, critic Henry Arnold wrote:

> "Pianist Nina Kennedy left Nashville not long ago a starry-eyed teenager with a promising talent and has returned an elegantly beautiful young woman with a prodigious artistry at the keyboard.
>
> Kennedy brought her hometown audience to its feet Friday night with a glowing performance of Rachmaninoff's *Concerto for Piano and Orchestra No. 2 in C minor.*
>
> There was great strength and tonal beauty in her playing and Kennedy revealed a poet's heart in her reading of Rachmaninoff's inspired, romantic score. Arpeggios rippled with reckless abandon, trills had an electrifying intensity and melodies soared with exuberant passion."

At that time, the *Musical America* was the bible of classical music. Virtually all concert managers purchased pages of ads in the annual publication called "A Directory for the Performing Arts." With my New York Debut under my belt, I decided it was time to buy my own page. Many of the graphic designers I consulted wanted way too much money for the job. Finally, I found a man who offered to do the work for the right price. While he was at it, I decided to go ahead and have flyers printed with the same design. That graphic designer was Michael Murphree. During our first meeting we established that we were "family." Thus marked the beginning of a long friendship. Michael, his boyfriend Jack, Susan, and I, would meet for cocktails, dinners, Broadway shows, etc.

Michael also filled me in on the gossip flying around about some of the gay men in classical music. He told me tales of gay male power-brokers in the biz – one of whom was notorious for slipping date-rape drugs into drinks he would give to messenger boys. This man died of AIDS within a year of my introduction to him. (It is a sad fact that many male members of my graduating class at Juilliard – who won competitions and artist management contracts and fat contracts with conductors and orchestras – are no longer with us because of AIDS.)

Unfortunately, *Musical America* is no longer being published. But if you ever find the archives, my full-page ads can be seen in the directories of 1989 and 1990.

14

One of Susan's last nagging worries was that I would be thrown out into the streets if and when she died. She had been struggling with her landlord to get my name on the lease for years, to no avail. When she finally begged her father to call some of his friends and he finally agreed, the matter was solved within days.

Susan had seemed well for several months. She had gone back to work and we were taking our annual vacations. That year we went to the Côte d'Azur in the South of France. We flew into Nice and rented a car for day trips to Cannes, Saint Tropez, Saint Paul de Vence, Monte Carlo, and Genoa in Italy. Driving a car around those hairpin curves all along the cliffs above the Mediterranean, after having shared a bottle of wine with lunch, I understood how so many "accidents" have happened on those old Roman roads.

It was in Nice where we visited the ancient Greco-Roman temple to the goddess Nike. It was the first time I saw stone tablets engraved with prayers to the goddess in the three ancient languages: Greek, Latin, and Aramaic. Thus began my interest in goddess history and liturgy. Hearing the prayers coming from my own mouth, I wondered how my life would have been affected if I could have prayed to a female deity as a young girl. Just reading the words "Praise Her" stirred something deep within my soul.

It was mid-way through our vacation when Susan developed a bad cough. She coughed the whole way back to the United States where we discovered that the cancer had metastasized to her lungs. This meant more chemotherapy, and that the fluid in her lungs had to be drained periodically. New Year's Eve of 1990, she was in the hospital. I brought her a bowl of my traditional homemade black-eyed peas and rice and after visiting hours were over, I walked home through the streets of Manhattan while revelers were celebrating and blowing horns and yelling "Happy New Year!" I've never felt so alone in my life.

On January 27th, 1990, around 2:00 am., two years and nine months after the initial cancer diagnosis, Susan died. I held her hand while she crossed over. I saw the look of ecstasy in her eyes just before *it* – the transfiguration – started to happen. I heard her last exhale, which sounded more like a huge sigh of relief.

I spent that night at Susan's parents' house, weeping the whole time. The next day, back at our apartment, several of our friends came over to make the calls to friends and colleagues to inform them of the funeral details. They fed me and put me to bed. I took a tranquilizer to get to sleep.

Again, I was alone.

But for the first time, I had a home. And a ghost.

That night, in the middle of the night while I was sound asleep, I was suddenly awakened by the sound of a crash and the television suddenly turned itself on. I searched for the remote control, which was always on the night table by the bed. Couldn't find it, so I groggily got out of bed to turn the TV off and promptly went back to sleep. The next morning, while I was rushing around getting ready for the funeral, I stepped on one of the batteries from the TV remote control. Then I remembered what had happened in the night. I looked down and there was the remote control on the floor. It had obviously bounced off of the wall and landed on the floor just in front of the TV. The back of it had fallen off and the batteries were on the floor.

Weeks later, a spiritualist would tell me that the energy of the recently departed rests in objects which they handled or touched frequently. She also told me to pay attention to the significance of the words "remote control."

There were also the usual signs of visitation – the flickering lights, a sudden wave of perfume or the scent of flowers, and other objects moving on their own. It was comforting to know that she was around and reaching out to me. But I still would have given anything just to be able to touch her again, to see her smile or hear her laugh. But the container – her body – was gone. Only the love remained.

Hundreds came to her funeral. From the front row, I hadn't really looked around to see how many were there but when the rabbi announced that we could be seated, I heard the sound of hundreds of bodies sitting down onto hundreds of chairs. I think many of her work colleagues had had no idea that she was that sick. The rabbi gave a lovely account of our travels and adventures, and even mentioned my name in the course of his eulogy. The whole day felt surreal to me. At one point during the service I heard myself wailing, but it felt like the sound was echoing from somewhere else. It definitely came from my body but must have been some sort of out-of-body experience. I had to take a tranquilizer to get through the day.

At the burial, each of us pitched a shovel-full of dirt into the grave onto the coffin. The sound of the dirt hitting the wooden box still reverberates in my head.

While working at Morgan on Wall Street, Susan had named me the beneficiary of her life insurance policy. At some point during the days after her death, I realized that my life had changed forever. Finally, for the first time in my life I could live without having to play concerts.

15

Unfortunately, I was still under contract for concerts through Black History Month, February, of 1990. That February I was engaged to appear as piano soloist with the Jackson, Tennessee Symphony Orchestra. The orchestra manager was a very sweet lady and was very attentive to my needs. After the concert and reception, she invited me to her home for a nightcap. I suspected that she might be "family," so I dared to share with her what I had just been through. She exclaimed, "Oh, Nina! No! NO!" Then she took me into her arms. In the following months, I became a regular guest in her home. She raised Tennessee Walking Horses so I got a little taste of farm life. It was especially interesting when one of the mares was about to give birth and my host asked me to go out to the barn twice a day and watch for droplets of milk from her teats, which would mean that birth was imminent and the veterinarian had to be called. The whole environment was a blessed relief from the stress of life in New York City.

During those months after Susan's death, I was invited to give a concert as part of the Dame Myra Hess Memorial Concert Series in Chicago. The concert would be recorded live for radio broadcast, so I was very excited. I had been a fan of Myra Hess' concert career and had incorporated her arrangement of Bach's *Jesu, Joy of Man's Desiring* in my programs. I played well and received an enormous ovation. The fee was minimal, but the director assured me that he would see to it that I would benefit via additional engagements. I never heard from him again.

I could not afford to break down emotionally until after the last concert of February. The breakdown started in the cab on the way back from LaGuardia Airport and lasted through the end of March.

I couldn't tell you much about my life during the aftermath of Susan's death. I remember a lot of dancing and drinking in nightclubs. My parents didn't even offer to come and help me in my grief. My apartment was a mess. I could barely order Chinese food or keep myself fed. The only thing that kept me going was the knowledge that Susan's spirit was watching over me and protecting me.

It was the year of the Gulf War. Young men were afraid of being drafted and being sent away to die. All of us were terrified of "The Bomb" being dropped on us. So we danced. We danced as if there would be no tomorrow. Sunday nights at The Pyramid Club in the East Village, we would be dancing so hard that you would see credit cards, flat keys, and foreign currency all strewn on the floor, having fallen out of pockets. But we didn't care. We were DANCING!

Suddenly, after six years in a monogamous relationship, I was single, lonely, self-destructive, and reckless. After spending so much time focusing on sickness and death, my body craved life. Sex was the only way I knew to grasp at the life-force. I didn't want conversation or idle chit chat. I didn't want to talk about how I was doing. I wanted to lose myself in another's body. Sex kept me alive.

I went on like this for months – dancing all night to Junior Vasquez on the turntables and drinking scotch until I had the courage to pick someone up, or coming home alone and watching the sun rise while blasting Wagner operas in my headphones. I played a few concerts during this time, but I really couldn't tell you much about them. I walked around in a daze, a fog of semi-consciousness.

One night at Henrietta Hudson's I met a sweet German girl (or rather she seemed sweet at the time). When I spoke a few German words to her, she had a look of absolute shock on her face. "Why do you speak German?!" she asked in disbelief. I told her that I loved Wagner operas and could quote most of them. She told me that she was from a little village in southwest Germany and that the Rhine River went right through the village. She would swim in the Rhine during the summers.

Susan had sent me a Rhinemaiden!

I was annoyed with shouting over the noise and invited her to my place. Thus began a dramatic affair that lasted for a few months. She was a painter and lived not far from me in the East Village. I took her to international parties where she quickly made "friends." Eventually she claimed she no longer had time for me. Years later, I would read online that this girl was wanted by the FBI for absconding with millions of dollars which she had stolen from her ex-boyfriend/employer. The online article said that she had even gone to the pope to get the Vatican involved in her "foundation." I could tell that she was not quite right in the head, but I had no idea that she was *that* crazy!

Later that year, I was invited by a friend of my mother's to give a recital at Morehouse College in Atlanta. That friend, Dr. Anna Harvin Grant, had been my mother's classmate at Fisk, and was then on the faculty at Morehouse. I knew that Atlanta had been the cradle of the Civil Rights Movement, and was proud to be able to share my art with the young men at Morehouse. I was also engaged to give a lecture and master class, so my familiarity with academic life served me well.

When I arrived at the Atlanta International Airport, I saw Dr. Grant waiting for me in the baggage claim area. I had brought with me the same beaded gown I had worn at Lincoln Center, and the weight of the beads made it impossible to carry it on board. Dr. Grant was chatting with a beautiful black woman whose face looked vaguely familiar from a distance. As I got closer, Dr. Grant seemed more occupied with chatting with her friend than she was with greeting me. I stood there awkwardly waiting for my chance to say hello and give her a hug. Then I saw that this beautiful black lady was none other than Coretta Scott King! She had just flown in from somewhere and they ran into each other at baggage claim. Dr. Grant introduced us and invited her to the concert. I gushed about how delighted I was to meet her, and felt that immediate pain in my chest when the memories of the pictures of her sitting at her murdered husband's funeral flashed through my mind. But on that day, she didn't look sad or like a perpetual widow. She had a very busy schedule representing her family and carrying her late husband's legacy into the future. It was one of the most memorable moments of my life.

16

A year and a half after Susan's death, enter Beth. If I hadn't been so vulnerable, I might have had the sense to walk – no, run – in the opposite direction. But I *was* vulnerable and she could smell it.

I needed an intermediary, someone who would act as a buffer between the rough business world and myself. I didn't know what to say to men. I didn't know how to talk to men. I had always let the piano do the talking for me.

Beth changed all of that.

I met Beth one Friday night at the Clit Club, where she was celebrating the end of her first year of law school with three other friends. When we kept finding ourselves in the same proximity on the dance floor, she introduced herself and offered to buy me a drink. She later told me that they all were going to an outdoor concert at Central Park the next day and invited me to join them. I accepted.

Days later, during our first dinner-date, she told me that she had been gang-raped when she was fourteen by a bunch of high school boys. She didn't know how many – it could have been five, six, or seven. She had passed out. She said that earlier that night she and her mother had had a fight and she left the house. She went to the home of one of her schoolmates, who had a sofa-bed in his basement. He had some friends over; they were drinking beer. When she asked if she could spend the night, he said "Sure." She said she didn't remember the details of how the rape actually started. She just remembers the superintendent of the building knocking on the door in response to her screams, saying he was calling the police. She said they all ran. She remembered running barefoot through the ice-encrusted snow. When she got home, her parents beat her up. Her mother punched and slapped her while her father held her in place. When she fell to the floor in a fetal position, her father picked her up and held her by the shoulders so that her mother could inflict more punishment. She eventually took a shower and went to bed. The police brought her purse to the house and asked her father if they wanted to press charges. Her father said no.

I had seen women go into flashbacks before during love-making. I knew the signs. I was determined to show her that this piece of information would not scare me away. She started a legal argument. I would soon learn that a legal argument for her was the equivalent of foreplay.

Days later we made love and she did go into flashbacks. But hers were the flashbacks of a three-year-old child.

Her father would call daily. She called him by his first name, so I didn't know who he was at first. It sounded like a conversation between lovers. I didn't ask questions. He called at all hours. Once he was calling obviously from his bed. Beth's mother was right there next to him. They made it clear that they had just finished having sex. Beth's mother took the phone and said to her daughter, "He needs a butt-plug. Where can I get a butt-plug?" Then he would call during the Anita Hill/Clarence Thomas hearings weeping. Everyone was watching the live broadcasts of the hearings. Beth told me that he was weeping, but she never asked why. It made me wonder what it was that he was so guilty about. How many black women had been on the receiving end of his "interest"?

I felt so sorry for this girl. She could be so loving and child-like when her defenses were down. It was truly heartbreaking watching her go into flashbacks. You never knew when they would surface. Once while we were making love, she started to cry like a baby. She put both hands on the back of her head.

"My head is bleeding," she whimpered.

I was used to her flashbacks by then.

"Let me see," I whispered calmly.

She turned over so that I could look. But just the sensation of the sheets on her skin brought her back to the present. I don't know if she heard me say that there was no blood. She just continued to cry and whimper.

Her mother was out of control when it came to physical punishment of her children. She broke Beth's nose when Beth was eight and repeatedly left both of her daughters bruised and scarred. Beth's father even claimed that his wife would beat him during the night while he was sleeping. He would awaken to showers of slaps and punches.

Here was someone who had been through as much as I had, if not more. I wouldn't have to censor myself out of fear that this person couldn't handle my recent experience. Morbid curiosity drew each of us toward one another.

I told Beth right from the beginning that I was a concert pianist and had been a child prodigy. She, too, had been a child prodigy of sorts. She had recorded commercial jingles as a small child and her voice was quite recognizable to the American public. I decided it was a common bond we shared. Few have known the kind of performance pressure that is forced onto a child. It can foster an early sense of discipline or it can result in feelings of exploitation. The difference is up to the parents' awareness and fulfillment of the child's needs. In both of our cases, our childhood needs were ignored.

She had made quite a bit of money as a child singing in nationally broadcast television and radio commercials. The money was supposedly being held in trust for her by her parents. After she finished law school, her father confessed that he had gambled most of her money away and had spent the rest on prostitutes.

Beth had grown up in the music biz. Her father, a frustrated composer, had started out as a drummer playing the nightclub circuit in the Poconos – or the "Jewish Alps" as they were called then. He went on to manage rock bands and eventually to compose film scores. By the time Beth was in law school, he was spending most of his time in lawsuits against music publishers and record labels in an effort to recoup lost royalties. When Beth and I met, she did not know what area of law would be her specialty. But after she overheard me on the telephone trying to negotiate a fee with a symphony manager in Vienna, she made an announcement.

"That's it!" she said. "You're never making another business call again."

From that moment on, she handled all of my business negotiations.

Soon after we were officially together, I had an engagement to appear as piano soloist with a southern orchestra. Beth asked to come along to gain more insight into the classical world. She had to inform her parents that she would be leaving town for a few days. An interrogation ensued: "Why? Where? With whom?" She answered them. The cat was out of the bag or rather, the Beth was out of the closet. Beth's mother insisted that she meet her for dinner before she left.

Beth asked me to be in her apartment while she met her mother as she didn't know what condition she would be in afterwards. Soon after she left, I settled into a TV show. Within ten minutes, she was already back. She rushed into the flat, slammed the door, and locked it. She called downstairs to her doorman.

"José, if my mother comes in, don't let her up," she said into the intercom.

I was all ears.

She said that her mother ordered their meal, then out of the blue came the following.

"I knew you were raped," she said. "I knew it while it was happening."

Beth responded, "Enjoy your soup." Then she got up and left her mother sitting there at the table.

That phone call which Beth overheard, I believed, was the prelude to my international concert career. Beth felt I should have held out for more money, but I was not going to risk hearing them say that they would have to find someone else.

A few years earlier, the manager who happened to be sitting in an office in Vienna – where I came to drop off my materials – crossed paths with the African American conductor Paul Freeman, who had already received my materials on several occasions. Both of them were on the planning committee for the Jeunesse Gershwin and Jazz Festival for that year. The opening night concert was being planned and I was invited for two performances. The first night at Vienna's famous Konzerthaus, I would appear as piano soloist in a performance of Gershwin's *"I Got Rhythm" Variations* and the second night I would perform the *Rhapsody in Blue*. The Chicago Sinfonietta was the orchestra.

This was my big chance, the break I was waiting for. I just knew that a European career would precede any American success, as had been the case for every other African American classical musician. I was on my way.

The second night of the festival was to take place at the Musikverein, Vienna's most prestigious concert hall. There was the portrait of Richard Wagner staring down on me from my dressing room wall. I warmed-up with the *Liebestod* on the beautiful Bösendorfer in my dressing room to honor him.

The African American soprano Wilhelminia Fernandez was invited to appear to sing a set of arias. Wilhelminia was to receive top billing in the publicity for the festival. She was already famous in Europe for her portrayal of the beautiful soprano in the film *Diva*. Tickets for the concert had been sold out, but most people in the audience came to see Wilhelminia.

Publicity poster announcing my Vienna debut at the Musikverein

When she finished her set, they would not let her leave. They called her back to do encore after encore. My performance had been during the first half of the program; hers was in the second. So at least I was able to listen to her and hear the deafening ovations. That ovation went on for what seemed like twenty minutes. What can I say? The Austrians LOVE their music! It was the first time I heard people in the audience stomping their feet to show their appreciation.

I don't like to blow my own horn, but I must admit that my own two performances were pretty fabulous. I received two standing ovations. The orchestra members gave me the ultimate honor by putting down their instruments to offer their own applause. I was so pleased and relieved that for this, certainly one of the most important performances of my life, I was able to do my best work.

But unfortunately, after this European triumph, no managers were beating down my door. No agents were waiting in line for meetings with me. I had crossed the Atlantic, given two amazing performances, and basically nothing happened. Only the woman manager who had recommended me in the first place invited me to participate in a piano festival in Munich later that winter.

The music of Wagner became a magical influence in my life. At first, I had wanted to learn the Franz Liszt piano transcription of Isolde's *Liebestod* after reading the autobiography of Arthur Rubinstein. The piece always provoked a huge ovation so I decided to put it in my repertoire. Imagine my shock and dismay when the associate conductor of the Philadelphia Orchestra told me after my audition, "Don't play the Liebestod. Play Mozart or Schubert. But not the Liebestod."

Oh, so there was something offensive about a female playing such blatantly sensual music, or what?

Eventually I became curious about the opera, but at the time it was only available for purchase on CD and I did not own a CD player. So for our first Christmas together, I bought a CD player and the Herbert von Karajan recording of *Tristan und Isolde* with the Berlin Philharmonic.

I watched Beth's emotional transformation take place before my eyes the longer she was exposed to this music. It was like watching layers and layers of thick walls of ice gradually melting away. She was a sensitive soul, but her sensitivity had had to go underground just so that she could survive her childhood.

Beth's family was Jewish. They never listened to any Wagner.

I remember being engaged to perform the Grieg Concerto with the Kingsport, Tennessee Symphony Orchestra. Beth came with me and sat in on my rehearsals. When I requested time to practice on my own, she repeatedly said that she didn't understand why I spent so much time and energy perfecting my technique. "No one can tell the difference," she said. But I could. I felt it was my job to go out there and give the best performance I was capable of, even if it was for just a few hundred dollars.

After the Grieg, I gave them the Liebestod for an encore. I felt the members of the orchestra especially enjoyed it. They put down their instruments to applaud me.

17

At that time, MTV was all the rage. I still didn't have a recording on the market, but I knew that recording artists had to think in terms of video if a product was going to sell. I had yet to see a classical music video on television.

Then I had a vision.

It all came flooding into my brain at once. I heard the music – Ravel's *Valses nobles et sentimentales* – and I saw the dreamy, sexy images. I told Beth my idea. As fate would have it, a few days later we ran into filmmaker Spike Lee who was shopping at Tower Records. Beth called his name and he didn't respond. Then I called his name and he either confused me with someone else – as he immediately came over for a hug and a kiss – or he was a lecher. In any event, I asked if I could call him about a project. He said "Sure!" and our contact was made. Now all we needed was a recording contract.

Beth called every classical label in Manhattan and could hardly get past the secretaries to speak to the male executives. Finally, she got ahold of one A&R director at one of the prestigious labels and gave him her spiel. He too was trying to figure out how to get classical videos on MTV. When she told him of our plan to generate publicity around Spike Lee, he scheduled an audition for me with one of his talent scouts. We booked a room at Steinway Hall. Evidently the excitement of this representative was too big to be ignored. I was given a top recommendation and was called in for a meeting.

By this point, I still didn't know how to talk to men or what to say to them. Beth did the talking. They went through the usual blah blah blah... Then she had the idea to pop a tape in the stereo of my playing. His whole demeanor changed. His face lit up. He sat back in his chair and relaxed. I even saw some teeth. He seemed convinced. He said he would discuss the proposal with his boss and would get back to us. Days later we had a second meeting, this time in the boss's office.

Beth thoroughly instructed me on what and what not to say, (for example: "Royalties? Oh, that's something they do in England. Right?") I was supposed to love making music more than getting paid and I was supposed to be willing to sign my life away just for another opportunity to play. But this time, it would be a performance for posterity. I had never really gotten what meetings with patriarchs were all about. Whenever I asked my father for anything, the answer was always no so I certainly could not walk in with any feeling of entitlement. Beth explained the basics: "Just go in, shake hands, look around, say 'Nice office. Nice view.' Then walk out with a deal."

The boss was a show-off. He bragged about his travels, his house in the country, his record collection. He was really more interested in trying to get Beth into his country house than in signing another classical artist. Beth played along, smiling and jiggling her breasts. I pretended not to notice. She had instructed me to dress like a pop star so they would get the idea of the kind of artist they would be promoting. This would not be their typical promotion for their traditional audience – the white-haired set. This was something new, something different, and something that would sell. We all shook hands and congratulated ourselves for being so hip.

We were barely home for an hour when the phone rang. It was the boss. He wanted to tell us personally that we had a deal. He was instructing the legal department to draft a contract. We were ecstatic.

Beth was still enrolled in classes while she negotiated this contract. She sometimes asked for help from her father's lawyer or from her Entertainment Law professor. But for the most part, she negotiated the contract herself. Meanwhile, I was practicing my ass off and starving myself to death for the video shoot. Spike Lee needed the master of the two and a half minutes of music before he was scheduled to begin shooting his next film. I was booked in the studio at least a month before his project was scheduled to start. We were sure we had plenty of time.

I should have been suspicious when we returned to sign the contract and our aging A&R director was nowhere to be found. The contract was signed *"in absentia"* by his secretary. But we were too excited. We had our tickets to fly to London, which was where the company's recording studios were located, and I was practiced and prepared to make history with what would certainly become a Grammy Award-winning CD.

I had first met Roberta Flack in Nashville back in the 1970s when she made a guest appearance with the Nashville Symphony. Through a strange chain of coincidences, I ended up contacting her fifteen years later in New York to ask if I might practice on her piano. She asked for some lessons in exchange. She still holds a place in my memory as one of the sweetest women I ever met in the music business. I began a regular practice schedule at her apartment in the Dakota on Central Park West on her beautiful nine-foot Bösendorfer. Whether she was home or not, the maid would let me into the apartment and I could make wonderful music on that wonderful instrument. Roberta was a real inspiration to me as a black woman pianist who had success in the industry. She showed me that it was possible.

John Lennon and Yoko Ono had lived in the apartment across from hers. "They're both still over there," she would say, years after he had been killed.

I told her I had my own personal ghost, too. But I didn't go into detail.

After my CD would be released, I was already planning to thank Roberta in my Grammy Award acceptance speech. I would not have been able to prepare so thoroughly for the recording session without her.

We did the photo shoot for the cover a week before we were to fly to London to record. I was the skinniest I had been since high school. Photographer Marc Bryan-Brown had been hired by my label to shoot the artwork for the album cover. Marc had been an official photographer for Whitney Houston back in the 1990s, so he was a pro when it came to photographing black women.

Photo Credit: Marc Bryan-Brown

An album cover photo by Marc Bryan-Brown

The night we arrived in London, we turned on the TV and saw that England's version of the Grammy Awards was being held that night in one of London's swanky hotels. I told Beth to get dressed. We were going.

There were representatives from my record label at the event, so I kept dropping names until security relented and let me in. (Saying that we had just flown in from New York helped.) All of the guests were seated at large, round tables, so all we could do was stand. I'm ashamed to admit that, at the time, I didn't know who Sting was. He was standing near us, waiting to go onto the stage to perform. Because I didn't know who he was, I was the only person who wasn't ogling at him. So he, in turn, felt free to look at me. He looked me up and down, admiring my outfit and seemed to want to introduce himself.

After he walked away, Beth elbowed me and whispered, "That's Sting! He was checking you out!"

All I could say was, "Who's Sting?"

The next thing I knew, champagne was being brought to us.

I asked around and found where the representatives from my label were sitting. We made the rounds, introduced ourselves, and told everyone about the recording I was making. None of them had heard about it, but they all said that they were happy to meet me. Maybe it was the champagne talking.

At Abbey Road Studios in London, my producer David Groves was a very kind man and was very attentive to my wishes. The Steinway in the recording studio was absolutely gorgeous and came with a technician who remained on hand to "kiss it and make it better." The studio had been booked for us for three days, but I was finished in a day and a half. The playing was perfect. The producer agreed; the performance could not be improved upon.

While I was recording, Shura Cherkassky – whom we had visited soon after we arrived in London – called the producer's booth to wish me luck. While on the phone he reportedly said, "Oh, vat is that beauuutifoool muuusic?!" in his thick Russian accent. I was in the middle of recording Ravel's *Valses nobles et sentimentales.*

We returned to New York expecting to receive the finished master any day. A week went by. Then two weeks. Beth called the producer to make sure everything was in order. He could not be reached. Three weeks went by with no master. Finally,

Promotional photo

Photo Credit:
Marc Bryan-Brown

Publicity photo for my CD

"We commonly hear complaints these days about young performers lacking in personality. No such charge could be leveled against Nina Kennedy, a fine pianist who made her debut last Sunday evening in Alice Tully Hall. Unlike so many of her generation, determined to assert their virtuosity even at the expense of the music, Miss Kennedy shaped her program with loving care."

John Rockwell
The New York Times

Nina Kennedy has appeared in recital and as soloist with orchestras throughout the United States, Europe, South America, and the Bahamas. Born in Nashville in 1960, she received her first musical instruction from her parents, Anne Gamble and Matthew Kennedy, who were members of the piano faculty at Fisk University for thirty years. She continued her studies at the Blair School of Music in Nashville where she was a recipient of the Myra Jackson Blair scholarship during her four years of high school study, and at the Curtis Institute in Philadelphia where she was one of three accepted from a field of 72 pianists. She received her bachelor's degree from Temple University, and her master's degree from the Juilliard School as a pupil of William Masselos, where she was awarded the prestigious Petschek Scholarship.

Nina was presented in her first complete recital at age nine. At age 13, she received a standing ovation from an audience of over 4,000 for her performance of Gershwin's *Rhapsody in Blue* with the Nashville Symphony. Her television and radio broadcasts include performances of the Beethoven 2nd Piano Concerto with the Jackson, Mississippi Symphony for PBS, and the Rachmaninoff 2nd Piano Concerto with the Chautauqua Festival Orchestra which was recorded live for broadcast on National Public Radio.

She is the subject of a video-documentary entitled, "Portrait: An American Concert Pianist."

Promotional flyer (back side)

After my recording at Abbey Road Studios

in a panic, Beth told the receptionist she would hold and wait
for the producer to pick up the phone. When he finally got on
the line, he told her he had not been instructed to finish the
master and that he had already begun recording a Pavarotti
opera. The New York office had booked him to record the new
project so he had no time to finish the editing of my recording.
Beth explained our situation, how we needed to meet Spike's
deadline, and he was waiting to shoot the video. He apologized profusely, but said there was nothing he could do. The
New York office had instructed him not, under any circumstances, to send the master to us. Beth began to smell a rat.

In the middle of all this worrying about when and if my
masters were going to be delivered, I got a call from Nashville.
Evidently my mother had had some kind of breakdown. It
began during a ceremony at Fisk when all faculty with emer-

itus status were asked to stand and be acknowledged. My father was faculty emeritus; my mother was not, even though she had composed and typed most of his letters for him, traveled as accompanist for the Jubilee Singers longer than he had directed them, concertized as a piano soloist, etc. etc. At the ceremony, she began to cry while he was standing. Soon she was sobbing and wailing uncontrollably. The whole ceremony was disrupted while people came to her aid, trying to establish what the trouble was.

She cried for days. Eventually she decided to put together a case to present to the president, demanding emeritus status for herself. She dug up old programs and articles, asked friends to send letters on her behalf, and spent hours composing her own letter to the president. She read the letter to me over the phone. From the tone of it, it was clear to me that she was having some kind of paternal transference with the president of the university. It was rambling and confused. At the end she asked for a meeting "with my husband by my side." I could just imagine the president's reaction to receiving such a confused letter.

I knew that my mother had not been given the opportunity to grieve her father's death properly. She was twelve years old when he was killed, and his firstborn – my mother's half-sister, Katherine – was claiming all of his property. She never got the chance to plead her case, to ask for some kind of inheritance or acknowledgement. When I delicately described this to her, along with the concept of emotional transference, she was silent for a few seconds. Then her voice, which had been childlike and quivering up to that point, suddenly was hard and cold.

"Well!" she spat. "It looks like you missed your calling in life!"

I was stunned. I thought of all those years she had forced me to practice, denying me the chance to have friends or a normal childhood. I thought of all of the tears and boohooing that went on whenever I wasn't practicing enough to satisfy her, so that she could yell out the right notes whenever I accidentally hit the wrong ones. I thought of all of the nausea and nerves and stress from all of the concerts I was forced to give when I was much too young to be put under such pressure. I thought of all of the energy I had wasted on trying to make her happy when she was so obviously miserable. But I said nothing. Something inside of me snapped. She obviously had no concern for what I was being subjected to as the result of her "encouragement." The sense of betrayal was so overwhelming. I was numb. But I was still her dutiful daughter and said nothing.

After weeks of begging London for the master, then Spike Lee for an extension and the secretaries in New York for an explanation, it became clearer that Beth and I were being screwed. We finally approached a famous pop star who had just announced in the press that she would begin to direct music videos for other artists since she had been directing her own videos for the past eight years. That pop star was Cyndi Lauper. She was sold on the project and offered to call the label herself to let them know.

Of course, she got right through to the executives. But the boss made the mistake of telling her that they were not going to release my project. When she asked why, he hemmed and hawed and said there were other priorities. But he then tried to interest her in directing someone else's video. She called us immediately.

"I don't know what's going on over there," she said. "But you're getting screwed. Get your masters and get out."

We followed her advice. Of course, the company was holding my masters hostage. We had to threaten to sue for tortious interference just to get *my* masters – the music *I* had recorded – into my hands. Beth was a bitch on wheels. Eventually they caved in under the pressure. I had to sign a contract stating that they would be reimbursed for their expenses before I began to see profits from a release with another company. The contract also stated that I agreed not to discuss the matter in the press. We hired a music recording editor in Manhattan to do the post-production. Months later, the recording was finished but we were right back where we started – without a deal.

Our relationship did not survive the ordeal. Beth became increasingly frustrated and I became the target of her frustration. Even Spike Lee didn't want to hear from us anymore. He, too, had been jerked around by those assholes. I couldn't understand how, after all my training and preparation, everything could be turning against me. I had worked so hard, had followed the advice of my elders, had obeyed my parents, and I was being left with a worthless pile of tape. Where was the justice?

To make matters worse, Beth was eighty thousand dollars in debt from her law school loans. Her parents had not contributed a penny toward her education.

18

It seemed that whenever Beth was studying for her exams, her parents, like clockwork, threatened to divorce. It had gotten to the point where she asked me to tell her parents that she wasn't home when they called. Her parents were thoroughly disrespectful toward me.

Her mother would yell, "Put my daughter on the phone!"

To which I would politely respond, "Why, I'm fine, thank you Mrs. Cohen and how are you today?"

Joe Cohen was no dummy. Divorce was rampant all over their suburban Long Island neighborhood. Joe perfected the technique of staying in debt so that his wife, in the event of their divorce, would gain nothing but half of his debt. Mrs. Cohen didn't even have her own bank account. She had to sneak cash from her husband's wallet to give to her daughters.

Beth's father would pick the times when she was most worried about digesting information in her studies to call and start a fight. I heard her voice rising and the phone being slammed down. Then she would bellow: "If my father calls, tell him I'm not here!" The phone rang again, Joe asked for his daughter. I followed her instructions. Joe insisted that I put her on the phone. I suggested that he call again later. He refused to hang up.

"Don't you hang up on me!" he threatened.

I apologized, hung up, and then turned off the ringer.

A few weeks later, Beth's cousin from Florida called to ask how she was taking the news.

"What news?" she asked, genuinely bewildered.

"You mean you haven't heard?" he asked in disbelief.

It turns out that Beth's grandmother had died and no one from her immediate family had called to inform her. She had to find out the details of the funeral arrangements from her Florida cousins. She asked me to accompany her to the funeral to be a support for her. As soon as we arrived at the door of the synagogue, aunts and uncles and cousins started pulling at her, separating us. Beth's father waited until I was standing alone. He approached me.

"Get out," he whispered.

"Excuse me?"

"You think you can hang up on me? Well, I won't have you in here." He was getting louder. "I said get out!" He physically blocked me.

I couldn't find Beth to tell her that I could not come inside. Finally, I saw one of her cousins who recognized me. I asked her to relate the message for Beth to meet me out front. When she finally came outside, she claimed to have no idea of why I wasn't coming in. Joe was in his element that day. He even barred Beth from sitting with the family. She had to sit at the back of the room with her grandmother's maid.

I went to a friend's apartment nearby and telephoned the synagogue from there to leave a message for Beth saying where I was. By the end of the day, she was numb and in shock. I couldn't believe how out-of-control her father was. But no one else in the family dared to cross him. He was a big man.

To distract herself from her crazy family, Beth put full steam into trying to secure another record deal. She decided that it was my own fault that I could not get another deal (since she had heard my concerts and knew my ability) and that I was simply suffering from a lack of confidence, which could be cured via psychotherapy. She didn't want to listen when I spoke of racism. She said it wasn't helpful and nothing could be done about it, so why discuss it. Some friends had recommended their therapist to us. We decided to make an appointment. We had originally wanted to begin some sort of couples counseling but when we first met with Dr. Weiss, she suggested it would be more helpful to begin with individual therapy so that she could get to know each of us first. We went along with her suggestion.

I was shocked at how quickly Dr. Weiss tried to prescribe medication. She insisted that I stop drinking alcohol altogether to avoid the risk of a reaction with the tranquilizers she wanted to prescribe. Memories of my mother's night table flashed before me. No, I did not want to be tranquilized.

The best thing Dr. Weiss did for me was to insist that I seek out a support-group, such as ACOA – Adult Children of Alcoholics. When I told her that my mother had been an alcoholic and that I was an only child, she suspected that my emotional development had been frozen. She said with all the feelings that would be coming up in therapy, I would need another outlet where I could find support. The Lesbian and Gay Community Center was just the place. I called and found that they hosted at least three weekly ACOA meetings.

After a few sessions with the doctor, she began to suggest to each of us that we needed to spend some time apart from each other. She recommended at least three months. She told us that if our relationship survived after three months of separation, we could then rest assured of having a secure relationship. In her private sessions with me however, the doctor admitted that she was concerned about Beth's emotional instability. Since she grew up with physical abuse, she probably considered it normal and never developed the skills to control her own violent tendencies. I was suspicious. Since the good doctor had already tried to get me addicted to prescription medication, she probably wanted to get me away from Beth so that I would be totally dependent on her.

Meanwhile, Beth had begun to follow the doctor's advice by spending weekends at her parents' house in Long Island. They had a big house, a swimming pool, a well-stocked refrigerator, and a housekeeper. I wished there was a place where I could go to relax and recoup.

I was thoroughly confused. I loved Beth when she was calm. Somehow, when she lost control of her emotions or became violent, I thought that her emotion was proof of her love for me. I immediately talked myself out of my hurt and humiliation by focusing on how sorry I felt for Beth. My true feelings would kick in three days later, when it was safe. At those times, I would proclaim that I would not be afraid in my own home and that she had to move out. But she had no money and I certainly did not want to force her back into her parents' house. My pity would win out. To top it off, Beth had me convinced that I could not make a professional move without her. She had me over a barrel. The girl was a damn good lawyer. She was just an emotional basket-case.

Meanwhile, I had to come up with ways of filling time outside of the apartment while Beth was making her business calls. I had observed the career of Daniel Barenboim and decided to see how far I could get as a conductor. While at Juilliard, I had taken all the conductors' courses and passed them with flying colors. The conductors were the ones who determined the repertoire and guest artists for symphony orchestras. It seemed like a natural conclusion.

Kurt Masur was the music director of the New York Philharmonic at the time. I decided to call and enquire about the apprenticeship program offered by the Philharmonic. It seemed easy enough. I received a concert schedule with repertoire list, purchased the complete orchestral scores and accompanying CDs, and by the time I actually sat in on the rehearsals, I had the score virtually memorized. Luckily, I had been blessed with an excellent ear.

Maestro Masur was a very nice man. He simply wanted to share his pearls of wisdom with anyone who would listen. During my short apprenticeship, I studied Beethoven, Brahms, Mahler, Mozart, Schubert, and Shostakovich symphonies, as well as tone poems by Debussy and Ravel. It was widely believed that his Beethoven was the best in the world. Being an official conducting apprentice meant that a pass would be waiting for me at the stage door entrance before all of the Philharmonic rehearsals, and I was able to sit in the first box to the left of the stage – with score in hand – and observe the rehearsal. I purchased all of the works we covered and amassed a large library of orchestral scores. Usually after a rehearsal we would gather in the Maestro's office to discuss the score of the piece we had just heard. Leslie Dunner – then Resident Conductor of the Detroit Symphony Orchestra – and I would sit at Maestro's coffee table, with scores opened and ask questions. He was always very pleasant and seemed happy to answer any questions we had.

One day when I walked into the Maestro's office, there was the score of Strauss' *Alpine Symphony* on his desk. I already knew the score quite well and asked a few questions designed to reveal my thorough knowledge of the score. The Maestro was impressed.

Being an official conducting apprentice also meant that, when the Philharmonic would perform in other venues, the Maestro might walk to the back of the hall or cathedral so that he could hear the acoustics. Unfortunately, Maestro only handed his baton to Leslie on those occasions. But I was ready, willing, and able. (And by the way, to avoid confusion, Leslie is a man.)

One day, however, I had a very uncomfortable experience. Leslie and I were seated on the sofas at the coffee table as usual, when suddenly the door flew open and Maestro's secretary came in. There was an emergency phone call for Leslie from his symphony's office, and Leslie ran out of the room.

Maestro and I were left alone in his massive office. I looked around to see that Maestro had walked over to his closet and had taken his shirt off. Granted, I knew that he was sweaty from the rehearsal and wanted to change into a dry shirt. But I suddenly felt embarrassed and jumped up to walk out of the room. He would have continued to discuss the score with me, but I assumed he wanted his privacy at that moment. I heard him giggling at me under his breath and felt ashamed that I couldn't have done a better job of pretending to be "one of the boys." I also knew that I slightly resembled his Japanese wife. Whatever was going on in my head, it pulled me out of my seat and pushed me out of the room.

To be fair to Kurt Masur, I never heard of any rumors of inappropriate advances on his part, unlike James Levine. We had heard *those* rumors for *years*.[1]

Being a conducting apprentice with the New York Philharmonic also meant that I was able to converse with and ask questions of the various guest conductors who came to town. I remember an interesting conversation with André Previn on Debussy's *L'après midi d'un faune*. At that time, he was in the public eye because of his personal life. The Woody Allen child abuse scandal was all over the media and Previn had been previously married to Allen's then wife Mia Farrow. I could imagine his frustration at putting so much effort and energy into his career only to be asked by the press about his ex-wife and her current situation.

---

[1] In 2018, the Boston Globe published details of allegations of sexual abuse by seventy-four-year-old conductor and pianist James Levine, as well as chronicling "cult-like" behavior that he allegedly cultivated among his devotees while he was teaching at the Cleveland Institute of Music (CIM) in Ohio between 1965 and 1972. Levine denied the charges.

Posing in Paris

Years later when I moved to Paris, I soon learned that Kurt Masur was the music director for L'Orchestre National de France, so we simply picked-up where we left off in New York as Maestro and apprentice. It turned out that the orchestra's summer festival took place at the Basilique in Saint-Denis, which was literally around the corner from my apartment. There I continued to digest more repertoire and establish a rapport with the members of l'orchestre.

As Maestro Masur was German and had spent most of his adult life in Europe, he did not have an awareness of the sub- tleties of American racism. America was still cleaning up the mess created during its shameful past. Unfortunately, Maestro

Masur did not know that it was the responsibility of the music director of the New York Philharmonic to ensure that the population of this organization reflected the population of the city it represents. New York City may have been built to be a segregated town, but the New York Philharmonic cannot and will not survive as a segregated orchestra. Even during my apprenticeship in the last decade of the twentieth century, there was still only one person of African descent in the Philharmonic, and he had been appointed by Leonard Bernstein.

There was a lot to do. But one ism at a time.

Time passed. I would spend my afternoons surrounded by glorious music in Avery Fisher Hall, and return to my apartment in the evenings to a moody, depressed Beth.

Unknowingly, I had recreated my childhood home.

19

Every February I could count on being hired by orchestras for Black History Month concerts. The concert budgets for February were the smallest of the year but African American artists and musicians were able to get some work at least. When the Jackson Mississippi Symphony invited me to appear as piano soloist, I told them I would do the Brahms D minor Piano Concerto. I felt the rhythms were funky and totally appropriate for a Black History Month concert. (And looking at some photos of the hair piled on top of Brahms' head, there was probably some African blood in that mix.) It also called for a full orchestra.

For the same concert, the Mississippi Symphony had invited the composer Anthony Davis to give a talk on his work. They had programmed his piece *"Notes from the Underground."* It was the first time Anthony and I actually met. I had been in the audience for his opera *"The Life and Times of Malcolm X"* at the New York City Opera, but we weren't introduced then. Beth insisted on coming to Mississippi for the performance. She had chosen my clothing from Soho stores and had decided that my marketing image had to be consistent, even in Jackson, Mississippi.

The day before the concert, Anthony and I were invited to speak before the Mississippi State Legislature while in session. There was a group of black children on a field trip from school in the building. Anthony spoke first. He thanked the Mississippians for inviting him and performing his work. Then it was time for me to speak. I walked up to the podium. Suddenly, the countless numbers of lynched black men whose bodies had been fished out of the Mississippi River flashed through my mind. I spoke.

"As some of you may know, I grew up on the Fisk University campus. Running around as a child I would hear strains of Bach and Beethoven coming from my mother's piano studio, and then around the corner I would hear strains of the Spirituals as sung by the Jubilee Singers directed by my father. And I learned then that *music* [I paused for dramatic effect] was the *vehicle* for bringing the races together."

Suddenly I was interrupted by loud applause begun by one of the black male members of the legislature. The applause spread throughout the room. I guessed I was finished. I thanked everyone and relinquished the microphone to the conductor. Even Beth was impressed. She didn't know that I was also a public speaker.

The concert was a success. Anthony even complimented me on my hip clothes. Beth and I flew back to New York and I had a nice little check in my pocket.

The next day while unpacking, I turned on CNN to see what was happening in the world. And then came the announcement: "The Mississippi State Legislature voted today to officially abolish slavery in than state, more than one hundred and thirty years after the signing of the Emancipation Proclamation by Abraham Lincoln..."

Slavery was still legal in the state of Mississippi while I played the Brahms Piano Concerto with their state symphony? In 1995? I had no idea.

• • • • •

The winter following my Vienna debut with the Chicago Sinfonietta, the same concert agent who booked the gig for me at Vienna's Musikverein invited me to give a concert in Munich as part of an international piano festival. Shura Cherkassky was also performing that night, right before me. As I had written earlier, Shura was a friend of my Nashville patron, Dr. Lee Minton, and had heard me play at the concert in London. We became good friends (in spite of our sixty-year age difference) and I always took it upon myself to introduce him to handsome young gentlemen whenever he was in New York.

I learned when I arrived in Munich that the piano festival was being held in the Herkulessaal – the concert hall in the King's Residence. Granted King Maximilian had several residences throughout Germany, but this was his home in Munich. Years later I would learn that this was the same concert hall in which Wagner's *Tristan und Isolde* had its world-premiere. I performed the Liszt transcription of Isolde's *Liebestod* on the program, completely ignorant of the fact that this was the place where the public first heard the glorious music of *Tristan and Isolde*. It's a good thing that I did not know! I might not have been able to function if I had. (It would be another twenty years before I would be able to sit in the audience for a live performance of *Tristan* at Wagner's own opera house in Bayreuth, Germany.) Renate Perls was in the audience for the concert that night. She had moved to Munich from New York and invited me and Beth to her apartment for dinner a few days later.

That night in Munich, Shura's Russian flag hung behind him and the Stars and Stripes hung behind me. I love the way the Germans give voice to their approval. I ended the program with the Rachmaninoff Second Sonata, after which the crowd rose to its feet and gave shouts of "Bravo!" I was called back for an encore, which I really did not want to play since I was thoroughly exhausted. Shura sat in the audience for my portion and again was full of compliments.

Afterwards we settled for cocktails at the Vier Jahreszeiten (Four Seasons) Hotel because there were no restaurants open at that hour. We were hungry, but had to make due with peanuts. Shura and I were discussing how difficult it was to prepare for these concerts and how we were expected to be perfect regardless of how tired or jet-lagged we were. "It's slavery, isn't it!" the old man said to me. I didn't know how to respond. Was this a test? Was I supposed to say, "Oh, no no! I love practicing my ass off to play these little jobs that pay no money!" Or was I simply supposed to smile and agree. I just looked at him thoughtfully and said, "Hmmm."

Meanwhile, I saw that Shura was paid three times more the number of Deutschmarks than I was paid. The concert promoter paid us in cash and I saw the amount of cash that was placed inside of Shura's envelope. On top of that, Shura was staying at the five-star Vier Jahreszeiten Hotel and I was in a little flea-bag. I changed my Deutschmarks to dollars before I left the country and took a photo of my pile of money when I returned home. It was my first cash payment for a European gig, so I was very sentimental about it. Before leaving the hotel however, the boss of my concert agent called to demand that I leave his cut at the front desk when I checked out. These Germans weren't playing around! The manager who booked me for the concert was thrilled with my performance and with the audience response. But soon afterwards, she was appointed executive director of a German orchestra and was no longer in a position to engage me for concerts.

The day after the concert we went on the tours of Ludwig II's castles in Bavaria. My fascination with Wagner was simply intensified as I saw the effort and attention to detail given to the murals depicting scenes from his operas throughout the castle of Neuschwanstein. After returning to the United States, I purchased a book of Wagner's correspondence with King Ludwig, Liszt, various managers and agents, etc. His struggles in the concert world helped me to perceive my own struggles in a new light.

A few years after the concert in Munich, I treated myself to four tickets for four nights at the Metropolitan Opera House for their fabulous production of Wagner's *Ring of the Nibelung (Der Ring Des Nibelungen)*. Those of us who bought all four tickets were invited to a champagne reception before the opening night performance. I had my fill of bubbly and wondered why some of the more elderly patrons did not partake. Well, the first opera *Das Rheingold* began, and by the time of the entrance of the Giants, my bladder was about to burst. I quickly exited and did my business, but when I tried to re-enter, the doors were locked. One of the ushers explained to me that since *Das Rheingold* is in one act, the doors remain locked for the entire performance. He got on his walkie-talkie and found a place for me in the first box to the right upstairs. I entered the box, took my seat and saw that I could barely see the stage, but I had a full view of the orchestra in the pit. I watched and listened. I witnessed the weaving of that magic spell – that special *Wagnerian* magic – and was transfixed. I saw it as a sign that one day, I will conduct this wonderous music!

20

Shura and I would cross paths for years afterwards. Whenever he would perform at Carnegie Hall in New York, I would meet him backstage and we would celebrate after the concert. Shura claimed to be interested in my career. He claimed that he had told his manager about me and that I should schedule a meeting at their offices. When I followed his advice and called the office, the secretaries had no idea of who I was. When I related this to him, he feigned shock and anger and swore that he had practically arranged the meeting himself.

In London, we met for lunch the day before our flight back to New York. He seemed to get it that we were a couple, and he wanted to reveal his own ambivalent inclinations. He spoke of a South African man who wanted to have an affair with him, but claimed to only be interested in men who were circumcised. Shura himself was not circumcised, though he was born Jewish. His mother had been so terrified from persecution of Jews in Russia that she wanted to spare her son from further persecution via this visible trait. It stated in Shura's Will that he wished to be circumcised after his death. He remembered the times in Russia when homosexuality was a criminal offense. Some of his friends had been jailed and executed.

We returned to New York quite happy to have reached a new level of intimacy with Shura. In London he had wanted to introduce us to a friend of his from Malibu, (or "Molleebooo" as he would pronounce it). Maxine was a Gertrude Stein look-alike and had a house right on Malibu Beach, just next door to where Liberace had lived. Since we were friends of Shura's, she invited us on the spot to come and visit her in California. We took her card and promised to keep in touch.

Beth's father had an old friend in the biz who lived out in Los Angeles, who was a consultant for some of Hollywood's talent agencies. We decided to combine the two: to meet with this retired agent and discuss marketing strategies for the CD, and to visit Maxine.

The retired agent told me to lose weight. Juilliard didn't matter. Competitions or prizes didn't matter. Talent didn't matter. "Ya gotta be skinny if you wanna be a star!" he said.

Maxine hosted a party in my honor and what a party it was! She even rented a piano so that I could entertain her guests.

Maxine really wasn't interested in the show-biz goings on in Hollywood. She just enjoyed spending her money and pretty much stayed to herself. Her last affair had been several years earlier with a famous Hollywood actress. The drama had been enough to last her for a while.

We left Los Angeles the day the Malibu fires began. Maxine's house, fortunately, was unharmed.

A few weeks later, Shura called from Israel to say that he would be in New York to play Carnegie again, and asked if I knew of any single young men he could meet. I said of course and promptly went through my little black book to find a friend for him.

I knew a young composer who was very single and very shy. He had a very nice piano in his flat and would let me come in to practice on it when I had to prepare performances. I asked him if he would like to hear Shura in concert and to meet him afterwards. He was delighted.

Beth, David and I sat in the audience for Shura's performance and all three of us went backstage afterwards. I was quite surprised to see that Shura was surrounded by attractive young boys. But he seemed depressed. When I introduced him to David, his eyes lit up for a moment; but then he went right back into his funk. I waited until we were outside of anyone else's hearing-range and asked him if he were okay.

"I'm old," he grumbled. "None of them vant to be with me." And he walked off in a huff.

I felt terrible. Shura had just given a wonderful performance. But he was lonely. He had no one to share his life with. Beth and I were together each time we saw each other in recent years – in Munich, London, and New York. And each time we saw him, he was by himself. I took David aside and explained to him how down Shura was and asked if he would "act as an escort." He seemed to pity the old man and did what he could to try to make him feel better.

The after-party was at a trendy Upper West Side restaurant. Many classical managers, agents and conductors were present and all were salivating over David. Business cards were stuffed into his pockets the entire evening, and I was furious that no one had welcomed me so blatantly into these classical circles. It was a closed boys' club.

Shura was so depressed. He ignored David for the entire evening, in spite of the fact that David had dutifully sat next to him. We were saying our goodbyes when Shura whispered to me, "I'm so embarrassed. I hate leaving these parties alone."

Again, I took David aside and asked if he wouldn't mind just going with Shura in his taxi, so that he wouldn't have to leave by himself. He said he would go along.

Shura then made quite a spectacle of blowing kisses to everyone outside of the restaurant, with a bouquet of roses in one arm, as he got into his cab with his pretty young boy on his other arm.

The next day I called David to thank him for being so accommodating. When he answered the phone, I could barely hear him speak. I listened closely and could hear that he was crying. I asked what was wrong and he said he couldn't talk. He said to call again later.

My God! What happened?

Beth called him the next day. She can be very soothing and comforting on the phone when she wants to be – a law school technique used for clients. She finally got David to tell her what happened:

As the cab pulled in front of the Pierre Hotel (where Shura was staying), David said goodnight and thanked him for the evening. Shura begged him to come inside and just walk him to the elevators. David agreed. Once they were in the lobby, Shura's personality changed. He started screaming at David, "Well, why on earth do you think I invited you here if you aren't coming upstairs?! Are you STUPID?!!" David was dumbstruck. He didn't know what to say and meekly walked along behind Shura into the elevator and to his hotel suite.

Inside Shura's room, he told David to sit down while he disappeared into the back room. He soon reappeared and was stark naked! The man was over eighty years old. It was a scene David did not wish to describe. Suffice it to say that it was the most disgusting thing he had ever seen. Shura then stood in front of David and said in a thick Russian accent, "I vant you to geev me a blow-job."

David was about to be sick. He stood up, apologized and left the room. He then ran out of the hotel and up Fifth Avenue.

Later I would learn that Shura's favorite vacation spot was Bangkok, where he frequented places that provided "entertainment" by very young boys – children, in fact. This man was a success! He had the kind of career everyone envied. And this was the truth of his private life. I really began to wonder about the kind of field my parents had pressured me into.

Beth could not handle the news of Shura's preference for children. I, too, was outraged; but I was even more furious at him for deceiving me, taking advantage of my goodwill and hurting my friend. I didn't know how I could ever speak to him again.

Within two years, Maxine called to tell me that the old man had finally departed this earth. I read in his obituary that his wife had divorced him because of "mental cruelty." I hadn't even known that he had been married.

And I suppose he is finally circumcised.

21

Beth's sister, Rachel, was extremely sexually promiscuous. She would pick up a stranger and bring him home for sex in her tiny studio apartment, even if Beth or a female cousin was visiting at the time and sleeping next to them on the floor in a sleeping bag. But one of these strangers, an Israeli who wanted his American citizenship, decided that he was going to marry Rachel. They eloped.

When the Cohens were informed of the elopement, they decided to throw an elaborate dinner party for all their friends and relatives. From the looks of the expensive spread under a large tent on the lawn of their Long Island home, no one would have guessed that this family was teetering on the edge of bankruptcy.

At this party, the same man who threw me out of his mother's funeral danced the *Horah* with me on the lawn of his home.

Rachel, too, had made quite some money as a child singing commercial jingles. When her voice began to mature, the studio executives who still wanted a child's voice started calling in her younger sister to sing the jobs. Rachel, too, thought about suing her father for the money. But once she was married and pregnant, she accepted her parents' gifts: an apartment, a job for her husband, a car, medical insurance, computers and stereo equipment, clothes and furniture for the baby, etc.

Beth watched as her parents lavished gifts and cash onto her married sister. It soon became clear to her that if she wanted financing from her parents, she had to be heterosexual. And being eighty thousand dollars in debt at twenty-five years old, it was something to consider.

After the baby was born, something happened to Beth. She became obsessed with that child. She wanted to be around him all the time. She revealed to me that she was beginning to have more of her childhood memories, but she didn't say exactly what it was that she remembered. We were no longer having sex by this point.

I know now that it was Beth's fear of going into flashbacks that made her so uncomfortable with sex. But at the time, all I felt was rejection alternated with waves of pity. As it was usually up to me to initiate sex, she would go along with foreplay until it became unbearable. Then she would break into uncontrollable fits of laughter, claiming that she was ticklish. In the beginning, she would wait for the laughter to pass and would be willing to try again. Toward the end, after I had been on the receiving end of her violent outbursts, I got sick of trying.

Some of the worst scenes involved her need to lash out against her imagined abuser and flee the scene. She had no explanation for this behavior since she usually claimed not to remember it. She had adamantly denied that she had ever been sexually abused by her father, but cousins had confided in me that they had suspected it. The man was sexually compulsive. He had taken her out on "dates" to New York discos when Beth was fourteen and specifically instructed her not to call him "Dad" or "Daddy." In some of her photos from that time, she looked much older. When some of Joe's rock band clients were at the house doing drugs and hanging out in the pool, Beth remembers Joe instructing her to sit on their laps. She remembers being asked by a drunk rock band member, "So... have you been fucked yet?"

One evening, early in our relationship, I thought we were about to make love when she suddenly jumped out of bed and screamed, "*You just want me to be your little slut!*" Then she got dressed and ran out into the night. Later, when I asked her to whom she really needed to say these words, she denied ever saying them.

The girl was deeply tormented.

Still, the bigger question was why I felt I deserved such treatment.

But then, there were the little hand-written notes left by the bed when she went to school, reading, "Promise me you'll always love me. XXOO"

Beth's father was born into poverty in Manhattan's Lower East Side, but his older brothers became quite wealthy. Both were successful real-estate moguls – one in Manhattan, the other in Florida. Both men had spent quite some money setting up their sons in their respective businesses. I was well acquainted with the Manhattan uncle since he loved the piano and would frequently invite us to his parties so that I could entertain his guests on his Steinway. His daughter, Laura, would call Beth occasionally and sometimes the three of us would go out to dinner.

It had been more than a year since our first meeting with the aging record executive in Los Angeles. Since then, Beth had finished law school, passed the New York Bar exam, and technically was ready to practice law. But she was still too young to have had enough experience to make her attractive enough for a law firm to want to hire her. She had sent out countless resumes and job-applications, all of which had been rejected. I had asked Laura about the nature of her brother's business and how it came about that her father footed the bill. She seemed uninterested and bored by such "male" subjects. All I knew was that Beth was becoming increasingly impossible to live with the longer her job-search went on. I had asked her about the possibility of asking Laura's father for work, at least to help her get her feet on the ground. He needed lawyers. He had hired men outside of the family to do his legal work. But to Beth, such a request was out of the question. She never fully explained why. But I assumed she was determined to prove that she could get on her feet on her own, without any help from the family.

Weeks dragged on and Beth still had no job – not even an interview. After countless evenings of watching her moping and sobbing on my couch, dismissing and laughing off my suggestions as if they were the most ridiculous ideas she had ever heard, I knew something had to be done. The air around her was toxic. Of course I had my own struggles, but I wasn't free to share any aspect of my own life in my own home with my own lover. The feeling was vaguely familiar. But I did all I could to keep her calm, fed, and healthy.

We were nearing the end of the NBA finals between New York and St. Louis. I couldn't sit in the living room anymore just to watch Beth mope. I had resorted to spending my evenings out – anywhere – just to be out of her toxic space. But this night, come hell or high water, I was going to watch the final. The Nicks had been behind for most of the game. But in the final minutes of the final quarter, we began to pull ahead. The windows were open and you could hear people from neighboring buildings cheering and screaming for the Nicks. After an amazing three-point shot which clinched the game for New York, I even heard myself whooping. A second later, Beth burst into the bedroom. Her eyes were blazing.

"How can you whoop and yell like that when you know what I'm going through?!" she screamed.

I was dumbfounded. Here we were in *my* apartment, for which *I* paid the rent, where she is living for free, poisoning *my* space and she has the nerve to try to tell me what I can and can't do in my own home? I stood up.

"No, I'm not staying here and taking this." I started to walk out.

"Don't you walk away from me!" She was screaming at the top of her lungs. "DON'T YOU DARE WALK AWAY FROM ME!" Then with the palms of both of her hands, she pushed me in the chest with a force that knocked me back down onto the bed.

In the shock and confusion which followed, I simply didn't know what to do. My first thought was, *I must have done some-*

thing really terribly wrong to cause this kind of reaction. My second thought was, *Well, if I just sit here and don't say anything, the storm will pass.* She cried and moped some more. I sat and tried to make myself invisible. Then she seemed to come up with a plan of action, which got her all excited and hopeful again. She took out her legal pad and started making notes for the next day's telephone conversations. Soon she was happy and child-like again. When it was safe enough, I spoke.

"By the way," I stated as calmly as I could. "Don't you ever hit me again."

"What are you talking about?" she laughed. "I never hit you."

The discussion was closed.

The next day marked an escalation of violence which for me was the official beginning of the end. Of course, all of the planned telephone conversations resulted in nothing. She still couldn't get past the damn secretaries. By the time I returned home from killing time on the streets, she was in a mood again.

I had gotten in the habit of being out while she was making her business calls, stemming from the days of trying to figure out what was going on with my recording. She couldn't handle hearing me sigh or breathe while she was on the phone, so she instructed me to be out during the afternoons. I obeyed.

As luck would have it, the phone rang. Since I was not allowed to answer my own phone, she collected herself, put her notes in place, and picked up the receiver. It was Laura. I heard the sigh of relief and saw her shoulders relax. They chatted with Laura doing most of the talking about the children of their cousins and the cute little things they did and said. After several minutes of relaxed chitchat, Laura evidently asked for me. Beth handed me the phone. She was still sitting at the desk while I stood next to her.

I didn't realize how much I was still smarting from the incident of the previous night until I heard Laura's voice asking, "How are you?"

I changed the subject.

"How are *you*?" I said.

"I'm okay. So how's it going with Beth's job-search?"

She knew she wouldn't get the truth out of Beth.

"Listen," I said. "Ask your father if he needs any legal work done. Beth needs the experience and I know she won't ask you herself, but she…"

The wind escaped from my lungs. I couldn't speak. The pain in my stomach began to seep into my consciousness. Beth had punched me.

"Fuck you!" she spat and stormed out of the room.

"Yeah? Go ahead." Laura's voice reminded me of where I was and what I had said. I cleared my throat.

"Well, maybe if you could mention it to him and let us know what he says."

"Sure, I'll ask him." She had no idea of what had just happened.

After hanging up with Laura, I walked into the living room. Beth was already on the couch in her moping position.

"I won't have you interfering with *my* family!" she yelled.

I didn't make eye contact. I put on my coat, picked up my keys, and walked out the door. I knew there was an ACOA meeting at the Community Center so at least I had someplace to go.

That night at the meeting, I heard myself say to a room full of concerned listeners, "My girlfriend just hit me."

That made it real. There was no going back. I had to do something.

22

I had no memory of being physically abused in childhood. When I suddenly found myself in an abusive relationship, I truly had no idea of how this could have happened. My father had told me that when I was little my mother was spanking me because she thought I had lied to her about something. He said that he had to stop her because he felt it was enough and that she had lost control. I have no memory of this incident.

When I told Dr. Weiss that Beth had started hitting me, she was clear.

"One of you is going to end up in the hospital and the other one is gonna end up in jail," she said.

Beth and I had to separate.

All my life I had been searching for a reason, a justification for all the practicing, all the personal sacrifice, all the preparation for a field in which I clearly was not welcome. I thought I had found my answer in the work of Antonín Dvořák and his utilization of the melodies from Negro Spirituals in his *Symphony from the New World*. Naturally I concluded that there must be an appreciation among the Czech people for African American classical musicians. So I decided to pack up the repertoire I had chosen to memorize during the summer of 1995 and fly to Prague.

Some friends of my parents' had friends who lived in Prague. The daughter was studying in the United States, so they wanted to rent out her room for a very reasonable price. I had wanted to spend some time in Europe. Prague was still cheap enough and centrally located. It seemed to be as good a time as any to spend some time abroad and see what kind of connections I could establish. Beth also thought it was a good idea. She thought it would be easier for her to get another deal for me without the added pressure generated by my presence. She was already spending more time at her parents' house than at my apartment. We were practically already separated.

When I informed Maestro Masur of my plans to spend time in Prague, he was very happy for me. It was much easier to get work and make a living as a musician in Prague. He promised a rewarding experience, told me to enjoy my trip, and said that he looked forward to my return in the fall. The opening concert for the fall season would be an all-Wagner concert with Jessye Norman singing Brünnhilde's *Immolation*. I couldn't wait.

I called a travel agent and booked a roundtrip ticket with the return date scheduled for a month after the departure. Beth would continue to book engagements for me while I was away and she would fax the contracts to me. I could devote my time to practicing and clear my head of business frustrations.

The O.J. Simpson case was going on during this time. America was obsessed with this spectacle: a black, former football hero accused of murdering his white ex-wife and her white male companion. Every afternoon, every nationally syndicated television network broadcast the court case live. I had a feeling that Beth was obsessing on the gruesome police photos of the bloody crime-scene; she was having even more nightmares and flashbacks. And there was that chilling audiotape of Nicole Brown calling 911, desperately trying to get the police to come to her house while her ex-husband was heard flipping-out in the background. Americans were glued to their TV screens while the sordid details of this murder-mystery were played out. I was looking forward to getting away from all this mess. Of course, the American media latched on to this opportunity to show what happens when black men marry white women, to hold O.J. Simpson up as an example of black male madness.

At least I would be free of this in Prague.

When Beth and I said goodbye to each other, I thought we would use this month apart to re-evaluate our relationship and focus on ourselves. She had other plans in mind.

● ● ● ● ●

While on the plane to Prague, I saw an article in the Czech newspaper about a gay men's chorus from Texas which was scheduled to give a concert in the Dvořák Hall the following night. A cocktail party was scheduled for the evening I arrived, to which the gay community of Prague was invited to meet and mingle with the boys from Texas.

My host met me at the airport and we took public transportation to his home in a green, suburban area of Prague. His wife was very friendly but spoke no English. I dropped my bags, showered, and changed and somehow, tired and jet-lagged, I got myself to the party.

I hadn't been aware of how unhappy I was with Beth until I got away from her. All of a sudden I was free to mingle, to make friends, and socialize. To be on a riverboat in Prague surrounded by dozens of American gay boys from Texas with an open bar, I was in my element. This was my first introduction to the local Czech liqueur Becherovka. The locals taught us to down a shot of the stuff and chase it with a beer. We all got very friendly with each other very fast.

There weren't many women on the boat. Those who were present were political-types and organizers for the concert. But the few women on the boat who were out to have a good time were the fag hags. Some were out to catch an American man, not knowing that they were gay. After a few Becherovkas, I developed the technique of asking a woman to pose with me for a photograph taken by one of the boys. Of course, we had to pose cheek to cheek with our arms around each other, while my partner in crime struggled to focus the camera. She didn't speak English and seemed genuinely to enjoy the attention. Later we stole away together for a few kisses and hugs. It had been so long since I was held like this.

The concert was the following afternoon at the Dvořák Hall, which was practically sold-out. It served as a benefit for AIDS research as well as an opportunity for members of the local scene to make new friends from across the ocean. The concert was delightful and fully appreciated by the audience. I'll never forget swaying and singing "We Shall Overcome" linking arms with hundreds of gay people (mostly men) as an encore. The Czechs knew all of the words. Half of the chorus was in tears.

At the lavish reception following the concert, I met more local lesbians and some American expatriates. Sal, a former fashion designer from Los Angeles, had been living in Prague for several years with his young, beautiful Czech boyfriend. We exchanged telephone numbers. As it turned out, Sal was planning a benefit concert/fashion show for Prague's Costume Museum. Later we would schedule a meeting to discuss his plans.

Schlepping photos and recordings of the Fisk Jubilee Singers with printed explanations of their ties to the Czech national hero Dvořák, I talked my way into the state-run TV station. Before I knew it, I was invited to return for a live interview with a translator the next day for their version of *Good Morning, America!* (or Good Morning, Czech Republic! in this case). They even rolled out a grand piano for me. I had heard that African-Americans were chic in Prague but this was ridiculous!

Meanwhile, my hosts were most generous and hospitable. The lady of the house prepared local dishes with loving care and always had my plate of eggs, potatoes, and sausage waiting on the table for me in the morning. She was very proud of her homemade jams and preserves. There was a lovely grand piano in the living room so I learned copious amounts of repertoire and dusted off old warhorses that I hadn't played in years. I took advantage of the time to memorize Rachmaninoff's *Variations on a Theme by Paganini*. It was a most productive summer!

The women's scene was a bit disappointing. I had thought I would find Martina Navratilova look-alikes running around, but no such luck. Czech women were poor. The meeting-places were small, dark, and dingy, but the women were friendly. I usually ended up buying drinks for everyone since I couldn't bear to watch five women sharing one beer. Besides, the average price for a beer – for an American – was about a quarter. At times I wished I had brought along cases of de-odorant. You couldn't even go into some dance places because of the body odor. I would open the door, the smell would hit my nose, and I'd close it right away.

I made my way up the hill, in the oppressive heat, to Prague Castle. The statues lining the entrance gate were shocking to me: nude men in poses depicting wrestling scenes, brutal violence and brute force between men of the same race. One figure is poised to strike his victim in the head with a wooden club. Are these images supposed to be comforting? Or are they a constant reminder of what men are capable of?

I tried to schedule meetings with symphony and artist managers, but had much difficulty. It seems these men were only willing to talk business with other men. As I was a female, it seemed they were expecting me to try to interest them in dating me, which made me no better than a prostitute in their minds. Even the secretaries were threatened by my presence. If anyone was going to date the boss, she was (even if he was already married). Here again, I needed a male representative and was reminded of how useless my father was.

Prague was not the safest place to be at the time. Pickpockets were everywhere. I saw women being molested and fondled in public. My host argued that one generation of Communism was able to wipeout the influence of centuries of Catholicism. "Men need to be raised to fear punishment in the afterlife for sinful behavior. You can't tell them they are free to do whatever they want without consequences," he would say. During our dinner conversations, I would ask him about his memories of the Second World War. He was a young boy, maybe five or six, when his mother put a note in his pocket one day and sent him to live in the countryside with relatives. He never saw his mother again. He had never told his wife about this.

Lo and behold, on the television screen in my hosts' dining room, there were images of the O.J. Simpson trial, with Czech translations relating what had transpired that day. Evidently the Czechs decided that, since this case was receiving so much national coverage in America, it must be something of importance. The concept of a "media circus" was foreign to them, I guess. Everything American was cool and hip to them. They did not question the motivation behind such obsessive journalism. They believed the propaganda. My hosts had not been taught about American segregation, about the systematic oppression of black people since the so-called emancipation of the slaves. They almost did not want to believe that America was not the "land of the free" that they had dreamed of. They were not pleased to hear my perspective.

Of course, I had planned a pilgrimage to the grave of Dvořák. The Vyšehrad section of the city was not easy to find. The State cemetery where Dvořák was buried also contained the graves of Smetana and Janáček as well as famous military leaders and political figures. When I finally found the grave of Dvořák, a feeling of awe came over me. This man had validated the music of African and Native Americans in his European-style compositions at a time in American history when most whites were trying to dehumanize non-whites. It took courage to incorporate this music in his *Symphony from the New World*. There at the gravesite I felt the pain of my struggles and invoked the help of this spirit whose music had touched the hearts of millions. After all, I had grown up as a daughter of the director of the Fisk Jubilee Singers. This music was in my blood.

My meeting with Sal was scheduled for that afternoon, so after my pilgrimage I began to make my way toward town. I could not find my way to the main street where I could take public transportation, so I asked for directions from a large young man who was standing near the wooded area just outside the cemetery. He didn't speak a word of English but he pointed me toward the wooded area and a street just beyond it, down the hill. I thanked him, walked in the direction he indicated, and didn't realize until it was too late that he was following me. When I looked around and saw him again, I actually felt relief since I recognized him. Then he grabbed me.

There is a moment during a physical attack when one is so involved in surviving that the body goes into automatic pilot. With adrenaline rushing through my veins, I think my attacker was quite surprised by my strength. After he grabbed me and felt me up, he tried to throw me onto the ground. But my feet seemed to have a life of their own. They kept me from actually hitting the dirt, and then he ran. He had gotten his thrill and then went off to continue with his wonderful life.

The relief of it being over was my first response. I had sur-vived. I was not hurt. All I had to do was get out of those woods and get into town for my meeting with Sal. While Sal and I sat over lunch at a beautiful restaurant in downtown Prague, he had no idea of what had just happened to me. Later that night it occurred to me that I could have been killed. My life easily could have ended there at Dvořák's grave.

And what did I bring back from my experience of this pil-grimage? I guess the message was that I'm just another female, regardless of how trained I am, how qualified I am, how com-petent I am. Black or white, American or not – I'm still just an-other female, and as such, I can be just as easily assaulted, raped, or abused by any male.

I needed Beth.

My last night in Prague, the Wynton Marsalis band was performing in one of Prague's old, acoustically perfect concert halls. I had hooked up with some Americans who had tickets. These were white businessmen who seemed to have their pick of Czech girlfriends. Their company was one of the sponsors for the concert, so we all met for drinks beforehand. All of the professionals were male and all of the females were spouses or escorts. I felt terribly out of place.

The jazz band made me forget my isolation for a moment. *Blow, Wynton!*

The crowd loved the American jazz. The dozen or so black men on that stage blew the roof off the place. Afterwards, as an American, I was given easy access to the backstage area. Wynton himself was very friendly and welcoming and affec-tionate. I gave him a copy of my recording, knowing that it would be impossible to gain access to him in New York. It's funny how friendly Americans can be with each other as soon as we're outside of the country.

As luck would have it, the next day there were the members of the Marsalis band at the airport. We all hung out laughing and talking and drinking beer and shots of Becherovka while waiting for our flights.

With Wynton Marsalis in Prague

23

After being away from Beth for almost a month, I'm embarrassed to admit that I was actually looking forward to seeing her again. We had kept in touch via faxes and occasional phone calls. She was spending most of her time either at her parents' house or her sister's apartment. The baby was fine and she was thrilled watching him grow. I left a message on my answering machine giving her my flight arrival information. I vaguely hoped that she would be at the airport to meet me, but when she wasn't there, I assumed we would have our private reunion at home.

I took a cab from JFK to my flat. Though I had my keys, I rang from downstairs to let her know I was coming up. The intercom system in my building is connected through the telephone lines so when someone rings from downstairs and no one answers, the answering machine would pick up. Such was the case this time, but Beth had changed the outgoing message on the tape since the day before. The message said that her new office number was in Long Island – her parents' number. I had a sinking feeling. I took the elevator upstairs, unlocked the door, and my suspicions were confirmed. Not only had she moved out but also the stereo, the VCR, the TV, and half of my CD collection were gone. Not only had she planned this wonderful homecoming – my returning to a nearly empty apartment – the bitch had ripped me off. She had even left a nice little nasty note for me on the coffee table, accusing me of being responsible for everything that was wrong in her life. At least she left the coffee table behind. That was it! She was a fucking psychopath. I still needed to get my keys from her but I was determined to stay as far away from her as possible. Who knew what she was capable of?

We finally spoke on the telephone. She had left several messages but I was still too much in shock to answer. She couldn't wait to see me. She wanted to have lunch. We would meet the next day at her father's store in the West Village after her therapy session.

I knew now that the girl was crazy, but I was still befuddled by her behavior. She seemed glad to see me. She talked and talked about the baby and about what had transpired with the CD. She had great plans for another music video involving RuPaul and violinist Vanessa Mae. I simply nodded while she went on. We went for a walk. As I listened to her, it seemed that she intended to go on with our relationship. As lawyer-client or as lovers, it wasn't clear. But she fully expected us to meet again and discuss her idea. At least it was clear in my mind: It was over.

"By the way," I said. "I was assaulted over there."

Her face went blank. She was silent for a few seconds. "Why didn't you tell me?" she finally managed to say.

"Because you bailed out on me."

I had had enough. This scene was ridiculous. I had my keys. I had been struggling the whole afternoon to contain my emotions. They were about to break through. My cheek started to twitch.

"I'll see ya," I said and walked away. (Just keep walking. Don't look back.) I knew where I was going. To Henrietta's.

Finally free of Beth, all of a sudden I had too much time on my hands. I had no more energy to waste on career pursuits. I began to spend more and more time at the Community Center. Even on days when there were no ACOA meetings scheduled, I copied the literature and offered to run the meetings myself.

To add insult to injury, the good doctor was sending bills to me for money I did not have. Evidently, her hospital did not accept my insurance as she had claimed that it did. It turned out that she was the one who orchestrated Beth's coverage within her parents' policy. Beth had gone without insurance since her graduation from law school. The good doctor must have smelled a fat insurance policy somewhere in that Long Island home. Without a therapist and without a lover, I needed ACOA more than ever. Just reading the literature aloud in the meetings was a comfort:

> "Many of us growing up gay, lesbian, or bisexual in alcoholic or otherwise dysfunctional homes experienced our own personal pain – the pain of feelings we could neither understand, share, or accept."

I knew I wanted to be with a woman when I grew up, but my mother had told me that it was "unhealthy" for two women to get too close. She scorned and ridiculed "queers" who were on the faculty where she taught.

"Isolated, alone within our families and alone amongst our friends, we experienced a profound solitude."

Not only was I isolated because I knew I was attracted to girls. I was even more isolated by being light-skinned at a black school, and by being a "nigger" at a white conservatory. Furthermore, I was an only child of parents who were old enough to be my grandparents. All of their friends had kids who were already grown.

"Today we have discovered that we are not alone as we once believed we were. We are not evil, sick, or even different from other people."

My own mother, during her drunken rampages, had called me "sick" and "evil."

"In the process of growth, there can be no denial."

How many times had my father said, dismissively, "Now, you *know* your mother was never an alcoholic!"

"We must not ignore the issues, conflicts, and pain we experience in being who we are. As ACOAs, we know that when we stuff our feelings, we can become increasingly tolerant of emotional pain. We can become numb."

So that's what was going on with Beth! I was numb. No wonder I had sexual problems. I couldn't feel anything. Besides, how many times had my father said, "Oh, you shouldn't feel that way."

"In these rooms we learn to accept, express, and feel our feelings in a new and powerful way. By sharing and listening to trusted others, we can develop a new acceptance and love of ourselves."

Some weeks, I was in those rooms every day. Thank Goddess for The Center.

I had read all the John Bradshaw and Alice Miller books, but it wasn't until I went into the rooms and heard myself speak the truth about my family – and saw the concerned, supportive, and understanding expressions from the other people in the room – that my feelings began to thaw. The concept of family dysfunction had been difficult for me to grasp at first. I had thought we were super-functional. But I came to learn that all the performing was designed to mask our individual pain from each other as well as from the outside world. Plus, all of the activity and stress served to distract us from our true feelings. My father did not have a functional wife. My mother did not have a functional husband, and I did not have loving, supportive parents. My parents expected me to play along with their denials, to build more walls around us to keep us more isolated. If I did not play along, then I was too much of a disruption to their precarious equilibrium. The emperor was naked! I couldn't lie to myself anymore.

But what to do about the fact that I had no comfort, no support, no siblings or spouse. I was alone, which is exactly why the rooms are so necessary.

I also learned why it was so important for the chemically addicted person to deny the impact of what she is doing to the family. For as long as I can remember, anytime I had been hurt either physically or emotionally, my mother had to laugh it off. I was either being "overly dramatic," or was told, "That little bit of blood doesn't do anything." Once during my adolescence when I developed an abscess in my breast, I actually heard my mother telling the doctor that I must have slept against the wall and caught a cold in my chest. She could not accept the idea of my being in pain because she could not comfort me. She could not be a mother. She was a critic and a teacher, but no mother. When members of my mother's social clubs began to imply (to *me*!) that they could smell the alcohol on her breath, I asked my father about detox programs. I knew they existed. There was help out there for people who needed it. But one Christmas, he finally admitted to me why it was that he refused to take any action.

"It's my fault," he said softly. "I'll change."

I had not told my parents that I had been assaulted or that I had been in an abusive relationship. My father loved Beth. She did some free legal work for him so he worshiped the ground she walked on. He had retired while we were together and his salary at retirement was below starting-salary at the school where he had taught for thirty years. Beth wrote a letter to the president of the university, threatening to sue for back-wages and for their retirement plan, which had been bungled by incompetent accountants. My father told me that when an envelope arrived in the mail from the president's office, he was shaking so much that he couldn't open it. Beth had calculated the amount due at nearly half a million dollars. My father fully expected a check in that amount to be inside the envelope. But it was just a letter from the president inviting him in for a meeting. Everyone on campus knew that they could talk Matthew out of wanting or expecting to be paid. He wasn't even capable of asking for a raise. But when a white person was sending letters on his behalf, he thought the Lord had answered his prayers. He would have wanted me to stay with Beth.

As for the assault, I could just imagine my mother's response: "What on earth were you doing there in the first place?! You must have been asking for trouble!"

No. It wasn't worth opening myself to more ridicule and accusations.

24

Meanwhile, Sal was organizing his plans for his extravaganza to benefit the costume museum in Prague. I received a steady stream of faxes from him outlining the details. I would be presented in recital but he wanted me to wear a dress from the turn of the century, for which I would be fitted when I arrived. He was getting corporate sponsors together, two of which were Czech Airlines and Hilton Hotels, meaning my expenses were covered. He also wanted me to give a recital at the American Ambassador's Residence.

My music career, it seemed, had survived my relationship with Beth, even though I had little energy left for it. I still had several contracts pending, in need of negotiation. I called one of Beth's gay male law school friends to ask if we could meet. Toward the end of our time together, Beth was adamant about not wanting me to call this guy. She made it sound as if he couldn't be trusted. But I was up shit's creek without a paddle. I needed representation.

We met at his flat and went to a gay club afterwards. I thoroughly enjoyed his company. It was such a pleasure to be able to relate some of the things Beth had put me through to someone who knew her. John had sat at our table for Thanksgiving dinners and numerous dinner parties. I considered him a friend. I admitted what she had said about him.

"She really didn't want me to call you. She had said, 'Under no circumstances are you to get in touch with him.' It seemed rather extreme," I said.

He was silent for a few seconds. Then he said, "I'm not surprised." When I asked why, he said, "She told me that whenever she was on the phone with me, you were standing over her with your finger on the button, threatening to hang up if you didn't like what she said."

"Come again?"

"Yeah! She said you threatened to beat her up if she said anything bad about you."

I couldn't believe it. How could I not have perceived what a liar she was? She had also told John that her grandmother had been killed in a concentration camp, when there were pictures of her smiling, healthy grandmother as a young woman in a bathing suit at Coney Island. She was already in the United States long before the outbreak of the Second World War. It seemed Beth had inherited her father's tendency toward compulsive lying. Suddenly I realized I had to re-evaluate everything she had ever told me. And I had invited such a person into my home, into my life!

John and I met several times after that to organize a plan of action. There was an impresario from South Africa who was interested in engaging me for a concert tour in addition to some conducting jobs. The proposals had to be composed, however, and the contracts drawn up and negotiated. Of course, there was no money yet. It was up to us, the Americans, to come up with the sponsorship.

I had also been inspired by Madonna's book *Sex* and had wanted to shoot a series of photos portraying me as a conductor and a nude woman as a metaphor for the orchestra – incorporating my Wagner scores, of course. We solicited the help of one of my old Bankers' Group friends who had experience in proposal writing. John called one of his photographer friends and we decided to check out a space that just opened for women that offered lap-dancing for the clientele. I brought my props, thinking the photographer would want some sample pictures. As luck would have it, the *Village Voice* was doing a story on the opening of this club and their photographers were clicking away while I demonstrated my idea with the help of a very willing lap-dancer. The following week, there was my photo in *The Voice*, along with my eager new friend.

Plus, I still had to play concerts. I was engaged to do the Rachmaninoff Paganini Variations with the Waterloo-Cedar Falls Symphony under the conductor Elizabeth Schulze. I had decided in advance that the Paganini Variations would be the final addition to my concerto repertoire. Elizabeth and I had already performed Gershwin's *Concerto in F* with the Kenosha Symphony in Wisconsin. It was such a pleasure to be able to work with a woman conductor! We could hang out over cocktails and go out to dinner at restaurants without raising eyebrows. We both felt that we had each other's backs as colleagues.

There was a Czech community not far from Waterloo-Cedar Falls, where Dvořák finished the orchestration for his

Symphony from the New World. I knew that he had supposedly composed the sketches for the Symphony in his New York home on Stuyvesant Square, where his student Harry Burleigh sang some of the melodies from the Spirituals for him. Stuyvesant Square was not far from my apartment. It seemed my life was inadvertently linked with Dvořák's in some cosmic way. The incident at his gravesite was etched in my memory forever.

A television crew came to the second rehearsal of the Rachmaninoff to shoot some footage for the evening news. I gladly did an interview with the reporter. When I caught sight of myself that night on television, I was truly surprised and saddened by what I saw. I looked exhausted. The camera revealed just how exploited and used I felt, but I thought I was covering up. And if that was how I came across on television, imagine how I must have looked in interviews, meetings, auditions, etc. It was suddenly clear I could no longer hide what was going on inside of me. It was time to re-evaluate things.

Elizabeth was also an assistant conductor for the National Symphony in Washington, D.C., and as such, she received a lot of media coverage. Then-First Lady Hillary Rodham Clinton was one of the many witnesses to her success, so when we came up with the idea to form the "Women's World Orchestra" (WWO, symbolic for world-peace, get it?), it made sense to inform our First Lady and other prominent women politicians. Little did we know that Mrs. Clinton would actually call us as soon as she received the materials. I remember hearing the phone ring and letting the answering machine take it since I was still in bed. When I heard that it was the White House calling, I was up and out of bed and across the room with lightning speed.

That summer, the Metropolitan Opera Guild was honoring Leontyne Price at its annual luncheon at the Waldorf Astoria. J. Franklin and Bertha Taylor, who were friends of my parents, were members of the Guild and flew up from Nashville to attend the luncheon. They invited me to meet them in the lobby beforehand. I knew that it would not occur to the white male organizers of the Metropolitan Opera Guild luncheon to inform notable black American women of Leontyne Price's honor. So I took it upon myself to send faxes to Oprah Winfrey and Maya Angelou. Dr. Angelou actually responded, sending a statement of congratulations which should have been read during the event. I forwarded the fax to the white male organizers.

The morning of the luncheon, I met the Taylors in the lobby of the Waldorf. When it was time for them to go in to be seated at the luncheon and they saw that their table was half-empty, they bought an extra ticket for me to join them. Many celebrities were on hand to pay tribute to Leontyne Price. Jessye Norman sang a group of songs, accompanied by James Levine. After Jessye finished singing, she and Leontyne embraced. There wasn't a dry eye in the house.

Maya Angelou's statement was not read.

After the luncheon, there was a cocktail party in an adjoining lounge. I recognized many celebrities from the opera world. I approached Miss Price in the receiving line and congratulated her. She and my father had attended Juilliard at the same time, so I asked if she remembered him. She did, and she went on to the next person. I was dismissed. Miss Price was in her element, surrounded by adoring aged white gay men. They were the ones who had crowned her queen of the Metropolitan Opera stage.

I saw Beverly Sills in a distant corner laughing and talking with admirers. At that time, she was the executive director of Lincoln Center. I knew that she had been instrumental in getting Anthony Davis' opera performed at the City Opera. I introduced myself and told her that I had seen Anthony recently, and that we were the guest artists in Jackson, Mississippi when slavery was abolished. She relished my connection of the two events. I went on to ask her if it were possible to send her information on my concert work, in hopes of securing a Lincoln Center contract. She was most amenable.

The next day, I instructed John to send a press package to Beverly Sills. A few days later I received a very kind letter from Ms. Sills stating that she had forwarded my materials to the executive director of the New York Philharmonic. I did not hear anything more from Lincoln Center.

Anyone else in her right mind would have said, "Fuck it! This racist, misogynist field is not worth the time, energy, or pain." But I had two little old black parents in Nashville, Tennessee who were just waiting for me to make their lives worthwhile via my success. They reminded me of how hard they had worked to keep me clothed and fed and to give me an education (even though I had scholarships during most of my time in college and grad school). What they really meant – and weren't saying – was that they had stayed together through a miserable marriage for my sake and it was therefore up to me to make them happy, to bring their inherited talent into the next generation, and enjoy the success which had been denied them in their day.

I am truly amazed at how desperately they needed to believe that the world had changed and that racism was no longer a factor. Such may be the case in other fields. But classical music? Here I was knocking on the same doors that had been closed in their faces and they still weren't opening for me.

25

Before I knew it, it was time to fly back to Prague. Sal had faxed me that my tickets would be waiting for me at the airport. I had practiced and prepared as well as I could under the circumstances, but my head simply was not there. There was no denying it. I hoped I could find pianos to work on after I got there. I faxed Sal to inform him that I would need access to practice facilities.

I also was afraid. I knew the Czechs spoke English and were well-acquainted with American culture, but they were also resentful of the strong dollar. Prices were suddenly doubled when they found out that you were American. Some cab drivers got pretty scary all of a sudden when they locked the doors and demanded that you pay three-times the fare indicated. I never saw any police around while I was there before. The criminal element was clearly in charge.

Thank goodness Sal was going to meet me at the airport. I was more aware of feeling a need for protection than ever before.

I took a taxi to JFK and was told to wait in the Air France waiting area for my Czech Airlines flight. I sat in front of a television and there was the "Million Man March" being broadcast live on CNN. Organized by Louis Farrakhan, the Million Man March was supposed to be a celebration of black manhood. At the same time, it was intended to show white Americans that black men were ready to come together and stand as an economic unit. Black American men from all over the country had brought and spent millions of dollars in Washington, D.C. that day. The amount paled in comparison, however, to the amount of dollars the U.S. government spends keeping black men incarcerated in the nation's prisons.

After all I had been through – being cheated by a white-owned record company, beaten by a white lover, assaulted by a white man, etc. etc. – I longed for a black hero, a savior who would come to my aid, protect and defend me, shelter me from harm. Even my own black father had never done any of this for me. He just sent me out into the white world to be used and abused by them as he himself had been. He carried no protective instincts toward his wife and daughter whatsoever. And by doing so, he instilled the message that I was unworthy of protection.

In those days, I was regularly consulting my Witches' Calendar, which indicated that it happened to be the birthday of Marie Antoinette. Black men had gathered at the Washington Monument – the great American obelisk, symbol of the power of Ancient Egypt – on the birthday of the woman whose life was taken at the site of the great obelisk in Paris, which stands in the spot where the guillotine once stood. That day in the Air France waiting room, on the birthday of Marie Antoinette, for a brief moment I had the feeling that my country and the men of my assigned race were finally getting it – that I could finally hope for protection and not be, yet again, disappointed.

After an uneventful flight, a smiling Sal met me at the arrival area. We embraced. He was clearly stressed-out but he was very glad to see me. We took a cab to the hotel – the beautiful, brand new Prague Hilton – and he checked me into my room. All of my expenses were covered, meals included. For that afternoon, he had scheduled a fitting for me with the fashion designer who was also a curator for the costume museum. The dress I would be wearing was an antique – multi-colored layers of silk in a nineteenth century design. The colors of the dress seemed to change depending on the intensity and direction of the light hitting it. There was even a matching hat. I had never worn such an elaborate gown.

After the fitting, finally alone in my suite, I wept from exhaustion, fear, and loneliness.

Sal had scheduled a press conference for the following morning. I had been using just my first name in all press releases for at least a year by that point, and Beth had changed the spelling of my name from Nina to Nyna, "because it was unique," she said. But for the Czechs, it was an issue. They did not want to be so presumptuous as to call me by my first name, so many of them solved the problem by referring to me as "Miss Nyna." I had prepared a whole shtick about why I did not use my last name, as it was a slave name and only reflected the name of the family that had owned my father's ancestors. My single name was a protest against American history. I also had planned to tie in the Fisk Jubilee Singers and their connection to Dvořák. But during the course of the press conference, Sal did most of the talking. I didn't even get a chance to use my speech.

I made up for this exclusion the next day on a morning television program, for which I was the invited guest. I had brought material on the Jubilee Singers for the translator to read in advance. I arrived at the studio and was asked to perform live on camera on a not-so-great piano. But we laughed and joked on camera while thousands of Czechs had their morning coffee and dressed for work. After my segment, they played a video of a Czech pop group with a small choir singing in the background. I smiled at hearing a definite imitation of black American gospel.

Even though I found pianos in the hotel to practice on, I still felt very nervous. I was under tremendous stress and felt utterly alone. I ate my meals in the restaurants alone. I didn't have anyone to share any part of my life with. Alone in my beautiful hotel suite, the pressure and anxiety would sometimes get to me. The silence was deafening. All I had was my work. My need for love went totally unfilled and unaddressed.

I decided to kill some time in the hotel lobby. There was a group of women who were obviously "open" for business. They were beautiful, well-dressed, and young. They were almost childlike while in each other's presence. But when a man approached, they suddenly became very serious and distant. One by one they would disappear into the elevators with clients and would return usually within half an hour or so. I was lonely. I thought about asking one if she would come with me to my room just for some company and maybe some snuggling. How much could it cost, anyway, for an American?

Costume museum benefit in Prague

Sal was really planning more of a fashion show than a concert. We spent the afternoon in rehearsals, mostly so that the dressers could practice getting the models in and out of their clothes on time. There was loud music, lights, and a catwalk.

Fortunately, Sal remembered to bring in a superb piano which was sitting on the stage, waiting patiently.

In the dressing rooms, I heard some of the women who were professional costumers discussing what to do about my hat. Evidently, this was the kind of hat that was made to sit on top of long, straight hair. My short natural didn't quite do the trick and the women didn't know what to do. Some of them pulled a little at my curls, obviously curious as to how this strange hair felt. They laughed a little, spoke to each other in Czech and then went searching for bobby-pins. Evidently my curls pushed the hat upwards on my head, and with the playing I was supposed to do, who knew if it would stay in place.

The evening went off without a hitch. Television crews covered the event. But the show was a bit too long. By the time I came out to play (which was supposed to be the climax of the evening) most of the audience was visibly tired. But I played through the entire Ravel *Valses nobles et sentimentales* and finished to receive a standing ovation.

There was a lavish reception following the show. My host from my previous visit had come to the event and was so excited. He came up to me at the reception and could not contain his enthusiasm.

"You were wonderful," he gushed, "Just wonderful!"

Sal was relieved and exhausted.

The American ambassador was in the audience for the benefit concert. Sal had made arrangements for me to give a recital at the residence two days later. I scheduled practice time at the residence for the following afternoon so that I could get acquainted with the piano and get a feel for the acoustics.

When I arrived at the residence, after passing through several security checks, I was admitted to a receiving area. The ambassador was in meetings that afternoon so she sent her secretary to greet me. The secretary first wanted to take me on a tour of the house, a beautiful, sprawling château complete with a marble swimming pool in the basement. The family for which the house was built had fled to America before the Second World War. She mentioned the family name: Petschek. It sounded familiar.

"Petschek. Is that P-E-T-S-C-H-E-K?" I asked.

"Why, that's right." She was used to having to spell the name for guests.

I had been the recipient of the Petschek scholarship for my study at Juilliard. This family already had a significant place in my life, and here I was in their home on the other side of the globe to give a concert. The world gets smaller every day.

She also showed me a large closet containing several orchestral scores, including full scores of Wagner operas.

The secretary showed me the way to the piano. The ambassador was still in meetings, but she said my practice would not disturb them. The piano was near the front entrance of the house. As I began to warm up, several military men in full military fatigues came to the door, were greeted by staff, and shown to the dining room. These men were big and loud and seemed totally at ease being waited on by servants. Some glared at me before continuing into the dining area. I don't know if these were scowls of disapproval or their natural facial expressions. I doubted that these men ever smiled.

A few minutes into my practice, I began to try out some repertoire. I heard the loud voices booming from the dining room in various languages, but it was not disturbing. The noises simply blended into the background.

Then I began to play through Wagner's *Liebestod*. This was by far the most beautiful music on my program for the evening. I had heard the men's voices rising in argument before I began. But after a few phrases, I noticed there was total silence in the other room. I decided to play through the entire piece without pause. When I was finished, the silence continued. It seemed the magic of Wagner's music had stopped their argument cold.

A few minutes later, one of the military men had to leave the luncheon early. He took his hat from the butler and gazed toward me for an instant. He nodded his head and definitely revealed his teeth. I guess that was as close to a smile as he ever got.

After rehearsing, I went back to my hotel for a short rest. I just managed to close my eyes when it was time to shower and dress for the evening.

The ambassador came to my dressing room soon after I arrived at the residence. I knew the new American ambassador was a woman but I was not prepared for how young she was. She came from a military career and did not know very much about classical music. But we had a nice chat and she soon left me to take her seat in the audience. Sal came to get me to escort me to the piano.

There were the usual introductions. Sal told the audience how we had met at the Dvořák Hall. The ambassador told the story that I had been the recipient of the Petschek scholarship at Juilliard and what a coincidence it was to give a concert at the Petschek home. When I was finally introduced, I was actually surprised by the size of the audience. The hall was packed. I gave one of my best performances. Sal was in tears.

After the concert, there was another lavish reception. The ambassador told me that she already had tickets for that year's Bayreuth festival in Germany. I had wanted to go to Bayreuth for years but so far had not had the opportunity. I was suddenly jealous of people in the American military.

When I finally got back to the hotel, I collapsed from exhaustion. I returned with several flower bouquets. The next morning, I decided to share one of them with the young woman who served my breakfast. I had seen her every day all week long, but we had not been able to converse since she spoke no English and I certainly spoke no Czech. The flowers almost brought her to tears.

That day I checked out of the hotel, made my way to the airport, flew across the Atlantic, and ended the day in my lonely New York apartment. My expenses had been covered, but I came home with no profit.

26

What was this fear, this pressure? I needed to have my success while I was young. There was the fear of ending up like my mother: frustrated, bitter, addicted, and trapped in a miserable marriage. She had been young and beautiful and hopeful, too. What happened? Had there been too much optimism among blacks during the fifties and sixties? Had blacks forgotten that they were living in America? Or had the black people of my parents' generation not been prepared for the emotional effects of watching younger generations enjoy freedoms which had been denied to older generations? Were they jealous?

This career was not working out. I could not understand how my parents could be so insistent that I prepare to enter a field where I was not wanted. Sure, I played concerts. But I was not making a living. In fact, there was no success in sight. Managers wouldn't sign me. Competitions wouldn't accept me. What the hell was I supposed to do? Admit that my parents were wrong? Or were they, in fact, sadistic? Did they set me up for failure so that I would have to return home to them with my tail between my legs to set up shop as their old maid? None of it made any sense. I couldn't even ask them for any more advice, since they had proven themselves to be unhelpful and uninformed. I was stuck. There was no way I was going to get those years back – those years of practicing, preparing, performing. All for what?!

"Suddenly I realized I had to reevaluate everything she had ever told me."

• • • • •

I received a letter from a recent appointee to the Office of Student Affairs at Juilliard. I regularly received requests for money from the alumni office, but I decided that I would give money to my alma mater when I started making some. So far, this was not the case. This letter from Student Affairs was different. The new appointee was a black man. He had observed some of the difficulties the black students were having with racist white faculty and decided to organize a monthly luncheon to which students, faculty, and alumni were invited. All people of color were welcome.

I was accustomed to the circle-atmosphere of the Twelve-Step groups, but I had never sat in a Twelve-Step group consisting only of people of color. I don't think the Student Activities director was prepared for how frustrated and angry the black Juilliard alumni were, myself included. Here we were supposed to be inspirations for the current students, but conditions for the current students were much better than anything we had experienced. I began to experience my parents' unacknowledged jealousy of younger generations of American blacks.

Students from all three categories of the performing arts were present – music, dance, and drama. The females in the drama department were the most oppressed. Some spoke of only being assigned roles such as the "Third Witch" or the prostitute or the maid. A black male student recently had been assigned the role of Richard III, and could not understand what all the complaining was about. The dance students were in a strange, precarious position. The all-white Juilliard dance faculty knew that these extremely talented black dancers would probably go on to have lucrative careers in television, film, music videos, etc. But this all-white faculty insisted that these students perfect European-style classical ballet – a field reeking with blatant racism. Many of these beautiful, talented students were threatened with expulsion for varied mysterious reasons. The truth was, most likely, that they were simply too good and as a result threatened their teachers.

It was a challenge for me to keep the focus on the future and to think in terms of what these young hopefuls needed to hear. But at times, my protective, maternal instincts would take over and I would feel the need to warn them about a certain high-ranking power-broker at Lincoln Center, who was notorious for not being able to keep his hands off of black boys. This was the age of AIDS. No job was worth risking one's life.

I also told the students to get standing room tickets or go to the rehearsals of *Die Walküre* at the Met. Jessye Norman was singing the role of Sieglinde, and it was an event to hear her body fill the entire Metropolitan Opera House with sound. There is a moment in the first act when Siegmund and

Sieglinde, twins separated in childhood who no longer recognize each other, are reunited as adults and gradually begin to remember the details of their separation. At one magical moment, big, black Jessye sings to big, white, Siegfried Jerusalem (that's his real name), "I looked into the lake and saw my reflection. And now I look at you and see the same body." Directors of opera houses all over the world had used this moment to justify not hiring black singers. But in New York in 1996, their racism was being defied right there on the stage of the Metropolitan Opera. Jessye Norman herself was a phenomenon, a force of nature, and even Jessye, with her magnificent voice, had to leave the United States and travel to Germany in order to start her career. And what a career!

I had already been to a performance of *Die Walküre* and stood in line to ask for her autograph. When she came out of the artists' entrance, the crowd parted to make way for her. She is so larger than life. I placed myself right in front of her, pen and program in hand. She came to me, took my pen and program, and began to sign. I was still under the influence of the spell she had cast on the stage.

"May I kiss you?" I asked.

She bent down to me and offered her cheek.

"You are wonderful," I gushed. "Absolutely wonderful!"

But she hears these things all the time. She must be numb to such worship. I did have to stop myself from falling to my knees; the effect of her voice is so powerful.

• • • • •

"Memphis in May"

The Memphis Symphony Orchestra gave an annual outdoor concert during a festival called "Memphis in May," and this year they invited me to appear as piano soloist in another performance of *Rhapsody in Blue*. John handled the paperwork. The concert was to take place during the re-election campaign for Bill Clinton and Al Gore. Gore was a son of Tennessee. He would be present at the concert. My history with the Gore family went back to the 1960s when the Fisk Jubilee Singers sang in Albert Gore Sr.'s office in Washington, D.C. back when Gore Sr. was senator. Somehow I managed to be right in the front of that photograph, right next to Senator Gore.

Fisk Jubilee Singers with Senator Al Gore Sr.

It was also the year of the summer Olympic Games in Atlanta. The Olympic torch was in Tennessee and the runner was scheduled to come through the stadium and light a cauldron on the stage in front of the orchestra. It was another huge extravaganza.

The Memphis Symphony had engaged me as a soloist several times before. I already knew many of the players by name. This was one of the largest audiences I had ever played for. Thousands! The concert was being broadcast live on local television. I hoped to be able to build up enough enthusiasm about the *Rhapsody in Blue* to rise to the occasion. The atmosphere was like a huge circus. I walked out on stage to shouts and whistles. The *Rhapsody in Blue* begins with a long orchestral passage. The piano isn't heard until the second page of the score. When I began to play, I noticed a sudden flurry of activity behind me but I was (of course) too busy to pay attention. The scuffling went on for my entire opening solo. When I finished my big build up for the entrance of the full orchestra, there was silence. I looked up at the conductor in a panic. It turned out that the stage crew had forgotten to turn on the microphones for the piano. The conductor decided to make a pause while the technicians got their shit together. I went backstage and waited. When I came back out, the audience was even more excited to see me. I struck a single tuning "A" to see if the mics worked. Everyone applauded. The performance went on, but more like a jazz concert than a classical concerto. The audience whooped and whistled after each of my solos.

What kind of sign was this? Here this was the largest audience of my career so far and my piano wasn't heard?! Television cameras, the vice president of the United States, a contingent of visiting diplomats, the Olympic torch... and my playing could not be heard. Was this karma? Or was this a sign that I should be doing something else?

I spoke to the vice president after the concert about a project I was involved with regarding an integrated youth orchestra in South Africa. My efforts resulted in my name appearing on guest lists for events at the South African Consulate in New York, where I made more delightful international contacts. He was very cordial and attentive and asked me to send materials by mail. Photographers clicked away while Al and I chatted.

I had met most of the ambassadors who were present for the conference they were attending at various cocktail parties and dinners to which I was also invited. After the performance, however, one of the African diplomats decided that he wanted to marry me. He was really smitten. He asked how to contact me in New York under the pretense of wanting to bring me to Africa for a concert tour. But as time went on and he only called me while he was in New York to invite me to his hotel, I soon got the message.

During the plane ride back, I saw a familiar face in First Class. The bald head, the telltale dark glasses, the dark chocolate skin. (What was his name? Shaft! No... the composer of the music for *Shaft*. That's who it was. But what was his real name?) I stared at him. He stared at me. Finally, I remembered his name: Isaac Hayes. I asked the stewardess to ask him if he were Mr. Hayes. When she did, he waved for me to come and join him. I did and he said, "I was just about to tell the stewardess to ask you if you were Ms. Kennedy!" He had watched the broadcast of the concert and told me he called all his friends and told them to watch. "That girl can PLAY!" he said to them. We chatted the whole way back to New York. After the flight, while waiting in the baggage claim area, Isaac Hayes asked me for piano lessons.

After "Memphis in May," I really didn't know what to do. I had no contracts. The masters of my recording were still sitting on a shelf. I had no record deal, no lover. John was turning out not to be as smart as I thought he was. He followed instructions but had no initiative. I still hadn't made any real money. These concerts paid small honorariums but it was not enough to live on.

The local TV station in Memphis made a point of sending a beautiful young black female reporter to cover the concert. While she interviewed me on camera, I said something about my work as a classical pianist in Vienna, the home of Mozart, and inevitably – when the Viennese learned that I was from Tennessee – they would ask me questions about Elvis Presley, who had made his home in Memphis. (From Mozart to Elvis. That's a stretch!) I guess the Viennese assumed that we were acquainted and I utilized this false assumption to my benefit as much as I could. However, Memphis was also the city where Martin Luther King met his untimely death. I think the reporter was nudging me to say something about Martin, but I couldn't think of a way to tie him into a conversation about Gershwin and the *Rhapsody in Blue*.

Privately, however, thoughts of Martin filled my mind. Memphis will forever be known as the place where the great leader of America's Civil Rights Movement was murdered –

the man who spoke of love, peace, and freedom. I have often wondered how the people of Memphis coped with the knowledge that this peace-loving, God-fearing man was taken from us on their watch. Years later, when I had moved to Vienna and spent much time there, I discovered that the Austrians really didn't know much about the history of African Americans. They weren't taught that much about slavery in school – especially the fact that slavery in America went on for nearly two hundred and fifty years. They certainly were not taught about Jim Crow and segregation, "Separate but Equal," or Brown vs. the Board of Education. Most of the Austrians I knew were shocked to learn of this history, especially since they practically worshiped African American athletes and entertainers.

After that concert in Memphis, I felt I didn't have any more energy to pour into this concert career. I felt depleted, exhausted, and disappointed.

The next chapter of my life began when I met Cathy – the cocaine-addicted actress.

Part 3

27

Cathy was a full-time student at New York University, and was enrolled at the Strasberg Actors' Studio as part of NYU's acting program. She had not been "out" as a lesbian for long. She had lost her virginity with a man while in high school "just to get it over with," then engaged in several sexual relationships with older men. By her senior year, she was in a relationship with a female classmate. They broke up after a few months, but Cathy was convinced: she was finished with men.

We met one Saturday night at the club with the lap-dancers. She was out for the evening as the third wheel with her ex and her ex's new girlfriend. Cathy had decided that she would hook up with someone that night, come hell or high water. The three of them happened to be sitting behind me during the show. Afterwards, I turned around and saw Cathy's smiling face. The next thing I knew, we were dancing close and kissing deeply. This was no flirt here. She meant business. She told me that her friends were spending the night with her in her NYU dorm room, but she invited me to brunch the next day. She made it clear that she really wanted to see me again; her space was just too crowded that night. It seemed fine with me. I was in no rush.

The next day she told me she was nineteen.

I must admit, I thoroughly enjoyed being with an actress. She was beautiful. She was stylish, looked great in her clothes (and even better out of them). She was theatrical and craved attention. The sex was terrific. There was only one problem: the cocaine.

Cathy was a gutsy actress. She went alone to men's apartments to read a scene or pose for photos or videos. She was searching for decent lesbian roles to perform but none existed. Some of the pitiful scripts she found were so ridiculous, even I had to laugh. Obviously there weren't enough lesbians out there putting their experiences on paper. I began to write short pieces for her to read, just for fun.

Cathy's father was a rich lawyer, which meant that she had unlimited funds to support her drug-habit. She had tried to commit suicide several times in high school. Whenever her parents grew suspicious that she might try again, they would call the local suburban police who had her on suicide watch. They could come to her house or to her school and take her away in handcuffs at any time.

In her NYU dorm, she immediately found the resident coke-dealer. She invited me to all-nighters where kids would snort, talk, write or paint, and listen to music. I was by far the oldest person at these parties, and certainly the poorest.

Sex with Cathy inspired some of my early erotica. We would sometimes read Anaïs Nin to each other as foreplay. Within our first week together, she told me she had had a memory. It was a vivid, detailed memory of being small and being forced to perform oral sex on an old man. She couldn't see the man's face. But she remembered the choking, the gagging, and the taste. She began avoiding sex soon after she told me this. Sometimes, when she was high enough and drunk enough, she would want to rush into sex before the memories had a chance to surface. She needed to take me by surprise. But eventually, the memories won out. She didn't want any more sex. All she wanted was to be taken out to eat and to do more and more cocaine. Her mood-swings became intolerable.

Again, I was having a relationship with chemicals. Her favorite phrase became, "You can find somebody better." And she was right. She was never there for me when I needed her. But I was always there for her. I knew she preferred to binge all night doing coke with her friends. The intimacy with me was too intense for her. All of the feelings she had put so much energy into pushing down simply came gushing out with me. She couldn't control it. But here again, I was with someone who put *my* feelings last. She wanted to be friends. We would go for weeks, months without seeing each other. Then we'd get together a few times for dinner or drinks and end up in bed. It pained me to watch her confusion. She wanted the closeness, the intimacy, but the bad feelings would surface and she would have to start a fight. The affair was over within a year. But my love for writing continued.

Little did I know, while I was listening to the operas of Richard Wagner and digesting the effects of his form of "Music Drama," that I was preparing myself to use similar dramatic, musical techniques in spoken-word performances. Music had trained my ear to the point where I could fully utilize musical structures and phrasings without the use of pitch. When the Norwegian soprano Kristin Norderval asked to improvise melodies onto my texts, I felt I had come full-circle artistically.

Kristin and I met one evening when we were both performing at the Women's One World (W.O.W.) Café/Theatre in the East Village. She sang a group of arias and I read some of my writings. Afterwards, she said that my words had brought tears to her eyes. She mentioned she had a girlfriend in Vienna. (Ah... Vienna!) It brought back memories of my former life as a concert pianist, when I had performed at the Musikverein and the Konzerthaus. I actually had not expected to meet anyone at the W.O.W. Café who would stir up these old memories. Kristin was the first classical performer I ever heard perform there. She told me she was preparing a parody on the sexist/misogynist operatic roles for women in the traditional repertoire. The piece would be called *Diva Construction* and in it she would sing her own compositions, present an installation of slides and photographs (shot by her Viennese girlfriend), and give a talk on how male composers had consistently portrayed female ecstasy as glorified rape. And in how many of these operas was the heroine murdered or killed by her own hand for the final climax? Kristin continues to call for new works by women composers and writers. We have lots of work to do.

And then, there was Anaïs Nin. I had read much of her erotica and diaries long before I knew that she was the daughter of a concert pianist/composer. I had even played some of the compositions written by her father during my teenage years. What is it about being a daughter of a pianist that fuels the need to write erotica? Before I knew it, I had a notebook full of erotic short stories. Since I was used to performing, it was easy for me to think in terms of getting on stage and reading to a room full of strangers. I had heard writer/poet Pamela Sneed read some of her writings at the Clit Club and was surprised that the writings she chose were memoirs without one word referring to lesbianism or sex. Several people in the audience started chatting or went to the other room where the music was still playing. If I was going to read for that audience, I needed a way to hold their attention. I needed a stripper. The combination was magic. All eyes were on the stripper while my words and voice went straight into the subconscious. By the end of my readings, the sexual tension in the room was so thick that the women would scream just for some sense of release.

I was reading all over town: at the Clit Club, the Women's One World Café/Theatre, Bar d'O, Velvet, Meow Mix, Crazy Nanny's, Henrietta's, 2i's, and even in some East Village restaurants. Television crews began to follow me around, partially because they knew I had strippers.

While working with strippers, my eyes were opened to a world of fearless women – women who opened themselves to being groped and grabbed by strange men all for a dollar tip. Most of the strippers I met were lesbians. Their experiences had made them sick of men. One of my dancers was a classically trained ballerina who couldn't get work in New York, so she stripped in an all-nude bar to pay the bills. I gave her a tape of my music, to which she choreographed and performed a ballet at the W.O.W. Café. When I presented her with her own copy of a videotape of the performance, she burst into tears. Before then, she did not have a videotape of herself dancing.

Why can't we live in a world where women don't have to prostitute themselves in order to survive? Why must men be so selfish and greedy? Do they really think so little of themselves that they need to hoard all of the world's wealth in order to be able to "buy" a woman? It is no accident that the majority of women and children live in poverty.

· · · · ·

Meanwhile back at Juilliard, the camaraderie among the students in the group for people of color made it possible for the Student Affairs director to propose an annual Martin Luther King Memorial Concert to the president of Juilliard. The president agreed and every year the concert was sold-out. Those beautiful dancers on stage simply confirmed my belief that their white teachers were jealous of their natural ability. The second year, a reunion was organized for alumni of color – including luncheons, workshops, cocktail parties, and dinners. By this point in my artistic pursuits, I was almost as well-known in New York City as a spoken-word performer as I had been as a pianist. The director of Student Affairs asked me to read the Maya Angelou poem "And Still I Rise" at the end of the program. I was assisted by a dancer who interpreted the words with her body. On the program, the reader of the poem was listed as "Actress, Juilliard Alumna." Evidently, I was a replacement for someone who had cancelled. A prophecy?

After my reading, all of the alumni were asked to gather on stage, join hands, and sing "We Shall Overcome." It was very moving. I already had begun to believe that I would never overcome the injustices and humiliations I had endured as a woman of color. But on that Juilliard stage, I sang the words anyway: *"Oh, deep in my heart, I do believe we shall overcome someday!"*

For the final monthly luncheon of the semester, I decided to read one of my dramatic pieces for the students and alumni at Juilliard. I picked my "Thank you, Mr. Whiteman" piece. It is told from the perspective of a woman of color going into a white man's office for a job-interview or to pitch an idea or request an audition. Some of the language is pretty raw and I realized after I began that some of the older female alumnae might have difficulty with some of the words. So I censored myself and "bleeped" out some of the worst ones. After I finished reading, the energy in the room was pulsating. I had never seen the students so animated. Some needed to argue with my point that we carry our ancestry and our ancestral karma into every interview. The whole time I was a student at Juilliard, my functionality depended on my ability to ignore my ancestry and ancestral karma. But what is art if not a song to, from, for, and of the ancestors? And in the realm of art, African-Americans have an utterly unique experience in this country. As karma would have it, as I was leaving the Juilliard building and walking through the Lincoln Center Square, a troupe of Australian Aboriginals were performing their sacred songs and dances. They spoke and sang of the ancestors, called to them, allowed themselves to become possessed by them, and danced as them.

When I got home, three women were on my answering machine. All three wanted me that night!

28

My friend Alberto Ferreras, who had a full-time position at HBO, wanted to pitch an idea for a comedy show on masturbation. He wanted to film comedians telling jokes about beating-off and asked if I would come in and answer his list of questions on camera as well as read some of my erotica. He told me to bring some of my writings to read while he adjusted the sound and focus. I read my short story about seducing a college girl.

A few days later, he called me. He had kept the camera rolling while I was reading, and while in the editing room he showed the footage to a straight male colleague.

"Whadya think?" Alberto asked his straight male friend whose wife was very pregnant.

"Shit, man! I got a woody," he said.

And so, Alberto's fantasy of spending hours alone in the editing room with this very sexually deprived, straight male with a hard-on began. We booked a day at an off-Broadway stage to shoot. Alberto copied my text onto cue-cards. We shot the footage in one afternoon.

Meanwhile, I had met and picked-up a woman at the Clit Club who was from Hamburg, Germany. She was filming a documentary on the tango. I knew that Kristin and I were planning performances in Europe for that fall so I made arrangements to visit this woman at her home in Hamburg. She planned to drive to Berlin for the weekend to shoot some footage at a tango school and to pick up a specially ordered, custom-made sex toy. It would be my first trip to Berlin. I would return there twice within a matter of months. I booked a triangle ticket with flights from New York, to Hamburg, to Vienna and back. It was outrageously expensive.

When we arrived in Berlin, I immediately felt the spirits of the disembodied. Many people had died here in a very short amount of time. I felt it in my bones as soon as we approached the city limits.

But dancing with the Berliners was not exactly what I would call a spiritual experience (or maybe it was and what I was feeling was the cold, stiff reserve of the German ancestors). The music was good. Everybody looked good and knew all the steps. But something was missing. I couldn't quite put my finger on it. Later it occurred to me that what was missing was joy. People were more concerned with looking good than feeling the joy of the dance. I felt surrounded by my ancestors from the other side of the globe. But the German ancestors did not come, as much as I tried to feel them. Maybe the history was too tragic. The pain too great, and too recent.

We went to the trendy section of East Berlin, where bombed-out buildings and their rubble stand as monuments to what happened there. Of course, many visual artists have taken over these spaces and turned them into museums. Bullet-holes are still visible on some of the buildings which once were large, private homes.

We had our dinner in a packed, trendy restaurant. After-wards, a fortune-teller offered to read my cards. My host was also curious as to what my future would hold so we agreed to a reading. My "ultimate outcome" card was the ace of wands, which meant there would be lots of powerful activity in my near future. Little did I know that all of this powerful activity would take place in Berlin. I interpreted the ace of wands as a symbol of the conductor's baton. I already saw myself conducting the Berlin Philharmonic in performances of Wagner.

Away from Berlin and safely in Vienna, I met the woman who would become my next long-term partner. Kristin's girl-friend, Manuela, had a cheap apartment not far from the Mar-garetengürtel and needed to go there to make some repairs. A friend of hers who was originally from Tyrol was living in that apartment. She had come to Vienna to go to college (which was free for Austrians). Manuela was living in another of her apartments not far from the Hauptbahnhof (train station), and she was also maintaining a neighboring flat for another friend who was temporarily living in the French countryside with her boyfriend. Manuela invited me to come along to the other apartment building so I could familiarize myself with the sur-roundings and the Strassenbahn (streetcar) map. When we ar-rived at the Margaretengürtel flat, Manuela knocked at the door. I was standing behind her. When the door opened, I heard the music of Tori Amos – (Cathy had *loved* Tori Amos) – coming from the stereo, smelled food cooking on the stove, and heard a full, melodious voice. They both spoke the Viennese dialect, so I didn't understand them. But I knew that I liked the sound of this voice enough to want to listen to it some more. Then Manuela stepped aside to introduce me, and then I saw her face. I had already decided; this was going to be my new home.

Helga fed me some delicious, hot pumpkin stew. The hot water for the whole apartment was regulated through an appliance over the sink, so Manuela had to fix it. The poor girl had been showering with cold water. But Helga was from the mountains, she could take it. It was a sprawling three-bedroom flat and Helga had just recently moved in. There wasn't much furniture, but she was in class all day and really just came home to sleep. Manuela was working the bar that night at the Frauen Café, so Helga said she would join us there.

Later I found out that Kristin and Manuela were definitely playing matchmaker for me and Helga, who had been announcing to her friends that she was a lesbian in spite of the fact that she had not yet had a girlfriend. And I was looking for a European base, so it was a foregone conclusion that we would end up together.

That night at the Frauen Café, I had arrived with Manuela who opened the place. The place soon was full of women of all ages. The walls were covered with feminist art and the music was soft enough so that we could actually converse. I loved the atmosphere, but the jetlag was kicking my ass. I could barely keep my eyes open. Helga arrived dressed for the evening and I got to listen to that lovely voice again. She kissed both of my cheeks as if we were old friends. Later in the evening I was sitting on a comfortable chair, which was actually too comfortable since I could not stay awake. Helga was sitting next to me. Then all of a sudden, a leg of the chair gave way and I fell to the floor. Susan strikes again! It was time to get out of that place and take Helga with me. She offered to escort me back to Manuela's apartment house. For the rest of the week, we spent most of our time there together, with Helga playing tour guide.

Toward the end of my stay, Manuela had arranged a concert for Kristin and me in a little mountain village called Hohenberg, where Manuela had friends. We made a cute foursome on the train – Kristin, Manu, Helga, and I. Kristin and I put together a program of arias and Lieder, and I played some solo pieces as well – some Chopin and Rachmaninoff, and then Kristin and I performed Isolde's "Liebestod" from Wagner's *Tristan und Isolde*. I had been performing the Liszt transcription for solo piano of the Liebestod in my concert programs for years but this was the first time I was supporting a soprano as her faux orchestral accompaniment. The audience was mesmerized and applauded wildly when we finished.

After the concert, while the concert goers were enjoying their wine and cheese and pastries, I went to the piano to run through some of the other Liszt transcriptions from other Wagner operas. During the transfiguration music in *Parsifal*, I noticed a low murmur emanating from behind me. I looked around and saw that the older men had formed a semi-circle behind me and were humming along to the music. Parsifal has one of the most famous men's choruses in all of opera, but I had no idea that this music was so special to these people. It was written in their Mother Tongue, after all, and its message is deeply personal and has a spiritual, almost ethereal quality. I was very moved and felt that I had found a home away from home.

It was after this concert that Helga told me that she loved me for the first time.

When I flew back to New York, a message from Helga was already on my answering machine. She wanted to know that I had gotten back safely so I called right away.

That month, I paid more for my telephone bill than I did for my rent. I had to plan another trip to Vienna, and the arrival date that I had scheduled just happened to be Helga's birthday. Manuela asked her to pick me up at the airport.

Our first official night together was All Hallows' Eve, 1997. Helga was a Scorpio (as Susan had been). In fact for six hours – the time difference between Central Europe and the East Coast of the U.S. – she and Susan shared the same birthday, and sometimes, even the same laugh.

The heating system for Helga's apartment was something I had never seen before. Many old flats in Vienna are equipped with oil heaters with flues that are connected to the chimneys of the building. She would buy the oil at the gas station and schlep it home in large, heavy jugs, then she would pour the oil into the heater and light the small flame. On very windy days, the wind would blow out the flame and puddles of oil would collect in the bottom. The only way to get the excess oil out was to burn it off, and sometimes the flame was so big we were afraid the little heater would explode. On some days when there was no oil and it was too damn cold to go outside to the gas station, she would turn on the gas oven and leave the oven door open to heat the apartment.

I wondered what my parents would think if they knew that I was schlepping gallons of oil – on foot, mind you, since we did not have a car – to have heat. Helga had also re-done the electrical wiring for the flat of the old pre-war building in order to be able to use the computer. Manuela and Helga had a large circle of female friends who were fully capable of handling all aspects of construction including electrical wiring and plumbing, because many women felt unsafe inviting Viennese workmen into their homes. These men were infamous for taking liberties when no husband or father was present to intimidate them. Their whole concept of sexual assault unfortunately lagged far behind ours.

After one of our early love-making sessions, I noticed and touched the scars on her wrists.

"What's this?" I asked.

At first, she quipped gruffly, "What do you think?"

After some hesitation, she told me the story of being a senior in high school – an elite boarding school for girls in the Alps. The girls were really being trained to be good wives and mothers and nothing more. Helga already knew that she did not want to marry. The last thing she wanted was to end up with another Tyrolean man like her father. Plus, the repressed memory of sexual abuse by a stranger during her childhood had not yet surfaced. All she knew at the time was that she had tremendous anxiety around being forced to have sex with a husband. So, right before her final exams, she decided to kill herself. She went to an idyllic spot in the mountains, cut her wrists, and then dove into Lake Constance.

Perhaps she was unprepared for the affect the adrenaline would have on her body. She is a strong swimmer so by instinct, she started swimming to the shore. Suddenly she felt overcome with the will to live. She got out of the water, walked to the main street, hailed a cab, and demanded to be taken to the hospital. The driver complained that she was bleeding all over his cab, but he took her to the emergency room. The doctors stitched her wounds and her parents were called. Her mother Frieda kept asking why she would do something like this. She really didn't have an answer. She severed the nerves of the first three fingers on her left hand. Luckily, she didn't finish carving her right wrist, but the scar is clearly visible. For the rest of her life she is constantly reminded of that moment in Vorarlberg when she was finished with life.

For me, the tale of this incident simply made me love her more. I had already witnessed the transition to the other side, the point of no return. Helga came close, but she survived to tell about it. For that, I was grateful.

Once Helga realized that she could live as a lesbian and didn't have to look forward to being forced to marry a man, she no longer wanted to die. Soon she severed her ties with the Catholic Church altogether, which is no small feat in Catholic Austria. After some therapy and extended preparation for her graduation, Helga went to Vienna to study philosophy, then architecture. When she realized the field of architecture was virtually closed to women, she studied and earned her certification to become an Austrian pastry chef. She still makes the best Apfelstrudel and Salzburger Nockerl I've ever tasted.

I had the feeling that I really hadn't experienced an authentic Christmas until I went to Vienna. The Christmas cookies, the carolers, the trees decorated with "honey candles" made from beeswax, the hot wine with spices, the sausages and potato pancakes served piping-hot at outdoor stands, the brass choirs that went from restaurant to restaurant playing for tips, and the fluffy snowfalls, all of it made for a delightful holiday experience in spite of the cold.

29

Helga and I cast a Wiccan Circle in her home in Vienna on New Year's Eve, 1999. It was the Full Moon in Cancer.

A few days later, Alberto, my producer, called from New York to inform me that our film was accepted and would be screened at the Berlin International Film Festival in February, which would be the world premiere. As the result of that screening, representatives from all over the world saw the film and requested it for their festivals. In a matter of a few months, I had more success as a screenwriter and spoken-word performance artist than I'd had in twenty-seven years as a concert pianist.

Meryl Streep, Glenn Close, Sean Penn, Woody Harrelson, and Steven Spielberg were at that year's festival, all presenting new films. Shirley MacLaine was also present as she was being presented with a lifetime achievement award. When we arrived at the largest cinema for our premiere, I thought all the paparazzi were lining the red carpet to catch a glimpse of me. But Sean Penn's film was going on upstairs at the same time as ours. They were there to see him.

I was used to waiting backstage, to walking out to a live audience, and being practiced and prepared to entertain these people for the next two hours. Sitting in the darkened cinema seconds before the beginning of the world premiere of my short film, my heart obviously did not know the difference. I grabbed Helga's hand and placed in on my chest so that she could feel what I was experiencing. She suppressed a giggle.

In the catalogue for the Berlin Film Festival I would be listed as the screenwriter and actress for the film *"Verbal Sex."* Alberto listed himself in the credits as the director and producer with Steve acknowledged as co-editor. Throughout the festival, the Germans usually waited until the final credit before applauding. But after the last spoken words of the film and with the appearance of the first credit, the usually stiff German audience was already in full-whoop. Our film was being followed by a Monika Treut feature about transsexuals, *Gendernauts.* Monika Treut is quite a celebrity in Germany. She embraced me as she approached the stage. It was the right audience for our premiere.

After the premiere we were able to calm down a little bit. I had no idea of how huge the Berlinale was. It seemed there were back-to-back screenings and parties. You just had maybe fifteen minutes to scarf down some dinner before you were off to the next screening. Many recognized me who had seen the film and complimented me. It was nice being recognized by strangers in the subways and on the streets of Berlin.

Suddenly I was a writing fiend. In one year I wrote two stage plays, a feature-length screenplay, a book of prose, and a memoir. It seemed all of that creative energy, which had been harnessed and restrained for so long in classical music, came bursting forth. My writing was still geared toward performance. I always heard the words spoken as I wrote them. Many of the international film festivals that were screening my short film also invited me to come and give a spoken-word performance or participate in a panel discussion. I became known internationally as a spoken-word performer and screenwriter.

I was doing most of my writing in Vienna, where I lived with my lover in domestic bliss. Getting away from New York also helped my creative juices flow. I didn't speak enough German to feel that I could fully express myself to people, which created even more of a need to express myself in writing.

It was Kristin who informed me about the international protests against the Vienna Philharmonic for refusing to hire female musicians. I began to do my own research on the subject, including uncovering details about Herbert von Karajan's history as a member of the Nazi Party. When the Vienna Philharmonic appeared in New York, under Riccardo Muti's baton, the protests made the front page of the *New York Times*. The Viennese were embarrassed, but not enough to do anything about it. It seems these men in classical music are as terrified of women as the men of the Catholic Church. But the light has been shed on that organization as well. Things are changing, albeit much too slowly.

When the Honolulu International Lesbian and Gay Film Festival asked to screen my film and invited me to perform, I was deeply moved. They offered me a free, all-expenses paid trip. As a child I had dreamed of going to Hawaii, of dancing Hula girls and steaming volcanoes. The fantasy of my childhood – inspired by television game shows that offered as their grand-prize "a fabulous, all-expenses-paid trip to Honolulu,

Hawaii!!" – was becoming a reality as a result of my own writing. While flying into the Honolulu International Airport, the tears of happiness streamed down my cheeks.

30

Back in Vienna, I thoroughly took advantage of the strong dollar against the shilling for purchasing cheap train and airline tickets. We took long-weekend trips to the Salzkammergut, Dürnstein, Willendorf in der Wachau (where the tiny statuette of the Venus von Willendorf was unearthed), and Reichenau an der Rax in Austria. Then we traveled to Venice in Italy (for which we stayed in the quaint little neighboring town of Treviso since we couldn't afford the hotels in Venice), and to the beach resort of Antalya in Turkey. From Antalya we took a day-trip to Ephesus, the city of the Goddess and home of the Great Temple of Artemis – the fourth Wonder of the Ancient World. (Ephesus was also where the Apostle Paul was imprisoned for blaspheming the Goddess.) There we bought a little statuette of Artemis to include in our Full Moon rituals. Helga and I also flew to Málaga in Spain where we relaxed on the Costa del Sol, and took day-trips to the Alhambra in Granada, and to Marbella (which was where the King of Spain had been purchasing properties when I spoke to him on the telephone).

My time in Europe was more about learning to enjoy life than pursuing my piano career. My parents hadn't even en-

At Ephesus

couraged me to enjoy life. I had to learn this from scratch. In America, they taught me that life was about work and striving and being accepted by whites. In Europe, I learned that it was considered rude to ask a person "What do you do?" during a first conversation. Americans, by contrast, will ask what you do right off the bat. I thoroughly enjoyed and incorporated this new perspective. Conversations about which wines paired with which cheeses were much more important. And of course, you had to have that glass of delicious Austrian beer when you first sat down at the table. (*"Bier nach Wein, lass das sein. Wein nach Bier, dass rat Ich Dir."* Beer after wine, let that be. Wine after beer, that I advise you.)

I was hardly prepared for just how seriously the Viennese took their waltzing. Helga had told me how they waltzed in the streets at the end of the Second World War, and I had seen for myself how they danced at the stroke of midnight on New Year's Eve to the amplified radio broadcast of Johann Strauss' *The Blue Danube* – (a recording of Herbert von Karajan conducting the Vienna Philharmonic, of course). But at the annual Rainbow Ball I caught a glimpse of how important the waltz is in the Austrian culture.

The Rainbow Ball is a gay event, a benefit for gay organizations. But at this gay event in the beautiful, plush Kaiser Ballroom of the elegant five-star Schönbrunn Park Hotel, even the lesbians were wearing makeup and formal attire. The drag queens were dressed to the nines, of course. There were white tablecloths, champagne, caviar, and virtually anything else you wanted to eat or drink (to be ordered a la carte). I should have known I would be in for a major event when I saw all the television cameras present, the opening greetings from various politicians, and the full string orchestra on the stage. But when the mistress of ceremonies introduced the first dancers onto the floor, the magic began. These dancers were professionals. They were the advanced students at a waltzing school, complete with their waltz master who gave instructions via hand-signals. Formally dressed couples began to dance, their movements free and effortless. The entire audience began to applaud the grace and elegance of the dancers. Then, with a wave of the master's hand, the couples switched partners. Men danced with men and women with women. The audience shouted its approval and appreciation.

When the professionals finished their routine, the master waved other amateur students from the waltz school onto the floor. All were formally dressed with coordinated rainbow-colored ribbons attached to their costumes. The dances were thoroughly rehearsed and well-executed, with only a few slip-ups here and there. The dancers were already full of champagne, so all mistakes were laughed-off and easily corrected. Some of the steps were obviously part of old social rituals in which families (i.e., parents) introduced their sons and daughters to the sons and daughters of other families. There were gestures of introduction, acceptance, coquetry, even refusal. But all were accepted parts of the ritual dance which served its purpose by introducing and binding families.

When this routine was done, the master waved his hand again and all of us were invited to join in the dance. This was not an easy task – let me tell you! Many of those watching on the sidelines had rehearsed, were dressed to be seen, and had been itching to get out there since the opening speeches. They also had been quenching their thirsts the whole time. Bodies pressed onto the floor in a rush to claim a prominent center space. Helga and I were among them. I soon learned that you couldn't just dance the way you wanted to. You had to follow the direction of the crowd. Couples were waltzing in a circular motion while simultaneously spinning counter-clockwise around the dance floor. If you didn't follow the crowd, you would have been trampled by drag queens in stilettos. There was quite some bumping and vying for space. If you needed a break or were overcome by dizziness, you quickly had to make your way to the sidelines all the while making sure that you weren't on a collision-course with a macho-type. Waltz at your own risk!

Out Scottish singer Jimmy Somerville was the guest star who later performed with his band. At the time he was most famous for his rendition of the disco hit "Don't Leave Me This Way." All of the dancing stopped for his performance and he was in rare form.

Socially-speaking, the Viennese Balls served a specific function. For those who weren't dancing, there were opportunities for chatting and catching-up. Business deals were made, recipes exchanged, gossip was circulated, and all of this went on while much wine and champagne were consumed. I felt rather jealous as I watched groups of old friends crowd around tables and share stories. One's dialect is also very important, as a listener is able to tell immediately which region one's family is from. But we did have our small, developing circle of lesbian friends, many of whom were present at the ball. Helga also saw some of her work colleagues. In such a relaxed, friendly environment, I began to feel that we were indeed solidifying our social bonds. It was a feeling I had not known in New York. Yes, there are women in New York who are always at the club when I am there, who join in the circular, social dance. But as soon as we leave the club, that is the end of our social contact. I doubt that we would even recognize each other on the street in the daylight.

I caught a glimpse of my reflection in one of the elegant side windows and saw an old, wise Native and African American spirit looking back at me. Her expression was stern and slightly sad. I thought of the traditional dances of the Native American people and how that culture had been dismissed, uprooted, and virtually destroyed by the European invaders. I longed for the inherited legacy of my own traditional, cultural dances. I had heard that Native American religions incorporated dance in their forms of spiritual expression. Use of naturally grown peyote and coca leaves were also part of Native American ritual practice. And of course, we all had heard of the peace pipe. But I really did not know much more. It was easier to find information on North American native tribes in Europe than it was in the United States. But everyone says, "Past is past. Time to focus on the present." So, I threw myself into this cultural experience and tried to ignore the feeling of being an outsider. There were several foreign guests dressed in their traditional formal costumes – visitors from African countries, from India, and the South Pacific. I certainly was not the belle of the ball, but it was great fun being able to live out my Cinderella fantasy with my beautiful Austrian princess.

• • • • •

The year was 2001 and Helga and I were determined to find a home. We were still in shock over the discovery that Jörg Haider – the right wing, conservative, second-generation Nazi – was going to be participating in forming the Austrian government. Haider seemed to make a career of making one faux pas after another. It seemed the conservatives were coming out of the woodwork in Austria. Feminism was advancing much too slowly for our taste, even within the gay community. It was not a safe place for us. But after the votes were cast and Haider's rise to power imminent, thousands of Viennese came out to protest in "Widerstand" (translation: resistance) and "anti-racism" rallies. I seriously wondered if so many white Americans would come out in protest against racism.

And then there was the bigger shock of watching the election of the American president from overseas, watching helplessly as George Bush II claimed the presidency, though he was not elected by the majority of the American people. Bush was the former governor of the state of Texas, which was infamous for executing more black men than any other state. How was I supposed to feel safe in a country where the president, on his first day in office, signs his first bills into law with Strom Thurmond (a presumed former Ku Klux Klansman) standing behind him? How could the Democrats have allowed this to happen?

We needed to find a home.

We had been abroad during the whole Monica Lewinsky affair. The Europeans couldn't believe all of the fuss in the American media. Of course presidents are going to have affairs. Why else would they want to have so much power?

We had thought about Germany since Helga already spoke the language and I had enjoyed more success there – both as a musician and screenwriter – than anyplace else. The Germans are cool, especially now since they actively want to overcome their shameful past. Plus, it was possible for us as a gay couple to marry (sort of). We had Viennese friends who had already moved there who had invited us to visit. We just needed to get there somehow. But it was cold as hell in New York in January, and Germany was even colder. I needed to get my black ass to the tropics.

During our leisurely winter mornings, we would usually sit over a breakfast of Kasmuas (literally translated "cheese mousse"), fresh bread, and lots of coffee. I had never known any American white folks who knew what to do with grits. But Helga's grandmother would make a huge pan of Kasmuas for the whole family on cold mornings. It was a breakfast for working in the fields: fried pieces of bacon, the water for the grits poured directly into the same pan, then grated cheeses stirred in at the end of the cooking. The stuff was heavy! But we would sit and enjoy cup after cup of coffee during our long philosophical discussions that went well into the afternoon.

Helga had begun to see a therapist in Vienna the previous year. One of her issues was that her family forbade any display of emotion during her childhood. Her parents would lock her in a basement even if she was justifiably angry, and her older sister would beat her over the head if she cried. Her parents did nothing to curtail the sister's beatings. They thought it was funny. As a result, Helga was pretty blocked emotionally. She would say that during her adolescent years and early adulthood, she felt nothing. This kept her from knowing what she wanted in life.

I too had been severely emotionally blocked by my parents, but being a musician, we learned to go through the motions of feeling, enough for a sense of catharsis at least. It was after Susan's death that my emotional walls crumbled. For a while after she died, all I could do was listen to Wagner operas and sip single-malt scotch. Being out in the streets was next to impossible, as I could succumb to a fit of crying at any time. But as long as I was in my flat, with Wagner blasting on the stereo and a scotch in my hand, I was all right. I eventually got some help for incorporating my emotions. I found a bereavement group at the LGBT Community Center, and a therapist. My bereavement simply revealed what I had known all along, but was unable to confront: the fact that I had no emotional support from my parents whatsoever.

My parents expected me to live out their dreams for them. Instead of having a childhood, I was a child prodigy, which of course nurtured their fantasies. Each of them had hoped for careers as concert pianists and each had felt discriminated against because they were black. They therefore had zero tolerance for any human frailty or weakness on my part. They didn't want to hear about the sexism I was facing at Juilliard or the misogyny that runs rampant in the classical music world. This was the post-Civil Rights era. I was going to have the career that they had felt was denied to them.

Susan's death also marked the beginning of my financial freedom. She had been a system's programmer at the Morgan Bank on Wall Street and had named me the beneficiary of her life insurance policy. Suddenly I had more money than I ever imagined I would have in one chunk. It gave me the freedom to re-evaluate my life.

Helga had had no such freedom. She had worked and worked since she was a small child – first in her parents' hotel in Tyrol, in hotel kitchens, in bakeries, on a tobacco farm in Switzerland, in more hotels in Vienna, and finally at telemarketing firms. She had enrolled at the University in Vienna to study philosophy, then architecture. But after too much stress, exhaustion, pressure, and not enough support, she broke down. She still carried around the resulting feelings of failure.

Those winter mornings in my New York apartment were really amateur therapy sessions. We would pick a topic, thoroughly examine it and pick it apart, have our emotional catharsis, and then record the session in our journals. Needless to say, we learned a lot about ourselves and each other.

New York is a busy place for an artist. I found it to be virtually impossible to clear my head enough of all the noise and dirt to write anything substantial. I was doing more journal writing than anything else. Helga was also writing quite a bit in her journal, in her own language of course. But she had gotten quite used to expressing herself emotionally in English. English is a much better language for the emotions, she would say. She spent most of her time looking through the want ads, modifying her resume, and sending out job applications. She had quit her job in Vienna before we left the last time and had no intention of going back.

We were regular fans of *The Oprah Winfrey Show*. Early in the year there was a special program on the up-coming V-Day celebration at Madison Square Garden organized by Eve Ensler, author of *The Vagina Monologues*. Evidently the play had toured most of the northeastern college campuses and had a huge following. Madison Square Garden was sold out, without any additional advertising. But if you weren't regular watchers of the Oprah Show, you might not have known about the event. Many of our New York friends, who are too busy with day jobs to watch Oprah, had no idea that V-Day was happening.

It was intense, beginning with the hanging hand-painted t-shirts on clotheslines in the entrance hall... t-shirts painted by women telling their stories of sexual-abuse and rape. Some shirts were just big enough to fit a baby. Then, once we got inside, there were more horror stories of incest, genital mutilation, forced prostitution, treatment of women in Afghanistan, etc. etc. How was it possible for so many women from so many different places to be treated so horribly in a "civilized" world? The numbers of women who stood when Eve invited all the survivors of sexual assault to stand... It boggles the mind. Both of us were both standing.

I had asked my friend Kristin Norderval, the Norwegian soprano, if she had wanted to collaborate on a performance-piece that could be tied into the V-Day celebration. At the time, she was busy preparing the title role for the new opera on the life of Aileen Wuornos, the lesbian serial-killer/prostitute. The premiere was to take place in San Francisco. Kristin also had not heard about V-Day. She didn't watch TV.

The energy between us after V-Day was heavy. We wanted to do something. But what? I was frustrated over not being published, over having my screenplays collecting dust, over having absolutely no income as an artist. Helga was frustrated over not knowing what kind of career she wanted to pursue. She had been living with this indecision for years but she always managed to find a job. Wherever she was in the world, she could open a newspaper, look through the want ads, apply for a job, and get it. Wherever she went, she knew she could get paid. I had no such knowledge. My experience was that I would work and work and work and have it all be for naught. Such had been the case for my short film – my first international success. Since the world premiere in Berlin, it had been requested and screened all over the world. But where was the money? So I just resigned myself to believe that, as long as I wasn't starving, I would put my energy into expressing myself artistically and the Goddess would provide.

We were very active spiritually. We did our Full Moon Circles and burned our intentions. We repeatedly saw proof of the power of the Universe to affect and change our lives. It just wasn't our time to be rich yet, I guess.

The swaying palm trees. The blue water.
The open sky. Here we come...

I knew I wanted to write but I needed a friendlier climate, a warm climate. During our Full Moon Circles, I would repeatedly ask for a beach house – a place where I could write in peace and commune with the ocean goddesses. Before we had left Vienna, I had met a diplomat who could make this dream a reality. There was the possibility, a slight possibility, that we could spend some time in the Caribbean for free. But the people involved were Austrian, which meant that Helga would have to make the contact. This would be difficult, since Helga was not comfortable with diplomats or ambassadors. I had given many free concerts in embassies all over the world, so I had no problem with reaping the benefits of personal contacts with diplomats. They owed me.

It was freezing in New York. Time to make our way south.

31

I had first met the wife of the Austrian Consul General for the island of Barbados in 1988, during my second trip to Vienna after being a guest of former American hostage in Iran, Kathryn Koob, who was living in Munich. Olive Moorefield and I remained friends for years. When we first met, I had no idea that Vienna would become such an important destination in my life. I would live there, on and off, for close to four years. Toward the end of my last year in Vienna with Helga, Olive was hosting another affair. Diplomats had come to Vienna to discuss the Middle East crisis, and Olive decided to sit them all down at the same table in a Heuriger and stuff them with fried chicken and wine. Before the affair, she had asked me to meet them at their home so that we could drive there together. She had also invited the ambassador from Belize to her home. I had heard of Belize, but I could not have told you where it was. I just knew it was somewhere in the Caribbean.

I was immediately struck by how comfortable the Belizean ambassador was with making demands. He was quite large and obviously consumed large amounts of food. He had just recently arrived in Vienna and was searching for a residence.

He was very clear about his requirements. Olive's husband fell all over himself looking through his address book, looking up names and numbers of people who could help the ambassador. I knew that I would have been thoroughly uncomfortable being so demanding. But this was power in action. This man knew how to fight for what he wanted and get it. I silently wondered if, in all our years of acquaintanceship, our hosts had ever put as much energy into helping me as an artist. Olive was always full of promises, but nothing concrete ever materialized.

As it turned out, introducing me to the Belizean ambassador was one of the best things Olive ever did for me. I stayed in touch with him via e-mail and asked for information on possible destinations in Belize. He gave me the name and e-mail address of his favorite yacht club, which was owned by an Austrian. That winter, when Helga and I looked up the website from our cold flat in Vienna, we were awestruck by the images of swaying palm trees, red sunsets, and blue ocean that flashed onto our computer screen. That was it! Somehow, we were going to get ourselves to Belize.

Helga was pretty much finished with Vienna and was determined not to return to Austria. I sent an e-mail to the Belize Yacht Club to inquire about availability, prices, etc. A night there was much too expensive for us. I begged Helga to write to the owner in her language so that the message would not be intercepted by front desk personnel. She was reluctant, but finally conceded. She even asked me what to write. Later I would learn that Helga had had quite enough of the tourism industry. Whether it was in the Alps or on a Caribbean island, it was all the same to her. She also carried around the fear of ending up like her parents.

The suggestion worked. The Austrian owner tried to telephone the day after he received the e-mail, but Helga was at work. So he sent an e-mail response, which was waiting for her when she got home. She didn't even want to read it right away. I insisted. As fate would have it, the yacht club owner and his wife were looking for someone to take over the management of the club as they wanted to spend some time at home in Austria the following year. I was ecstatic. I had never been in the Caribbean for more than a week at a time. But this time, we were going to *live* there indefinitely. I couldn't wait to get there.

But there was a slight problem. Helga's three-month tourist visa was about to expire and we needed to cross the border soon for another stamp in her passport. The Austrian yacht club owner had difficulty making decisions and was "not going to be pressured into rushing into something." Later we learned that he had had a heart attack several years before and therefore took things slowly. But we couldn't wait for him to make up his mind. We had to leave the country immediately or risk future immigration problems.

Helga had been determined to do something about her visa situation the last time we left Vienna. She inquired about applying for a student visa and learned that she had to be accepted by a college before she could even begin the application process. So she spent a fortune in college application fees, payments for translations of transcripts, postage, etc. etc. But even if and when a college would accept her, how on earth was she going to pay these exorbitant American tuitions? There was little financial aid for non-U.S. citizens. University study was free in Austria; the thought of having to pay to go to college seemed outrageous. Asking her parents for help was out of the question.

We had met two Canadian lesbian filmmakers while standing in line for the premiere of our film in Berlin. Laurie and Dominique were also presenters at the Berlinale that year. We stayed in touch and promised to get together soon, and now seemed like the perfect opportunity since we needed to cross the border for Helga's tourist visa. We called them. They were happy to hear from us but were in the middle of filming their next project, which involved trips back and forth to Sri Lanka. They offered to let us stay in their flat, which was sweet. But the more I thought about it, the more I realized that going to Canada does not really constitute a border-crossing. I made a few calls and found it was true. Helga would not get a new stamp in her passport coming back into the United States from Canada. We had to think of something else. And fast!

I grabbed the "cheap tickets" section of the *Village Voice* and booked two seats to Cancun, Mexico. Then I called a Holiday Inn and reserved a room for the next five days.

Traveling together across international borders is always stressful since, at any time, an ambitious immigration officer can say "No" to either of us and force us to separate. But in the meantime, we decided to forget about the stress and enjoy our five-day holiday in Mexico. (Leaving the U.S. was decidedly less stressful than trying to get back in.) Helga had never been to the Caribbean before. It was late February, so we flew with empty carry-on bags into which we could stuff our coats and sweaters when we landed. I prepared her for the waft of tropical air when the door of the plane is opened and one suddenly feels the need to strip. For an Austrian mountain girl, the heat was extreme. We cleared Customs without incident, made our way through aggressive cab-drivers to a city van which made all stops along Cancun's overly-developed row of beach-front hotels. Since our reservations were with Holiday Inn, my expectations were low. We were the last two riders in the van when we pulled up to a very nice, recently built Holiday Inn a little further away from the beach, complete with swimming pool and pool-side bar. (The bar was actually inside of the pool so that you could sit in the water while enjoying your cocktail.) We would have to take the city bus to the beach, which gave us a chance to mingle with the locals. But we were saving a fortune. After drinking two beers and lighting some incense in our slightly mildew-scented room, we fell into a deep sleep.

A holiday in Cancun was exactly what we needed. The Caribbean ocean was the bluest, clearest water Helga had ever seen. Both of us are prone to maintaining high stress-levels. Four days of relaxation, forgetting about the stresses that awaited us at home, made it possible for us to go on. We returned to New York armed with the power of the Mayan goddesses and a new stamp in Helga's passport.

32

Since our Austrian yacht club owner had not heard from us in a few days, I guess he began to worry. I imagine his wife got all excited about being able to return to Austria with an Austrian at the helm of their Caribbean hotel. He had made disparaging comments about the "locals" and how unreliable they were as workers. They wanted someone from Europe to teach the staff how to bring the level of cleanliness up to European standard. Not an easy task since Caribbean real estate is vulnerable to hurricanes and invasions of various life forms – crawling, flying, and swimming.

Five days of no contact definitely worked to our advantage since the yacht club owner was willing to pay for Helga's ticket to Belize, and to offer her free stay at the hotel while they discussed the arrangements. Since the ambassador was my friend and had inquired as to whether the yacht club owner had heard from me, it was easy to convince him to extend the invitation to both of us. I had to pay for my own airfare, though.

The night before we left for Belize, while we were packing and running around my New York apartment, I turned on PBS and happened to find the beginning of Wagner's *Tristan und Isolde*, which was being broadcast live from the Metropolitan Opera. I had never seen a production of *Tristan und Isolde*, though I practically knew the entire score from memory. Of course, I needed to watch the entire seven-hour production. The first act takes place on a ship. I saw it as a sign that we were in store for a wonderful adventure.

The yacht club in Belize was located on one of the Belizean islands, Ambergris Caye. When our plane landed, we quickly made our way through Customs, thinking we had enough time to catch a 3:00 ferry to the island. During the taxi ride to the water, I found the landscape to be rather disappointing. Later we learned a hurricane six months earlier had severely damaged the land and the coral reef. Belize City was hot – not a place where we would want to spend very much time. There was much poverty, several drunks. Even finding a pay phone was difficult. The taxi dropped us off at the dock for the ferry where we waited in the heat for three hours. (There was no 3:00 ferry.) At least during the wait, Helga was able to call the Webers to inform them of our anticipated arrival time on the island. They would pick us up.

As soon as the boat left the area of the mainland, I began to see what all the fuss was about. Belize consists of many small islands, some of them private, in addition to the mainland territory. The country had been an English colony until the 1980s, so English was the official language but many spoke Spanish and/or a Creole patois. After an hour-and-a-half-long boat trip we arrived at the dock of Ambergris. We were exhausted, hot, thirsty, and no one was there to meet us. But several taxi drivers offered to take us to our destination. We waited in the heat and dust for about fifteen minutes and then decided to take a cab. We drove for ten minutes down the beach and arrived at the front desk of the yacht club. About ten minutes later, the Webers arrived, apologizing and claiming that the boat was early. After short, polite introductions, we were shown to our suite: a fully equipped flat with an ocean view. We had arrived in paradise.

The Webers invited us to dinner that evening, but I was too exhausted to attend since I had stayed up the entire night before to watch *Tristan und Isolde*. Besides, I thought the three of them would prefer to speak in their native language while working out the details of Helga's employment. It was just as well. I slept while Helga accepted her position on a month-long trial basis. The Webers would reimburse the cost of her ticket. She returned pleased and slightly tipsy (Herr W. had opened a bottle of Austrian wine for the occasion), sat on my bed, and opened a Styrofoam container of fresh red snapper and fries for me. She even remembered the beer.

We enjoyed four blissful days in our ocean view flat, having breakfasts on the terrace of the freshest papayas and pineapples, and orange juice so delicious it had to have been squeezed that morning. We gradually got acquainted with the area. People on Ambergris mostly traveled on foot. Motorized transportation consisted of bumpy and sometimes dangerous rides in golf carts. If you needed to get from one end of the island to the other, the quickest way was via water-taxi. In our area there were expensive shops and delis for the tourists. But the locals shopped in town, which was a half-hour walk on the beach from the yacht club. Walking such a distance on the street a block away from the beach was impossible. Without the ocean breeze, it felt like you were dying of heat stroke. Plus, you would end up covered with dust kicked up by the golf carts. But if you had lots of groceries and just stood on the road long enough under the shade of a palm tree, someone would eventually come along in a golf cart and invite you to hop on. You still ended up covered with dust, though.

Then there were the scuba shacks. We didn't know it before we left, but Belize is one of the scuba capitals of the world. Each dock held two, maybe three little huts where tourists went to be fitted for scuba gear, were taught to put it on, and sat and waited to be picked up by the motorboat which stopped at several docks along the way. We decided to sign up for a snorkel trip offered by one of these shacks. The boat was scheduled to pick us up around 2:00, so we figured we could pick up some lunch before waiting on the pier.

Belizean food was a cross between Caribbean and Mexican cuisines. We found a cute little place not far from our pier that offered a take-out menu. We picked out some seemingly harmless goodies: chicken enchiladas wrapped in banana leaves, tortillas filled with beans and cheese and spicy sauce. We brought our purchases to the beach and sat munching contentedly under the palm trees. We were still wiping our mouths with napkins when the boat arrived for our snorkel trip. The instructor told us to grab our gear and hop in the boat.

A few minutes after we pulled away from the pier, we began to realize that eating such spicy food had been a big mistake. The waves were two and three feet high. The boat was going against the direction of the waves to take us out to sea. By the time we anchored and jumped overboard, we were relieved to be free of the rocking motion of the boat. But the rocking motion didn't stop. The waves continued to pull our bodies up and down, up and down. What I would have given at that moment to stand on solid ground. I had to wait until we reached a stretch of shallow water where I could put my feet on the bottom, but balancing myself in my flippers and trying to stand on clumps of choral made it difficult. Helga and I avoided each other, each of us not wanting the other to see how sick we were.

But in between waves of nausea, we witnessed some of the most beautiful underwater spectacles in the world: brightly colored fish, all sizes and shapes, stingrays that recognized our guide and attempted to embrace him. The guides had warned us that the stingrays love humans and like to brush against your skin. I was grateful for the warning when I felt a soft brush against my thigh and turned around to find a new friend passing above and below my legs. Ten to twenty stingrays followed us around the reef, inviting us to participate in their choreographed social dance. Even a mother and her new baby joined in the dance.

There were two destinations during the snorkel trip: The Hol Chan wildlife preserve and "Shark Ray Alley." When we climbed back into the boat to head for the second destination, we both had had quite enough. But there we were, back on this furiously rocking boat, for another bumpy ride over high waves – up and down and up and down. As soon as we pulled into Shark Ray Alley, sharks surrounded the boat. That's right.

Sharks! They wanted to be fed. All of the tour guides would throw pieces of fish off of one side of the boat while we were instructed to jump into the water on the opposite side. I was skeptical. But after watching other tourists successfully jump in and seeing that the sharks were preoccupied with their feeding, I eventually took the plunge. Swimming with sharks is an experience I will never forget.

On the beach at Ambergris Caye

When we were back on the boat, after swallowing mouthfuls of seawater, our condition was even more precarious. I encouraged Helga to sit with her back to the wind. She just wanted to sit far away from everyone. I focused on the shoreline with all my strength and prayed for an end to this constant movement. We couldn't get back to land fast enough. After the other tourists were dropped off at their hotels, Helga leaned over the side of the boat and gave her lunch to the fish. She was so embarrassed. But the boat driver said not to worry, the fish love it. When we stood on the pier, which still felt like it was moving, we must have looked like zombies. We simply handed over our equipment and zigzagged along the beach back to the yacht club. Plans for the rest of the afternoon were decided: Nap!

33

One of our first nights on the island we decided to have dinner at the beachfront restaurant of one of the neighboring hotels. The menu was not at all fancy: grilled chicken and ribs, beans and rice, potato salad and coleslaw, and a refreshing local beer. We savored our meal under the stars, the ocean breeze cooling our skin. I was saying something about ancestry, about the funny feeling I had that my Native American ancestors must have migrated north from Central America. Since I never had access to any factual information about my Native American ancestry, the details were always a mystery. I simply resigned myself to going on hunches and guesses, stemming from feelings in my gut.

But at the very moment when I said, "I always had a feeling my ancestors migrated from here," a ball of fire shot through the sky. "What the fuck was that?!" I exclaimed, as Helga turned around to look. By the time she turned, the light was gone. All she saw was the shocked expression on my face as I gazed into the night sky. At first I thought fireworks, but there were no more. Helga said it must have been a meteor entering the atmosphere, but the brightness was so big for something that would have been so far away. I just happened to look in that particular corner in the sky when this thing appeared.

A sign.

• • • • •

Needless to say, some of the staff at the yacht club were rather threatened by Helga's sudden arrival. The Webers had a reputation for firing employees at the drop of a hat. Some feared that they were being replaced and therefore were not at all helpful or willing to give information. She had a tough time learning the ropes. But eventually, her warmth and smile won over most of the other employees, and many appreciated the fact that she was efficient and that her presence seemed to put the Webers at ease. They were finally able to speak their own language – their own dialect, even – with an employee. There were usually two other staffers who rotated shifts at the front desk: one rather arrogant closeted gay man and a nicer, friendlier young woman. One day the woman came to work wearing an interlocking women's symbol on a thin chain around her neck. Helga was so happy to see it. Finally, there was someone who would have some information about the scene in Belize.

"Oh! Are you a lesbian?" she asked, point blank.

The woman cleared her throat and hesitated, then whispered, "Well, I know some people who are *like that*."

"'*Like that*'? You mean gay?"

It turns out this young woman in her early twenties shared a home with her lover, who was a mother of three. She had five mouths to feed on her minimum-wage salary from the yacht club. Even though she and the arrogant closet queen were supposedly hired to do the same job, he treated her like a secretary. She may have worn a lesbian symbol, but she couldn't say the word. However, she was able to give us some information about the scene and told us there was even a Gay Pride Day on Ambergris, which was the gayest island in Belize. We couldn't believe our luck.

Spending so much time in the outdoors, I became quite athletic: long ocean swims in the afternoon, evening jogs on the beach. I remember, for the first time in my life, feeling free to swim with my whole body, to stretch my arms and legs to their maximums with each stroke. The water was clear, the tide calm since the island was protected by the reef. The pier at the yacht club was built to accommodate many boats, and many fish decided to make their homes there also. With all the algae growing on the wooden logs supporting the pier, there was always something there in the area for the fish to eat. For their protection, there were prominent signs on the dock that read "No Fishing." The fish had even grown accustomed to being fed by swimmers. I risked being attacked by a swarm of hungry, friendly, curious fish whenever I jumped into the water. I was enjoying my new-found freedom and comfort level in swimming in the waters around the yacht club's pier one evening, when I looked off into the distance and saw something large and black moving in the water. *Don't panic*, was my first thought. But I swam faster than I ever thought I could back to the steps to the pier. Upon further inspection, the swimming phantom turned out to be a huge stingray, larger than I. Such sightings were commonplace, but I did not know it at the time. I just remember the shock of seeing this USO (unidentified swimming object), bigger than me, eerily gliding in the distance.

But there would be more USOs. One of the resorts closer to town had a dock that went further out into the water and had a circular gazebo at the end. On a clear day, one could almost see from one end of the island to the other from the outer edge of the wooden structure. Late one afternoon I had gone out onto the gazebo to contemplate whether or not I would have a swim. A few adolescent boys were splashing around, jumping into the water from the railing. The wind was strong that day; the tide was rough. Even though the water was warm, I decided against swimming since the wind made the air-temperature feel cooler. But I enjoyed my time in the gazebo, gazing out into the ocean, when again I saw something large and long moving through the water. As the USO approached, I saw the telltale fins, the menacing gaze. Yes, it was a shark. I watched it as it swam under the gazebo and out again on the other side. It seemed to move in a circular direction when lo and behold, there was another one! They were both at least seven feet long. Since most of the boat trips had been cancelled that day because of the rough surf, it seems the sharks had missed their feedings. So they decided to come toward the shore to see what they could find. I just kept thinking, *I could've been out there. I almost jumped in.* But there were no shark attacks that day. In fact, shark attacks around Belize are quite rare.

34

I began to see the performance of *Tristan und Isolde* as a more significant sign as we spent more time at the yacht club. On windy days, it would be rather unpleasant sitting directly on the beach with the sand blowing around. So I would sit on the yacht club pier, watching the boats come and go. Act One of *Tristan* is set on a ship, and toward the end of the act we hear the seamen yelling to the men on land to assist with tying the ship to the dock. As I witnessed for myself, this actually happens. When the larger boats come in, the sailors yell for anyone who is on the dock to come catch the ropes and pull the boat to safety. The bigger the boat, the more men who come running from other boats to make sure that their boats are not hit in the navigation. The scene is very exciting. I had always thought of yacht-owners as rich snobs. But during my time in Belize I learned that owning a yacht calls for a lot of hard work. Surfaces need constant cleaning to prevent damage from rust, salt, and mildew. Long-distance travel means paying close attention to weather forecasts, since a storm at sea can be life threatening. I met some very nice people on those docks who were very liberal and open-minded, and who enjoyed good company and lively conversation. I begin to think of life at sea as something I could really get into – water sign that I am.

The immigration officers made frequent surprise visits to the yacht club to make sure that all the new arrivals on the boats in the marina had paid their taxes, and that all visitors had visas. Occasionally there were boat inspections to make sure that no illegal substances were being smuggled onto the island. And what became of confiscated illegal substances? Your guess is as good as mine.

We learned to make our way in this tropical paradise. The Webers soon told us that our room was booked for the following week and it was necessary for us to move to a different room. We packed our things and waited for the golf cart to transport us to a different room, not quite as nice, but equally equipped. This time, however, we had to sit outside and strain our necks to see a little piece of ocean. We were also on the ground floor. The Webers informed us that we could have this room for a few days but the entire hotel was booked for Easter week in two weeks' time. This meant we had two weeks to find an apartment and settle in while Helga learned the ins and outs of the club.

We moved into our second flat at the yacht club and looked through the kitchen equipment to make sure everything was there. There was a pantry next to the refrigerator which contained pots, pans, dishes, etc., on a few shelves. Some of the pans had little black specks in them, but I didn't think anything of it. We just washed them out and put them back. There was a strange toilet smell in the cabinet though. I just attributed it to plumbing that ran behind the wall.

Later, when it was time to cook dinner, I reached in the cabinet for one of the pans and there were new, fresh black specks. Then I had a sinking feeling. I had lived in New York City for over ten years, after all. I knew what cockroach poop looked like. But these pieces were larger and differently shaped from the roach poop I was used to. I put the pan back. We had sandwiches for dinner and used plastic cutlery.

Later that night, Helga needed a knife from the cutlery drawer. She pulled the drawer open, screamed, then slammed it shut. "What was it?" I asked. She wouldn't say. I kept asking. Finally, she said she wasn't sure. It was a beautiful bug about three inches long, brown with stripes of green and blue, and it was sitting on the silverware. Okay, I don't care whether we're in the tropics or not, a cockroach is a cockroach and I'm a New Yorker. It was war!

The next day Helga informed Frau Weber that the flat was infested and needed extermination. Later we would learn that most of the flats at the yacht club were in the same condition, and in some cases were infested with termites as well. Frau W. gave us a can of weak bug spray. I went to the store for the good stuff. Armed with two cans, the massacre began. After life in New York, I knew where they came from, where they hung out. I started with the drains, then I emptied the contents of the kitchen closet and drawers into the sink. And then, starting at the furthest distance from a possible exit, I sprayed every corner, every nook and cranny, every crack and hole. Then I closed the cabinet doors and drawers and waited. The sound of scurrying filled the kitchen. Tiny feet scrambled to carry small bodies to safety. Dozens didn't make it and simply crawled out into the open air to die. After about an hour, I sprayed their entrances and exits (usually around the pipes carrying water under the sink) and then sealed them with Spackle. The scurrying went on through the night. For the next three days, dazed, disoriented roaches wandered aimlessly around the floor, begging to be put out of their misery. I would never squash one with a shoe or newspaper. It would just get a direct hit of spray, flail around helplessly, and gradually die twitching in its last death-throes. These were some of the biggest roaches I had ever seen. Some of them needed enough spray to kill a small mouse. But even if it managed to crawl behind something or into something where it remained hidden, inevitably, after a few minutes, there he'd be out in the open, dead. These may have been tropical creatures who lived in the grass, unlike the sewage-dwellers in New York City. But still, I was not going to share my space with them.

The extermination was successful. We didn't see another cockroach in the flat for the rest of our time there. There may have been an occasional salamander, but no bugs. Such a traumatic experience gave urgency to the need to find a new flat. The search was on.

Our Caribbean experience got even more exciting on those days when we would get up, turn on the faucet, and nothing would happen. We'd call the front desk and would be informed that there was a power-outage. Since the water pumps were powered by electricity, this also meant no water. At first the power-outages were just for a few hours. When the water came back on, we would fill empty gallon jugs to keep them on hand for bathing, and in such heat, hot showers weren't always necessary. Later we were informed that a huge power generator on the island had blown. It took several days for the replacement parts to reach the island. When they finally did, power was out for hours daily during the repairs. We found public toilets in the newly constructed convention center of the yacht club, which did not use electric water pumps. Some of the guests, however, didn't seem to care if their full toilets went without flushing all day. The maids were the poorest of all. They still had to wash and press dozens of sheets and towels somehow. Easter, one of the resort's busiest weeks, was just around the corner. We still needed to find a place to live.

35

Searching for a flat was not easy. Helga was working all day, six days a week. We went to look at a few rooms but Helga asked me if I could take on the responsibility of finding a place, as she had no time during the day. We hardly saw each other while she was working. Even though I would sit on the beach that was on the yacht club property, her duties were primarily inside the buildings. Occasionally, she would have to supervise the gardeners and I could see her from a distance. But when she had her work-face on, this was no time for socializing. She would have an hour break for lunch. Once I found my favorite spot on the beach, she would come there to meet me and I would bring lunch for both of us. We lived off of sandwiches or tortillas stuffed with cheese, fresh avocados, and tomatoes. Then we would eat the freshest mangoes and papayas I've ever had for dessert. It was cashew season and men would walk along the beach carrying baskets of fresh cashews to sell. Eventually, after a few first pitiful attempts, we learned to make the perfect beans and rice. Cooked items were reduced to dishes that could be eaten cold or at room temperature. In that heat, you certainly did not crave hot food.

We learned to live without butter. By the time we would have carried it from the store to our flat, it would have been totally melted. We would enjoy our lunch while gazing at the water under the shade of a hut built from palm branches. The time flew and each day it seemed like the time for her to go back to work came earlier and earlier.

I had brought for reading material the Anaïs Nin diaries and Richard Wright's *Black Boy*. Anaïs always inspired me to write but when I would try to sit and write on the beach, the wind would invariably blow my papers away. I had to confine my writing time to the moments I spent indoors, which were few and far between. Later, as the rainy season approached, I would have an hour or so in the afternoon to record my thoughts. The brief cloud-cover and short showers were blessings indeed. There was even relief from the dust for a few minutes.

Sitting alone on the beach grew more difficult, as the local men seemed to think it was improper for a woman to be by herself. Every day, at least three times a day, some man – a total stranger – would decide to sit with me or walk along the beach with me. I was afraid of angering these men or of provoking their taunts and insults. I'd heard them all before.

"What?! You too good to talk to me?"

"You can't speak?!"

It was even more insulting if Helga was with me and we were engaged in conversation. The inevitable "Hello, ladies!" would be shouted and repeated from behind, until we responded. As if we had nothing better to do than to wait for this man's attention. The harassment was intensified during this time because in the aftermath of the hurricane, men were being shipped from the mainland to Ambergris to work at various reconstruction sites. Some of these men seemed almost desperate to hook up with the tourists. The fantasy of the "rich sugar mama who can take me away from all this" ran rampant. But one day the usual "Hello Miss, you all by yourself?" turned out to be a blessing. I was sitting as usual, trying unsuccessfully to read, when he sat down.

"You new here, right?"

I nodded.

"How long you stayin'?"

"I don't really know."

"Yeah? Well, if you need any herbs or anything, I got some great herbs, natural healing stuff, you know, for the skin or for the back. I got oils to rub in… anything you need."

"Really?" My curiosity was piqued. "And what about to smoke?"

"I got some really nice home-grown. No chemicals or nothin' added to it. It's totally pure."

"Oh? And how much?"

"Fifty Belize dollars. You want some? I can go get it right now."

That was a bit quick. I told him to come back in an hour and I would get the money.

"Great! I'll see you right back here, in an hour." He held out his hand. "I'm Elton."

Elton kept his promise and sold me a small bag of nice, mild herb with lots of seeds and stems. It was very fresh.

Elton was big and black and it was good to know that he was there if there were any signs of trouble. But most of the other men who talked to me definitely wanted more than to sell me herbs. I soon realized I was even more fearful of these men because we had to wear such skimpy clothes. It was way too hot for long pants or sleeves. I would wear a tank top and shorts over a bathing suit, which they interpreted as an invitation. Only the tourists walked around like that. The local women either walked in groups or covered themselves. But most local women on Ambergris were not free to walk around during the day (except on Sundays). Most of the local women worked as maids in the hotels on the island and, as Helga learned from her work at the yacht club, many could not read or write. She realized this when she handed a list of items to be cleaned to one of the young maids. The woman looked at it, nodded her head, and took the list. Then at the end of the day when the room was inspected, only half of the tasks were completed. Helga asked in distress, "Didn't you read the list?" The woman looked down, pulled the crumpled piece of paper from her pocket, looked at it and nodded her head. Helga followed her eyes. Then she saw. "You can't read, can you." The woman, still looking down, shook her head no.

It seemed the local women were even more oppressed by the local men, who had to maintain a level of respect toward white female tourists. But their misogyny was released on their own kind. One day Helga heard voices rising between one of the older male gardeners and a maid. The woman was a grandmother, but maintained a youthful appearance with her long black hair. The argument was in Spanish so Helga couldn't decipher the details. But later, the woman went out of her way to avoid being in the gardener's space. When

Helga asked what the disagreement was about, the woman just said she would not speak to "Mr. G" again. After further prompting, she finally admitted that he had threatened to beat her, to "teach her to respect a man." There was no feminism on this island.

Most of the staff at the yacht club was Hispanic or black. The Hispanics looked Mexican or Mayan with strong Native features. In their eyes, Helga was still a white woman who had to be respected, therefore. So Helga found herself in the position of having to explain to "Mr. G" that it was unacceptable for an employee to threaten another employee with violence. He may have nodded to her, but it was clear that her words were not going to change his beliefs.

She developed a plan. The security guards who were on duty for the night-shift used walkie-talkies. During the day, those walkie-talkies sat collecting dust in the storage closet. She asked Frau Weber if it was okay to use those walkie-talkies during the day for communication between the maids and "mission control." Frau W. agreed so Helga had to teach the supervising maid (who, by the way, was the grandmother whom Mr. G had threatened) how to use a walkie-talkie. This way the women in the laundry room could know exactly which rooms were finished and when, as well as which rooms still needed clean sheets and towels and when. The plan seemed to work except for the fact that – during the first entire week of the new high-tech mission – whenever Helga called into her walkie-talkie asking the maid-supervisor to respond, all she heard on the other end was giggling. Then the supervisor learned to push the button before speaking, but she forgot to hold it down. So Helga would hear the beginning of a report on her end, then silence in mid-sentence. The men just looked at these women using walkie-talkies and laughed. Meanwhile, I had flashbacks of *Charlie's Angels*.

36

Luckily for us, there was a medical school on the island. This meant that there were several apartment houses away from the resort areas which were intended to house students and faculty. We had arrived at the right time of year – in between semesters. Our only problem was that many of the landlords only wanted students in their houses so that they could be guaranteed rent for three months at a time. Helga was working on a trial basis and her contract could be terminated at any time. I had to think fast. Helga was getting desperate to leave the yacht club since the owners had no respect for her boundaries. They knew where she lived and could knock on the door at any time. We saw an ad in the weekly paper for a small ground floor flat in a private home directly behind the yacht club. It was on the opposite side of the street, which meant that the dust from the road being carried on ocean breezes went directly into the windows. We made an appointment with the owner of the house.

The Asian woman who greeted us was quite friendly. Her husband owned the house. She invited us into the flat. I took one look around at the rusted, old plumbing and appliances and the worn, dusty furniture and was ready to leave. Helga, on the other hand, was making approving noises. Then I knew she was desperate. We thanked our host and told her to expect a call from us the next day. I spent the rest of the afternoon on foot, walking from house to house in the blistering heat, asking anyone who would answer if they had a room to rent.

I found several flats, but all of them were taken. So I was up and out early the next morning to continue my search. Finally, I found a sweet three-story house about two blocks behind the yacht club. There were still piles of earth and planks of wood in the front, but the façade was freshly painted in a bright pink with newly planted little cacti lining the front wall. Construction sounds filled the hall. I asked one of the workers if the owner was around. He yelled to the top floor for his boss. A young-looking shirtless blond man peered over the balcony, answering to, "Yo, Mike!" He seemed nice. I asked him if he had any empty flats. He said there was one but he wanted a medical student. I explained our situation and told him we would know in approximately a month's time exactly how long we could keep the flat. I was begging, in my tank top and little shorts and pouring on the sweetness. It worked. He offered to show me the flat.

Mike talked about preferring medical students as he jingled his keys and opened the door to the ground-floor studio. But he said there was a young couple in the room he was showing me who would be leaving in two days. My expectations were lowered when I saw it was another ground floor flat, so I immediately looked under the sinks and along the floors and windows for cracks. The bathroom was beautiful: clean with new fixtures, a huge shower with bright, gleaming tiles. The bathroom window looked out onto the neighbor's yard and flower garden. He said the front windows usually stayed closed with the curtains down because of the dust factor. Besides, you didn't want people to be able to see in from the road. Since he was supervising the construction (which was actually post-hurricane reconstruction), I showered him with compliments on the house and told him I would take it right then and there. Helga's lunch break was soon, so I could bring her by that day. He said a few medical students were coming by that afternoon but if they decided not to take it, he'd give it to us. Later when I brought Helga, she said she liked it, but she would have liked anything by that point. I think Mike was pleased by the fact that one of us was employed since the island was crawling with beach bums who started out as tourists and never left. He told us to call him in the morning. By then he would know if the place was free or not.

As fate would have it, the medical students never showed up. We moved that night.

As Helga settled into her work schedule, I settled into my daily routine. We were both up before sunrise. We would sit down together for a light breakfast with crappy instant coffee and powdered creamer. Then we would walk to the beach together. I dropped her off at the yacht club usually on my way into town for the morning shopping. I was always in a rush to get into town before the sun was too hot. By the time I shopped, brought the groceries home, and did a little morning writing, it was soon time to start preparing lunch to bring to the beach.

Being on an island, we had to pay for import costs on everything. Even Bacardi wasn't cheap. But we soon discovered that Belize had its own local rum. With plenty of fresh pineapple juice and even fresher supplies of cream of coconut, we were set! Even without a blender, we shook our concoction in a Gatorade bottle and left it in the freezer. Delicious!

The heat was not exactly conducive to lovemaking. We would start to sweat as soon as we got out of the shower. But there was an air-conditioner in the flat. We wanted to conserve energy, so we would just turn it on for an hour or so in the evenings. It also served to drown out our noises and the creaking bed springs.

One night I was on my own for the evening. Helga was working late, so I decided to enjoy some of Elton's herb. The next thing I knew I was walking on the beach in no particular direction. So... here I was at the yacht club. I sat in the marina for a while and then I went toward the reception area. Who knows? Maybe I'd catch a glimpse of my sweetie. I sat at the pool-side bar. I had already had a couple of rum-and-pineapples. But the young black bartender insisted that I try one of his specialties.

"It's called a pontireepur," he said.

"A wha?"

"Pontireepur!" he repeated.

"Okay," I said.

It was a delicious drink of coconut rum, pineapple juice, a splash of cranberry juice, and something else I didn't catch. One of the waitresses came over. The two of them were giggling about something. She looked at me.

"Howdya like the drink?" she asked.

"It's great. What's it called again?" I was hoping I could understand her accent a little better.

"Pontireepur," she said.

It didn't help.

"Wha?"

"Ponti-reepur!" she repeated slowly.

Oh. I finally got it. They were saying "panty-ripper." The bartender was aware of my sudden enlightenment.

"Makes you wanna take your clothes off," he grinned.

"I see."

Helga suddenly appeared. In the chain of command, she was this bartender's superior. I handed her my drink to taste.

"Mmmm. It's nice," she said. "What is it?"

I looked to the bartender. "Tell her what it's called," I said.

Suddenly he got all shy. He smiled and then giggled. He looked to the waitress as if to ask what he should do. Finally, he decided to cover up his embarrassment and talk like a man. His face became stern.

"Pontireepur," he said seriously.

"Wha?" Helga asked.

"Panty-ripper," I repeated.

"Oh," she said. She was not amused. "I'll see you later," she said to me and walked away.

I sat and continued to nurse my drink. Then Herr W. came to the bar. He smiled and said hello to me. I was feeling especially chatty (as I usually do after having some herb), so I thought I would reminisce aloud about their homeland. I asked him if he enjoyed the opera.

"Yes, of course," he said, like a good Austrian.

"I have a good story for you."

I did have a wonderful story about an evening in the Staatsoper in Vienna. It was the first time I took Helga to the opera. Wagner's *Flying Dutchman* was the opera that evening.

"Just a minute," Herr W. said. Then he asked the bartender to open a bottle of Austrian white wine. He tasted it, nodded, "Ja, gut," and motioned for the bartender to pour me a glass.

"Where was I? Oh, yes. Flying Dutchman. Well, you know the story. The Dutchman sails the oceans of the earth, searching for a virgin who will love him. He is only able to come ashore once every seven years. Well on this particular night at the Staatsoper, at the moment when the virgin is anticipating his arrival, we feel his presence at the door of her room. The anticipation builds. He's coming. But the door won't open. He tries again. She's waiting. The whole orchestra is waiting. But the door is stuck. The poor Dutchman is trying so desperately to open the fucking door that the whole back wall of the set is shaking. But the door won't open. They had to close the curtain. The director of the opera house came out and apologized to the audience. He said, 'For two hundred performances the door has always opened, but on this particular night, we had bad luck. We're very sorry.' After a short pause, the door was fixed and the performance continued."

Herr W. was cracking up.

That night it had been seven years since Susan's death. The Dutchwoman had found her virgin, an Austrian Felsenfrau (mountain woman). The real drama that night was in the audience, not on the stage.

He suddenly jumped up to go inside. I think he did not want Frau W. to hear him laughing so much with another woman. I finished my wine and panty-ripper and continued my stroll along the beach.

37

Before we came to Belize, we had this wonderful fantasy of living off of fresh fish and rice. After we got to Belize, we found that it was virtually impossible to buy fresh fish. This could not be true. There must have been a trick we just hadn't figured out. The restaurants had fresh fish, so it had to be sold somewhere. Some locals advised us to look in the sky over the piers at the end of the day for birds hovering over the incoming fishing boats. The fishermen would clean the fish and throw the remains to the birds. During my evening jogs, I would locate the birds and run miles down the beach to the boats, only to be told by the fishermen that they weren't selling any fish.

The more we inquired, the more we learned about how vulnerable these people were to the whims of Mother Nature. Belize was the scuba/snorkeling capital of the world. Tourists came for the deep-sea diving. Men who had boats could make a fortune from taking a boatload of tourists for a deep-sea dive with each paying fifty dollars a head. Compared to what they made from selling fish, it simply wasn't worth it. Restaurants and hotels had their own boats and fishermen. Tourists who had timeshares still had to eat out if they wanted fish. It was the rule of the island.

But there was another factor governing the mood around fish and fishing: manhood. The island economy had been suffering since the hurricane. Much of the reef was destroyed. Fewer tourists and fewer boat tours all added up to a depressed economy. On some of my evening jogs when I would ask unsuccessfully to buy fish, I saw several men standing, watching while fish were being cleaned and filleted. The men were glassy-eyed, fresh from the bar. On some evenings, a group of fishermen would set up a grill and start grilling the fish. The smoke was visible all along the beach, signaling to other men a beach barbecue. Men stood and watched, chattering in Spanish and Patois, spitting into the sand and scratching their crotches. My requests to buy fish were repeatedly refused and I was told that they were simply having a party for some friends. I watched this a few times, thinking I could ask more sweetly or speak more politely. Until one evening, after an exceptionally long run, I came upon the same scene but this time there were two little girls watching the food preparation. The men laughed, cursed, scratched, and spat. I waited for a pause for my turn to speak. By now I was sick of being polite.

"How much for some fish?"

After such a long run, I really had a major itch. Why was I stopping myself when they were able to scratch themselves whenever the hell they wanted without being self-conscious? I scratched my crotch and spat at the same time. All eyes turned toward me. The sweet sounds of two little girls giggling filled the air.

Helga was so annoyed at not being able to buy fish that she went out and bought some hooks and a line. She soon learned that these fish were experts at eating the pieces of bait without swallowing the hook. They especially loved chicken hotdogs. One day she pulled her hook out of the water and saw a little crab desperately running after the half-eaten fragment of hotdog.

One evening after another unsuccessful fishing session, Helga walked into the flat barefoot. I was used to seeing the locals without shoes, but I thought I remembered seeing her leave the flat with her shoes on. It turns out that she had stepped onto what she thought was a secure patch of sand to retrieve her hook. The next thing she knew, she was up to her knees in sand and mud. The shoes had to go. It was all she could do to pull her feet out onto solid ground.

We had all but given up on the possibility of finding any fish when one beautiful evening, during one of our long walks on the beach, we saw the telltale sign of birds flying over a boat at the end of a pier. Next to the tied boat was a lone man, his head bobbing up and down as he cut apart his catch of the day.

"Let's ask him if he'll sell us some." I was still hopeful.

"Nooo..." Helga groaned.

She hated to beg. So, I left her behind on the land and trotted out to the end of the pier. The man seemed friendly, pleased with his catch. The fish was not the usual snapper I had seen. I asked him what kind of fish it was.

"Spanish mackerel," he said. The rainbow colors in the scales caught the sunlight. His knife clearly wasn't sharp enough as he struggled to separate the delicate flesh from the bones.

"Wow," I said, faking admiration. "How far out did you have to go to catch those?"

"Not far. Just a couple miles outside the reef. They practically jumped into the boat by themselves."

I was not amused. But Helga saw the conversation was lasting longer than usual. She decided to join us. As she approached, I could see that she had definitely caught his interest.

"Hi there," he called to her.

"Hi," she barely responded.

I made the introductions, "This is my friend Helga."

"Hi," he repeated. "I'm Javier." He then displayed his fishy hands as an excuse not to shake hers. Then the usual conversation started. "Helga? What kind of name is that?"

"I'm from Austria."

"Oh, really? Wow! That's a long way away."

"Yep, but I'm here working at the yacht club."

"Oh, that's great. So you'll be here a while."

I had it all memorized. He continued to struggle with his knife, cut himself a few times, and rinsed the wound in the ocean. While he was cutting, he would occasionally throw fish skin and body parts into the air for the birds to grab. They swooped down so low – within a foot of our heads. After a while he was obviously tired of cutting.

"You like fish?" he asked Helga.

"Sure. Love it."

"Well, I already have enough for my dinner. Here, you take the rest."

When we offered to pay him, he explained it cost him the same if he caught five or twenty by the time you calculated the cost of the boat, gas, and oil. He was cooking for one, so it would just go bad anyway. We skipped all the way home with our fresh catch of Spanish mackerel. We even took a photo of the beautiful fish frying in the pan.

One evening after dinner, we decided to take a walk on the beach since it was hot in the flat after cooking and there was a cool ocean breeze. It was a beautiful, clear, starry night. We walked along hand-in-hand and found ourselves headed in the direction of the gazebo. We went out onto the boardwalk approaching the structure and found our favorite seats waiting for us. The heterosexuals were partying at the bar so we were able to have some privacy. The breeze was glorious. As we silently gazed out into the water and imagined what was happening in the boats and yachts that were anchored in place, I noticed a small light in the distance just on the horizon.

"What's this, now?" Helga said with her classic Tyrolean cynicism. She thought it was a ship approaching or some sort of light-show.

As the light grew larger, we realized it was the moon. We had arrived just in time for the full moon-rise and had front row seats. Never before had we seen such a huge full moon with such shades of orange and bright yellow. We sat in silence and awe.

38

One month had elapsed, which meant that we had to apply for extensions on our visas. This involved a visit to the local Immigration Office at the airport. When we arrived at the office, through the glass door I saw the young officer and a younger woman sitting behind a desk. I knocked, opened the door, and asked if this was the place to apply for visa extensions. The officer looked flustered and told us to wait outside. "Oh, sorry," I said as I glanced at the woman. She was not a secretary. She wore large dark glasses and looked as if she wanted to hide. The officer soon came outside, went into another room, and emerged again holding a small brown-paper bag. He went back into the office, threw the bag down on the desk before the woman, and peered at her expectantly. She hastily picked up the bag and rushed out of the office, disappearing into the streets. The officer shook his head, then motioned for us to come in.

The visa-extension application involved paying our forty dollars and presenting our passports to be stamped. That was it! We were free to stay another month.

The swimming during our first month was wonderful. My strokes became stronger, my muscles developed. I was tan, trim, and strong. Then after a while we would see swarms of small brown disks about half an inch in width. The locals informed us these were jellyfish. They came in by the millions every year around this time to mate and leave their eggs behind. At low tide, thousands of their lifeless bodies would line the beach. It was a feast for the seagulls and crabs. Even the fish under the yacht club pier made snacks out of the horny jellyfish. The locals also told us that the jellyfish could sting. It was most unfortunate on hot days when we were dying to swim to come to the water and find swarms of these predators just waiting to sting us. But then on other days, when the tide came from a different direction, the water would be totally clear and we were free to jump in. Mating season for the jellyfish was just a couple of weeks long and we were quite relieved to be able to resume our swimming schedule.

But one evening, after a wonderfully long swim in what we thought was clear water, I noticed a slight itch on a patch of skin on my butt. I didn't think anything of it, attributed it to mosquitoes, and washed it thoroughly. But the itching increased. Then there were more patches. I kept scratching and the patches became quite red. Helga was scratching too. Both of us scratched our way through a sleepless night and hit the streets the next day in search of rubbing alcohol. The pharmacist at the tiny drugstore informed us that we had been a meal for the microscopic larva of the jellyfish, otherwise known as sea lice. The larva only bite when they get trapped in a bathing suit or under clothing, so it was best to wear as little as possible while swimming and to slather the skin with baby oil. But there was no cure for the itching. Alcohol gave temporary relief, but we would soon hear each other scratching again. After a while, itching and scratching simply became part of life. Even the locals were scratching.

I soon learned that sun-tanning the affected area gave the most relief. But since the itchy skin was under our bathing suit lines, we needed to find a place where we could sunbathe nude. This was not easy since obnoxious men were everywhere and we could count on big Elton walking by daily and stopping for a chat while his eyes traveled along our bodies. On our evening walks, we passed a pier belonging to a resort which seemed to be quite empty. It was a small resort with a few rather large apartments. I guess there wasn't as much booking from guests after the hurricane. Most of the time the pier was deserted. But there was a chain at the entrance of the pier and a prominent sign that read "Pier use for hotel guests only." We ignored the sign. The pier went far out into the water. We were able to feel that we had some privacy for the first time during our stay. There was a wooden structure at the end that kept anyone on land from being able to see us. But we would need to cover whenever a boat sped by, depending on the direction of the sun at the time. Of course, I ended up with a case of burned nipples at the end of the first day. But from then on, the pier at Xanadu was our favorite private spot. We swam (covered in baby oil of course) and lounged naked which gave us beautiful, unobstructed tans by the end of our stay.

• • • • •

The time came for Helga and the Webers to decide whether or not their working relationship would continue and under what terms. Helga had already decided that she really did not like working for them since he was unable to make decisions and she was... well, neurotic at best and down-right crazy at worst. There were many instances when it turned out that both Webers had not told the truth. They also were not shy about making disparaging and sometimes racist comments about the other employees. Helga was conflicted since she knew the Webers were planning to go to Austria and she would not have to deal with them while they were gone. She loved this tropical paradise, but she also had the sinking feeling that she was getting more and more entrenched in the tourism industry like her parents. The day before a decision was to be made, Helga arranged to get her second check and immediately cashed it at the bank.

The Mayan gods made the decision for her. An official from the Immigration Office showed up unannounced at the yacht club one day. He knew the Webers and asked who this new woman was behind the desk. Helga promptly disappeared to avoid answering any questions or saying the wrong thing. After the officer left, Helga met with Frau Weber and another staff member to plan out a strategy. Even though Frau W. worked all day every day, she still was not officially an employee of the yacht club and therefore did not need working papers. She was officially just the wife of the owner, who sat on his ass all day and did nothing. Helga, on the other hand, would need working papers. Herr Weber had promised to secure working papers for her during one of their telephone conversations before we arrived. Unfortunately, he seemed to have forgotten this.

Helga was understandably upset. The Webers had neglected to keep their promise and thereby subjected Helga to possible prosecution or deportation. She, Frau W., and the local staff member decided to inform Immigration that Helga was a temporary employee and to file the proper paperwork for payment of taxes. The official had scheduled a second meeting for later that day and was told of the situation according to plan. Unfortunately, Herr W. decided to take matters into his own hands when he walked into the meeting and recklessly announced that Helga was not working there. She was just a friend of the family, he said. The official knew immediately that he was lying. He told Helga to report to the Immigration Office the following day and left angrily. Herr W. had put his foot in his mouth again. The annoyance on all three faces was obvious. Helga walked out.

She returned to the flat earlier than usual and told me what had happened. We spent the rest of the afternoon deciding what she should say to the Webers that evening, when their decision-making meeting was scheduled. She hated working there by this point and was prepared to demand several changes if they wanted her to continue working. I advised her to be honest about her feelings, since she was afraid of breaking down under the stress of trying to swallow her anger. The Webers had carelessly put her in a dangerous situation and they should know how she felt about it.

She went to the meeting and returned within half an hour. Evidently, weeks-worth of pent-up frustration erupted as

Helga confronted the Webers on their mismanagement, their attempts to manipulate employees via in-fighting, and their dishonesty. Frau W. appreciated Helga's honesty, Herr W. did not. He growled that he would not be spoken to in this way and fired Helga on the spot. Helga was actually relieved that the decision was made. She handed over her papers and walked out while Frau W. watched the whole scene with her mouth gaping open. She didn't want Helga to leave. She was looking forward to going home and to having another Austrian handling their affairs. Besides, Helga was an excellent employee – the best they had ever had. I wished I could have been a fly on the wall of their bedroom that night.

Thank goodness Helga had gotten paid that day. We had just enough money to get us through two more weeks, maybe.

39

During our last two weeks in Belize, we actually had time to schedule trips to other islands. We had heard about the island called Caye Caulker, how it was a weed-smoker's paradise and a haven for people who liked to party. Since many boats carrying illegal substances went through the waters around Belize, some traffickers found themselves needing to throw bags of cocaine and marijuana overboard if they were being pursued by law-enforcement. So miraculously, bags of illegal substances would wash up on the beaches of Caye Caulker and other islands. Locals smoked openly, but the police frowned on tourists trying to do the same. Thank goodness we were warned.

But we were not warned about the rampant homophobia. When we arrived at the dock, we were greeted by religious graffiti – you know, the normal stuff: fire and brimstone and sinners going to hell. But we didn't think anything of it and continued walking along the beach. We saw caged roosters (obviously being held for cock-fights), drug-deals going down, and a few drunks here and there. There was much devastation on the island after the hurricane. Many buildings were barely standing, half of them having been torn away. I heard a loud male voice in the distance and ignored it, expecting the usual "Hello, ladies." But the voice grew louder and it soon became clear a man was following us.

"You can't do that on this island," he announced.

When we realized he was talking to us, I asked, "Can't do what?"

"That's not allowed here."

We still couldn't get an answer. All we were doing was walking on the beach holding hands.

"What's not allowed? Happiness?" I asked.

He smiled and shook his head. A few minutes later we heard a louder, more menacing voice booming behind us. "You take that shit to San Francisco! You don't do that on this island!!" He was following us, collecting a crowd of onlookers.

"You get off this island! You hear?! Do that shit in San Francisco."

We picked up our pace. Evidently the sight of two women holding hands was more offensive to these men than that of bloody cock-fighting, passed-out drug-addicts, or HIV-infected prostitutes.

Since several tourists had mentioned to us that the TV show "Temptation Island" had been filmed in Belize, we decided to take a day-trip to the resort where the series was filmed. Captain Morgan's resort was further north on Ambergris, but here again the landscape had been severely damaged by the hurricane. It blew my mind to see tourists who were staying on other islands, but who came especially to Captain Morgan's just to have photos taken of themselves in the same hot-tub that was seen on the TV show. (I had never seen the show.) There weren't many guests, but the water was beautiful. I positioned myself in a beach hammock and enjoyed one of the best naps of my life.

As we were nearing the end of our time in Belize, Helga decided that she wanted to take advantage of the opportunity to scuba-dive. She was already an excellent swimmer. She just needed to learn to use the equipment. I had been scuba diving once before and did not really enjoy it. I could not relax knowing that I was so far away from the surface, and I couldn't just take a breath if I needed it. We found a shack where the instructor agreed to provide a guide for a snorkel trip for me, while Helga did the scuba tour. This meant getting back into the boat for the up and down trip to Hol Chan. But this time we knew not to eat beforehand.

Helga suited-up and fastened and checked her gear. Since all I needed were a snorkel and fins, I decided to wear a T-shirt to keep away the sea lice. We both were well slathered with baby oil. Helga soon disappeared into the depths with her instructor and I swam along the surface with my snorkeling guide. Again, the fish were beautiful. My guide went out of his way to give me a wonderful experience, pointing out eels, starfish, and stingrays trying unsuccessfully to hide in the sand. At one point, I looked and saw a large bright green fish at least five-feet in length swimming along to my right. A few minutes later, there was another one. Then another. I looked behind me and there was a whole school of at least twenty of these big, bright green fish swimming along with us. Suddenly, I realized that these fish were almost the same color as the t-shirt I was wearing. They weren't swimming anywhere else in the wildlife preserve. They all came to swim with me. Some came quite close and looked right into my mask. I think one even tried to mate with me.

Helga was ecstatic after her dive. She said it was the best thing she had ever done. She had no fear whatsoever of all that water being between her and the next breath of air. She said she couldn't wait to do it again.

As our time to leave the island approached, we found ourselves quite restricted financially. We were living off of the money Helga had made at the yacht club, which was steadily running out. I was able to use my credit cards at some restaurants, but there was no cash machine on the island. Our plane tickets were valid for up to two months and we had already postponed the departure date twice. As the end of the two months grew closer, we decided to use the tickets and book the flight exactly two months to the day after our arrival.

We wouldn't even set foot in the expensive touristy restaurants. Since we were both such good cooks, it is especially annoying to pay thirty dollars for something we could prepare just as well, for a quarter of the price. Besides, we knew the cockroach situation on the island. There was no guarantee that you would not find moving creatures on the floors of most restaurants, regardless of how expensive they were.

But usually, for one night a week, most oceanfront restaurants would set up a grill and tables outside on the beach for a beach barbecue. They were easy to find: just follow the music and the aromas. For ten dollars you could sit down to a plate of grilled chicken or ribs, beans and rice, fresh potato salad, and some kind of cake or flan for dessert. And of course, there was all the beer you could drink for two dollars a bottle. Usually the music was pre-recorded. But sometimes a local band would be hired to provide the music. These were the only times when we were actually free to dance in public since the beach barbecues were mostly for the tourists, and the hotel or restaurant staff was instructed to keep the local men away from the females (that is, unless a couple consisted of a native and a tourist who arrived together).

There was a disco just two blocks from our house. But judging from the harassment we received during our walks on the beach, we decided it was not a safe place to be. Just walking past the entrance door on a Saturday night was hazardous, since there was a wooded area between the club and our house. We were repeatedly warned to make sure that we were not being followed on our way home past the club. But the music sure was soundin' *good*!

It was our last night on the island. We sat on the beach, each saying our own private goodbyes to the ocean goddesses. Lo and behold, here comes our herb connection Elton. We tell him it is our last night.

"No! Really? You leavin'?"

"That's right. First thing in the morning."

"Oh. Well here, have a trip on me." He hands me a fat, rolled joint. "I can't believe you leavin'. I just saw girls like you on TV last night. I like girls like you."

We thanked him for the herb. He leaned down for a hug and kiss but Helga pushed him away nicely. At least he left us to enjoy our smoke in peace.

Elton had given us way too much herb to smoke in one sitting, so the next morning, while waiting for the boat to take us to the mainland, I enjoyed some more of his gift. The boat ride was one of the peak experiences of my life: clear blue open sky, calm clear water, schools of fish jumping along-side the boat, private islands in the distance with no more than two or three houses and a single boat tied to the dock. As we approached the mainland, pelicans circled over-head. I knew I did not want to take what was left of Elton's gift through Immigration, so I decided to make an offering to the Ocean Goddess. Already having wrapped it in plastic, I dropped it and said a prayer as I stepped out of the boat. I'm sure it made someone very happy.

The trip back to the States was uneventful. We felt the normal anxiety going through Immigration at the airport in Miami, but our plan to stand in line for a female officer seemed to work. Later, after we had arrived back in New York and were busily unpacking, I noticed Helga taking a little piece of paper out of her wallet.

"Won't be needing that anymore," she said.

"What's that?" I asked.

As it turned out, from the time when we were still in Vienna, gazing at pictures of Ambergris on the yacht club website on the computer, Helga had written down on a little piece of paper that she wanted and was willing to receive a free trip to the Caribbean. Her wish had come true, and I believe she was truly surprised by her ability to manifest her fate. Her spiritual powers were working. The only question now was what to write on the next piece of paper.

A Postscript

Photo: Kathy Rey

At home in front of my wall

In the next book of memoirs, you will read of our adventures back in New York City where Helga enjoys success as a tele-marketer, and I struggle with my writings and other artistic endeavors. It was during this return to the U.S. that I received the call that my mother had passed, and Helga and I return to Nashville for the funeral and burial. It marks the beginning of a whole new relationship with my father.

Eventually we return to Europe where Helga and I visit with her parents, siblings, and grandmother in Austria. During this visit, Helga confronts the phantoms of her childhood and again feels the need to escape from her tiny Tyrolean village. After stopping in Vienna, we ultimately make our way to visit friends in Cologne, Germany, and decide to make our home there for a while. Luckily, we just happened to be living there during the terror attacks of September 11, 2001.

And after spending a few years in Germany, we decide to make our home in Paris. From there we fly to Africa for a holiday. It is an emotional "homecoming" that I'll never forget. At the end of my four years in Paris, (when Helga announced that she wanted her freedom), there was a young black senator from Illinois who had declared his candidacy for the presidency, whose success would spark my interest in returning to my country. There was also a documentary film I was in the midst of producing, which required that I spend more time in the United States. That film about my father titled *Matthew Kennedy: One Man's Journey*, went on to win several awards at international film festivals.

After enjoying success in the film world, I began to see my work as a pianist in a different light. It took some of the pressure off to "prove myself" and allowed me to perform for my own enjoyment. Thus began my return to the concert stage and a new level of success.

There is also a tale of seduction by an African diplomat and the story of my ultimate arrival into the arms of an African-American.

I also became the host of my own television show.

Stay tuned...

INDEX